EISENHOWER:
TURNING THE WORLD
TOWARD PEACE

Harold Stassen and Marshall Houts

Merrill/Magnus Publishing Corporation
St. Paul

Merrill/Magnus Publishing Corporation
One Merrill Circle
St. Paul, Minnesota 55108

Library of Congress Cataloging-in-Publication Data

Stassen, Harold Edward, 1907-

    Eisenhower—turning the world toward peace / Harold Stassen and Marshall Houts.

        p.   cm.

    Includes index.

    ISBN 1-877927-04-X (alk. paper) : $22.95

    1. Eisenhower, Dwight D. (Dwight David), 1890-1969. 2. United States—Foreign relations—1953-1961. 3. Stassen, Harold Edward, 1907- . 4. Presidents—United States—Biography. I. Houts, Marshall. II. Title
E836.S69   1990
973.921 '092—dc20   90-6452
                                                      CIP

ISBN 1-877927-04-X

10 9 8 7 6 5 4 3 2 1

Printed in the United States of America

Page ii: Excerpt from *The Hidden-Hand Presidency*, by Fred Greenstein, copyright© 1982, Basic Books, Inc.

Pages 29 and 30: Excerpts from *First in the Nation: New Hampshire and the Premier Presidential Primary*, by Charles Brereton, copyright© 1987, Peter E. Randall. Reprinted with permission.

Pages 37-38: Excerpt from *Mandate for Change*, by Dwight D. Eisenhower, copyright© 1963, Doubleday & Company, Inc. Reprinted with permission.

Page 55: Excerpt from *The Ordeal of Power* by Emmet John Hughes. Copyright© 1963 Emmet John Hughes. Reprinted with permission of Atheneum Publishers, an imprint of Macmillan Publishing Company.

Pages 100-102: Excerpts from *Reminiscences*, by General of the Army Douglas MacArthur, McGraw-Hill Book Co.,© 1964 Time Warner Inc. Reprinted with permission.

Pages 225-227: Excerpt from *At Ease: Stories I Tell My Friends*, by Dwight D. Eisenhower. Reprinted with permission of John S.D. Eisenhower.

Pages 243 and 349-350: Excerpts from *Where the Buck Stops: The Personal and Private Writings of Harry S. Truman*, by Margaret Truman, copyright© 1989, Warner Books. Reprinted with permission.

Pages 286-289: Excerpt from "The Peace Plugger" from *Affairs of State: The Eisenhower Years* by Richard Rovere. Copyright© 1956 and renewal copyright© 1984 by Richard H. Rovere. Reprinted by permission of Farrar, Straus and Giroux, Inc.

Photographs reprinted with permission of UPI/Bettmann and AP-Wide World Photos.

TO

ESTHER GLEWWE STASSEN

AND

MARY DEALY HOUTS

Acknowledgments

For help on this book, we express our thanks to:

RICHARD NORTON SMITH, Director, Eisenhower Library, Abilene, Kansas

DAVID J. HAIGHT and MARTIN M. TEASLEY, archivists, Eisenhower Library

KATHY STRUSS and HAZEL STRODA, audiovisual curators, Eisenhower Library

Researchers:

TOM KIRKER, Kansas State University History Department

CONNIE K. HARRIS, University of Minnesota History Department

Former Close Associates:

ROBERT MATTESON

G. EDWARD LARSON

Editorial Assistants:

MARTY PHILLIPS, Mission Viejo, California

MARY HOUTS, Dana Point, California

Merrill/Magnus Publishing Corporation:

NANCY LAKE-SMITH, President

MELINDA BOA, Editor

ROBERT LUNDEGAARD, Consultant

H.S.
M.H.

Contents

Preface

In three short years, Dwight David Eisenhower, thirty-fourth President of the United States, moved the world from the icy brinks of World War III to the hopes of enduring peace, with devotion to freedom, justice, and human rights.

When he assumed the presidency, many world leaders, military and political analysts, and people everywhere feared nuclear destruction within the decade. Looking back, I believe that it may well have occurred had we continued the stilted, confrontational policies of Truman-Acheson, on the one hand, or those of Adlai Stevenson and his followers on the other.

I can write this book now because critical documents classified originally as "Top Secret" and "Eyes Only" became declassified in the Eisenhower Library in Abilene, Kansas in 1985, 1986, and 1987.

I do it as part of the centennial of Eisenhower's birth October 14, 1990, and because I believe that his style of "openness" and "reaching-out" give valuable lessons to the people and to future Presidents of this great country.

My goal is to cut through the layers of media and academic misunderstanding, misinterpretation, and minimization of Eisenhower as President, and present the facts as I know them.

Princeton political science professor Fred Greenstein, former president of the American Society of Political Science,

i

recently confirmed my long-held views in his *The Hidden-Hand Presidency* (pages vii-viii):

> I could never have imagined in the 1950s that years later I would immerse myself in the study of Dwight D. Eisenhower's leadership. I had voted Democratic as a 1952 undergraduate majoring in political science and as a 1956 graduate student learning to teach and practice it. Before the decade was over I had my own students and was teaching them to view Eisenhower in the same fashion that most of my colleagues and all of the journalists I respected viewed him—as a good-natured bumbler, who lacked the leadership qualities to be an effective president.
>
> Events, speculations, and hard evidence changed my view. The events were the manifest difficulties Eisenhower's successors had in maintaining political effectiveness, even at the minimum levels of winning and serving out second terms. Compared to them he stands up well. . . .
>
> [T]he archives and the testimony of numerous former associates of Eisenhower's made it clear that he employed a well-articulated, and to a considerable extent, self-conscious approach to handling certain of the built-in dilemmas of American presidential leadership. It is an approach that needs to be explicated both for the record and because it provides potential lessons for future presidents. (New York: Basic Books, Inc., 1982)

It is my view that Eisenhower should be recognized as the most brilliant leader for world peace in this century. The 1955 Geneva Summit, the first ever in peacetime, pointed the world toward openness and meaningful international dialogue. He started the now irreversible movement away from a stubborn Cold War posture, promising hope for the individual freedom of peoples around the globe, a prerequisite for enduring world peace.

His other major accomplishments in these same three years include:

(1) The successful close of the Korean War, with the cessation of battle casualties;

(2) Negotiation of the Red Army out of Austria, that key country in the center of Europe, with fair agreements which still hold;

(3) With his brilliant Ambassador to Italy, Clare Boothe Luce, the settlement of the age-old controversy between Italy and Yugoslavia over Trieste, laying the foundation for peace and economic progress in the Adriatic area;

(4) The construction of the St. Lawrence Seaway which gives major cities in both the United States and Canada deep-port facilities and ocean-going ship service from the Great Lakes to the Atlantic;

(5) The construction of the Super-Interstate Highway System all across America which millions enjoy every day without appreciating Eisenhower's fight with special local interests to bring it about;

(6) The handling of the Senator McCarthy tragedy, based on Eisenhower's abiding faith in the constitutional doctrine of separation of powers;

(7) The decrease in violent crime, with emphasis on personal security for all the people, and respect for our unique Common Law system of justice;

(8) A strengthening of the United Nations as a prime instrument in maintaining the peace;

(9) The insistence that financial incentives should be in line with the social, cultural, and economic objectives of a free people, if they are to attain fulfillment in all these areas;

(10) An economic philosophy that stoutly opposed greed and corruption, and that gave full peacetime employment to all who could work (unemployment ran less than four percent), a prime interest rate averaging five percent per annum, zero inflation, and home ownership rising to an historic level;

(11) A domestic agricultural policy that provided long-term production with a high level of parity, insuring the continued prosperity of America's food producers, as well as a substantial decrease in starvation throughout the world; and

(12) An honoring of traditional values founded on a deep faith in a personal God who could be reached in daily prayer, while maintaining respect for all religious beliefs and freedom of conscience for the individual.

I write in conversational terms from notes and recollections, confirmed by official documents, minutes, and Eisenhower's own letters, especially to his lifetime friend, "Swede" Hazlett, to his brother Milton, and to his fellow-general, Alfred Gruenther.

Those years of full employment, good business, no American soldiers killing or being killed, balanced budgets and no inflation, new world openness, and progress in human rights, did not come easily or accidentally. They resulted from great leadership and difficult, controversial decisions by a superb, gifted, and greatly underappreciated Dwight David Eisenhower.

Harold E. Stassen
Sunfish Lake, Minnesota
March, 1990

Introducing Harold Stassen
by
Marshall Houts

This letter came hand-delivered from the Oval Office to Harold Stassen's office next door in the Executive Office Building:

THE WHITE HOUSE
WASHINGTON

December 28, 1956

Dear Harold:

As 1956 draws to a close, I want again to express to you my appreciation of your contribution to the affairs of our government. I realize that your latest post has been an extremely frustrating and difficult one, and I am all the more grateful for the enthusiasm and zeal with which you have tackled one of the greatest problems of our time. I am truly indebted to you.

With best wishes to you and yours for a fine New Year, and warm personal regard,

Sincerely,

/s/Dwight Eisenhower

The Honorable Harold E. Stassen
Special Assistant to the President
The White House
Washington, D. C.

STASSEN'S FIVE POSITIONS
IN THE EISENHOWER ADMINISTRATION

From Eisenhower's nomination in 1952 until Stassen resigned in 1958, Stassen held more sensitive posts and became party to more important discussions than any other member of the Eisenhower administration. At one and the same time, he served as Director of Mutual Security (later Foreign Operations Administration), member of the National Security Council, member of the group that later became the Council of Economic Advisors, member of the Operations Coordinating Board (formerly the Psychological Strategy Board), and Associate on Cabinet, with full cabinet rank and the duty to attend and speak out at cabinet meetings.

His input into both domestic and foreign policy proved enormous, carrying special weight since he and Eisenhower thought alike, saw most problems from the same perspective, and developed a working formula for getting things done, in spite of opposition from some of the entrenched Washington bureaucracy, and often dissent from other cabinet members.

In addition, Eisenhower at times asked Stassen to "sit quietly" in meetings and boards and committees. These were the President's code words for Stassen not to participate actively in the discussions, but to be available afterwards to report to Eisenhower on his analyses of the problems. He was then to assist in identifying the bottom-line questions and help chart out a course of action.

THE MANEUVER TO OUST STASSEN

Eisenhower's heavy reliance on Stassen's recommendations did not sit well with those interested in promoting their own philosophies and schemes.

At one point, Eisenhower called Stassen to the Oval Office and told him that Treasury Secretary George Humphrey, Defense Secretary Charles Wilson, and Secretary of State

John Foster Dulles had come as a "committee" to ask Eisenhower to "fire" Stassen.

"I'm not surprised," Stassen answered. "What did you tell them?"

Eisenhower reported that he told the cabinet officers that Stassen always followed his instructions better than anyone else in the administration, that Stassen's views and Eisenhower's almost always matched, and if the appearance of the three men constituted a threat to resign, he would accept their resignations then and there.

Stassen recalls Eisenhower's words, "They stared at me like I'd hit them with a two-by-four, and Charlie said that they didn't want it to go that far—only that they thought you spoke out too much in cabinet and National Security Council meetings."

Stassen responded simply: "I'll stay as long as you want me; I'll go whenever you tell me."

"Very well," Eisenhower snapped. "We'll say no more about it."

THE FREQUENT CANDIDATE

Stassen's frequent runs for the Republican presidential nomination cloud his substantial accomplishments as statesman on both the national and international scene. About these campaigns, Stassen says:

> Certainly, I never suffered any delusions that lightning would suddenly strike and I would be nominated. 1948 gave me my one real chance; but each time, when I announced that I would run for President, I got a temporary forum to expound my views on economic policies, foreign actions, and on the UN. Future world peace continues to be my most compelling interest.

These are the words of a man to whom issues, and not the office, are paramount.

THE "BOY GOVERNOR"

"Turmoil" is too weak a word to describe the political situation in Minnesota in 1938.

Labor strikes and retaliatory lockouts produced killings in the streets; thugs and gangsters controlled the powerful Teamsters Union; angry mobs marched on the capitol building in St. Paul and took over the Senate and House in a "sit in"; waste and political favoritism in government reached scandalous proportions. Businesses fled the state because of hostile laws threatened by the Farmer-Laborites in control of both the executive and legislative branches of state government.

Harold Stassen, then president of the Minnesota Young Republicans, formed an organization that startled not only the state but the nation by electing him governor in 1938, at age thirty-one. His "Diaper Brigade" included a lieutenant governor even younger—twenty-eight years—and the speaker of the lower house of the state legislature just under thirty years.

This group of novices produced an astounding legislative record:

(1) Minnesota's first civil service law "to raise the standards of public service and to improve the morale of state government";

(2) A new state purchasing system with a commissioner of administration to eliminate political graft and reduce costs;

(3) A program to develop low grade iron ore;

(4) A law "to curb the small-loan sharks";

(5) A single tax commissioner to equalize tax assessments and make tax collection uniform;

(6) Improved social security benefits;

(7) Liberalized old-age pensions;

(8) A balanced state budget; and

(9) A Labor Conciliation Law that provided a "cooling off" period in labor disputes, notification to a state labor conciliator ten days before a strike or lockout, and a thirty-day fact-finding committee in strikes or lockouts that threatened the public interest. The Stassen administration successfully abated the economic loss and human suffering that arose from the violent labor-management confrontations that plagued Minnesota during the preceding decade.

THE GRIDIRON DINNER SPEECH

Stassen's accomplishments as "Boy Governor" attracted national attention, especially when the Minnesota electorate gave him an eighty percent approval rating after his first legislative session.

This led to his invitation to represent the Republicans at the annual Gridiron dinner given by the Washington Press in December, 1939. Stassen first met Franklin Delano Roosevelt at this dinner.

THE 1940 REPUBLICAN CONVENTION

Stassen's record as governor and his successful Gridiron dinner speech led to his invitation to keynote the Republican Convention in Philadelphia in July 1940.

He explained his Minnesota philosophies and programs to the nation: "Enlightened capitalism"; governments free of corruption to act only for the best interests of all the citizens, not just for a limited few; labor-management programs to even up the equities on both sides and to protect the interests of the public; sound fiscal policies with mandatory balanced budgets; and on America's role in world events, "It is clear that the walls of isolation are gone forever."

Stassen became Wendell Willkie's floor manager in Willkie's bitter fight with Dewey and Taft. Willkie won the nomination, but lost to FDR's third term bid. Even in defeat, the Willkie race produced a lasting effect on the foreign policy attitudes of the Republican party. Stassen's convention and campaign roles further enhanced his reputation as a national Republican leader, but they also made him anathema to the Party's Old Guard, ultraconservative, isolationist leaders.

PEARL HARBOR AND NAVAL SERVICE

Stassen's reelection in 1940 proved impressive, his popularity with the voters holding firm; but Pearl Harbor changed his—as well as the country's—priorities.

"I am not only a young governor," Stassen told the voters before the 1942 campaign, "I am also a young reserve officer. If you reelect me governor, I will serve through the 1943 legislative session, and then resign the office to go on active duty for the remainder of the war. Have this in mind when you elect a lieutenant governor!"

Minnesotans responded with the election of Edward Thye as lieutenant governor (elected on a separate ticket in those days). Thye served ably as governor and later as a U.S. Senator.

In 1943, Stassen received a commission as lieutenant commander in the Navy and moved to active duty as Assistant Chief of Staff for Administration to Admiral William ("Bull") Halsey, Commander of the Third Fleet in the Pacific.

Stassen stood watch for the Admiral's command with six regular navy officers as the Third Fleet operated in the Western Pacific and China Seas; and he ran the Combat Information Center as the Fleet scouted, pursued, engaged, and finally destroyed Japan's naval forces.

UNITED NATIONS FOUNDING
CONFERENCE IN SAN FRANCISCO

In February 1945, President Roosevelt, remembering Stassen's stirring Gridiron Dinner speech six years earlier, named Stassen to the American delegation to the Founding Conference of the United Nations in San Francisco. Stassen flew to Washington and learned the names of the seven other members of the American delegation: Senator Arthur Vandenberg of Michigan, senior Republican member of the Senate Foreign Relations Committee; Senator Tom Connolly of Texas, Democratic Chairman of that same Committee; Democratic Congressmen Sol Bloom of New York and Republican Charles Eaton of New Jersey, ranking members of the House Foreign Affairs Committee; Edward Stettinius, Secretary of State; Cordell Hull, former Secretary of State and distinguished Senator from Tennessee; and Virginia Gildersleeve, Dean of Barnard College of Columbia University.

On the morning of February 21, 1945, Stassen met with President Roosevelt in the Oval Office to discuss Roosevelt's hopes for insuring peace in the post-war world. Stassen then returned briefly to Pearl Harbor.

Stassen sat in the editorial offices of the *San Francisco Chronicle* giving an interview on how he viewed the upcoming United Nations conference when the April 12 flash came that announced Roosevelt's death. In a matter of days, Truman reappointed the original UN team, and their negotiations began in late April.

At the end of the conference, thirty-seven reporters from all over the world voted Stassen as one of two delegates who made the most effective contributions to the development of the UN Charter; the other was Australian Foreign Minister Herbert V. Evatt. Stassen's tasks included prodding the Russian delegation to sign a Charter acceptable to the rest of the world, working with Molotov and Gromyko.

After signing the United Nations Charter, Stassen rejoined Admiral Halsey's staff aboard the Missouri.

THE JAPANESE SURRENDER

Stassen stood the Admiral's morning watch on the bridge of the *U.S.S. Missouri* on August 12, 1945, and wrote out the Admiral's official log in his own hand:

> Steaming as before. 0804 [R]eceived news flash that President Truman had announced that Japan had accepted surrender terms. Early morning strikes returning and landing at 0840 as directed. 0930 R. Adm. Badger left the ship, transferring to the destroyer Nicholas. 1020 All strikes have returned . . . . 1040 [I]ntercepted the wording of the Jap acceptance note on the San Francisco radio. Notified all hands that Admiral Halsey would broadcast a message to the Fleet at a time to be announced later . . . . 1055 Received Alpoa 579 to cease offensive operations against Japanese Forces . . . . Gave orders to Missouri to break Battle Flags . . . and sound whistle one minute. . . . Whistle & siren sounded for one minute . . . . Admiral Halsey and R. Admiral Carney on the bridge to witness the event. At 1113 the Admiral ordered the Flag Hoist "Well Done" to the Fleet run up. Promptly done. At 1125 one Judy splashed by T g 38.1. 1126 . . . [O]rdered alert . . . . Three bogies tracked. All tallyhoed as friendly. So closes the watch we have been looking forward to. Unconditional surrender of Japan—with Admiral Halsey at sea in command of the greatest combined fighting fleet of all history. There is a gleam in his eye on the bridge that is unmistakable!
>
> H.E. Stassen

[Note: "Strike" means attack force of U.S. planes; "break" means run up and unfurl; "Judy" a Japanese plane; "bogies" blips on radar; "tallyhoed" sighted and recognized.]

OPERATION "BENEVOLENCE"

Stassen left the Missouri temporarily before the formal surrender ceremonies September 2, 1945, to take on a special assignment, the supervision of "Operation Benevolence," the dramatic rescue of American prisoners from the Japanese home islands.

For thirteen days and fourteen nights Stassen and Commodore Roger Simpson supervised the "benevolencing" of 14,000 Americans before he returned to the *Missouri* to take part in the final arrangements for the historic surrender ceremonies on September 2. As the junior officer in an assemblage of one hundred U.S. and Allied generals and admirals, he watched from the deck behind MacArthur.

After winning the Legion of Merit and other commendations, including promotion to captain, Stassen returned to civilian life early in 1946.

THE 1948 RACE FOR PRESIDENT

Stassen announced in 1947 that he would run for the Republican nomination in 1948 as a Progressive Republican. In those distant days, party primaries amounted to little more than screen tests, the real nominations made at party conventions controlled by party "leaders" and "professionals."

Stassen criss-crossed the country—searching for delegates, winning some primaries, losing some. When the Republican convention opened in Philadelphia in July, 1948, the delegate count showed a split among Governor Dewey of New York, Senator Taft of Ohio, and Stassen. The wheeling and dealing in the smoke-filled rooms heated up. Dewey and Taft reached an agreement that gave Dewey the nomination and the party a losing Dewey-Warren ticket.

Dewey's upset by Harry Truman in November taught many Republicans a lesson that carried over to 1952.

THE UNIVERSITY OF PENNSYLVANIA

In August 1948, a committee of trustees of the University of Pennsylvania came to Minnesota to invite Stassen to become president of that prestigious school, founded by Benjamin Franklin. Penn faced serious challenges that the trustees thought could be met only by a strong executive from outside the usual academic ranks.

During his tenure as university president, Stassen became well-acquainted with another Ivy League president, Dwight David Eisenhower of Columbia.

Stassen's Republican party commitments did not slacken during his years at the University of Pennsylvania. In 1950, he gave the closing national address for the Republican congressional campaign. In early 1951, he assembled forty-one national Republican leaders to launch an effort to get Eisenhower to accept the Republican nomination in 1952.

THE RELUCTANT AUTHOR

Over the years, Stassen's reply to his friends who urged him to write of his years with Eisenhower always came out the same: "I am more concerned for the future than with the past. Besides, how can I describe my participation in the crucial events of the Eisenhower programs without sounding self-serving?"

His attitude changed several months ago when a group of us sat around a dinner table with our spouses, remembering law school and fraternity days, talking of "what might have been" in politics.

As always, someone asked about a facet of Stassen's work with Eisenhower. He described, with some prodding, his appointment as the country's only Secretary for Peace, his work as the first disarmament negotiator, the clashes with Secretary of State John Foster Dulles over the Secretary's "brinksmanship" concepts of foreign policy, the real genesis of the 1955 Geneva Summit, and Eisenhower's daring "Open Skies" proposal that Stassen wrote over Dulles' objections.

As one, we pounced on Stassen with our demand: He owed it to posterity to detail his historic experiences in book form because of their continuing relevance to world problems.

He finally agreed.

A NOTE ON FORMAT

His attitudes led us to decide that we would write only about those episodes which we could document from Stassen's own personal files, from the Eisenhower Library in Abilene, and from a few other safe sources.

We also faced the problem of how to handle critical conversations that are this book's personality. Recollections of conversations are always reconstructions—nothing more than summaries—whether placed inside quotation marks or not. Since no verbatim transcripts or tape recordings exist of Stassen's intimate and revealing conversations with Eisenhower, we dare not present them as exact quotes. Rather, we set them in a slightly smaller type size to let the reader know that the words attributed to Eisenhower are paraphrases— Stassen's accurate reconstructions of substance, based on his incredible memory and detailed notes. I can attest to his phenomenal recall.

Chapter 1
Eisenhower for President

In late 1951, the General and I shook hands as we exchanged greetings in the door of his NATO office in Rocquencourt, just outside Paris. Smiling, he motioned me to a chair at the right edge of his desk, while he walked around the other side to his seat.

I recall vividly my exact words in opening the conversation: "General, you should be the next president of the United States. It would be best for future world peace, and best for the national security and economic prosperity of the United States."

During the General's tenure as President of Columbia and mine as President of the University of Pennsylvania, we worked together on a number of Ivy League projects. All nine Ivy League presidents served as governing trustees of the Brookhaven Atomic Laboratory on Long Island, where we evaluated research projects. At other times, our discussions focused on reports of broad interest from the Wharton School of Finance and Commerce, research projects of Harvard Medical School, studies in public administration at the Yale School of Public Service, the new electronic media in journalism at Columbia, or public finance at Princeton. Eisenhower and I often talked together, enjoying each other's outlook. I arranged an appointment to meet him at his Rocquencourt NATO base without difficulty:

1

Supreme Headquarters
Allied Powers Europe
23 August 1951

Dear Governor:

While in Germany, I received both your telegram
[birthday greetings] dated the 15th and your note of the
7th. For both of them, I am grateful.

Of course, when you reach here in December, I shall
be looking forward to seeing you. I hope that you will
find it possible to give my office a few days' advance
notice so that I can reserve a period for a good meeting.

With warm personal regard,

Sincerely,

/s/Dwight D. Eisenhower
23 Aug

Honorable Harold E. Stassen
President
University of Pennsylvania
Philadelphia 4, Pennsylvania

Now, the General served as Supreme Commander of the
North Atlantic Treaty Organization. A row of small flags
stood behind him announcing NATO's membership:
Belgium, Canada, Denmark, France, West Germany, Greece,
Iceland, Italy, Luxembourg, the Netherlands, Norway, Portu-
gal, Turkey, the United Kingdom, and the United States. A
supporting base to his right lifted a much larger stars-and-
stripes toward the ceiling.

Article V of the mutual treaty signed April 4, 1949,
described NATO's chief purpose:

> The Parties agree that an armed attack against one or
> more of them in Europe shall be considered an attack
> against them all and consequently they agree that, if

2

such an armed attack occurs, each of them . . . will assist the Party or Parties so attacked . . . to restore and maintain the security of the North Atlantic area.

He looked at me intently, that boring-in look he used to analyze both a speaker and his words. Without a transcript, I do not presume to quote our conversation verbatim, but I remember its substance:

General, I am well aware that you are on active duty—in uniform—so you cannot engage in a political discussion. I'm not here to ask any questions, or seek any answers. I am here to give you my best analysis of the political situation at home, and to pledge my unconditional support, if a sound program can be worked out to nominate and elect you President next year.

The calendar on his desk read "December 12, 1951," not quite a year since he took over as NATO Supreme Commander, technically SHAPE (Supreme Headquarters Allied Powers Europe). I continued my argument:

Your election as President will provide the world with its best chance for a continuing peace. You have the best prospects to become President of all the people since George Washington; but you will not be elected without a detailed program to bring about your nomination as a Republican.

I stopped, and he replied in his clipped, midwestern staccato. He explained the problems in his tough fight to bring NATO members together in an effective defense force, and his promise to President Truman to see his mission through as long as he felt needed.

I told him that I fully expected this reply and congratulated him on the incredible results already achieved.

3

Eisenhower personally kept NATO from breaking up before it ever came together. Western Europe still ached from Nazi brutalities only six years past. Physical, sociological, psychological, and economic scars of the war disfigured the entire continent. Everyone dreamed of peace, but without the need for additional sacrifice. They prayed for "normalcy," whatever that term could then mean; and the threat of Communist takeovers, country by country, did not arouse the same stimulus for joint defensive action as actual war.

All Western European countries wanted the United States to become Big Brother and supply the bulk of the ground forces needed for defense, as well as money and materials. No nation would even amend its conscription laws to permit tours of military duty for more than one year, barely enough time to teach raw recruits the newer technologies of post-war weaponry. France feared a rearmed Germany, and some in London balked at a strong United States role that would reduce England's international voice. Centuries-old prejudices and rugged nationalism flared on all sides as Europe moved into what many feared would become a new "Dark Ages."

In less than a year, Eisenhower worked out the plan called the European Defense Community that provided control and leadership of NATO's armed forces. The plan included joint strategic planning units, centralized procurement, political liaisons, training schedules, and field maneuvers. It also contemplated a Table of Organization of national divisions merged into international corps and armies under the leadership of a Supreme Commander whose staff came from the member nations.

My argument went on:

> In my opinion, General, you can best be elected President as a Republican, and you can best carry out the policies you believe in as a Republican.

At this stage, no one knew whether Eisenhower considered himself a Republican, Democrat, independent or none of the above; and try as they might, no researcher ever came up with a partisan political statement made by Eisenhower during his more than three decades of active military service.

During the 1948 presidential race, Eisenhower, then president of Columbia University, emphatically removed himself from political consideration by either party, although both made him continuing overtures. James Roosevelt, FDR's eldest son, remembers that he and a number of younger Democrats did not believe that Truman stood a chance of reelection. Rather than see an Old Guard Republican in the White House who would undo all FDR's work, this group delegated to James the task of visiting Eisenhower at Columbia to try to talk him into accepting the joint nomination of both parties if it could be worked out. Eisenhower thanked James, and told him he did not believe such a development possible.

I now talked of 1952:

> Senator Taft, whom I respect, but whose policies I do not agree with, is well in the lead to become the Republican nominee. He opposed the NATO treaty, is basically an isolationist, is considered anti-union and too conservative to ever get into mainstream thinking. In my view, he would likely lose next November, even worse than Dewey lost in 1948.

Eisenhower reached for a pad of paper, picked up a pencil, and started to doodle. I knew this as a good sign from my past associations with him. It meant that he listened intently, shutting out all visual images except his moving hand and the subconscious forms it created on the paper, concentrating only on the oral messages he received and not on the speaker's physical appearance or facial expressions.

I watched the General, his head down, his eyes studying the increasingly rapid motions of his hand, intent on what I said:

> If Taft is the Republican nominee, I will support him for election, as I believe that leaders should be loyal to their political party, but I will do everything I honestly can to prevent his nomination.
>
> Therefore, if you are still in Europe, I will enter the early presidential primaries against Taft. I will engage him on the basic international and domestic issues that are a concern for the future of our country and of world peace.

He never once looked up, his eyes following his moving hand. I must admit to some distraction as I wondered what figures his pencil strokes might be producing.

"I'm not here speaking for myself alone," I said, and I then described in some detail a three-day meeting I had called the past June 17-19, 1951, at the historic "Justice House" estate of Amos J. Peaslee. Peaslee, a lawyer, served as one of my strong supporters in my serious bid for the Republican nomination in 1948.

That meeting brought together forty-one Republican leaders from all across America, among them U.S. Senators Ed Thye of Minnesota and Fred Seaton of Nebraska; Eleanor Todd, Republican leader of New Jersey; Dorothy Peaslee, Swarthmore trustee from Pennsylvania; former governor Huntley Spaulding of New Hampshire; Governor Walter Kohler of Wisconsin; Bernard Shanley, New Jersey lawyer active in national Republican circles; Marjorie Howard, Republican Chairwoman of Minnesota; Republican National Committeeman Webster Todd of New Jersey; Republican National Committeeman William Linnell of Maine; Congressman Walter Judd; Lieutenant Governor Gordon Allott of Colorado; attorney Glen Lloyd of Illinois; Thomas S. Gates of Pennsylvania; and a brilliant young lawyer from Minnesota, Warren Burger.

All of these men and women supported me in my run in 1948. All feared Taft and his pre-war isolationist philosophies and the Old Guard's view of the domestic economy. We all searched for options to prevent our party from withdrawing from the real, post-war world.

We canvassed the question of how we should prepare for the 1952 convention and elections. Some said that I should mount a second all-out campaign for the nomination; a few thought Taft unstoppable and wanted to climb aboard his bandwagon in the hope that they could sway him to modernize his views.

Eisenhower's name generated more discussion than any other. Some opted for an early endorsement of his candidacy, some feared that he might jerk the rug from under them by taking himself out of the race, still others seriously worried whether a career military man without political experience should become president at all.

Our talks emphasized both foreign and domestic policy and finally brought this consensus: Taft could not beat a moderate Democrat because of his far-right views. But if General Eisenhower could be nominated instead of Taft, he would win the election in November and carry enough senators and congressmen with him to give the Republicans control of Congress. He could then put through sound, forward-looking domestic policies, strip away fat and corruption grown dangerous under the Democrats, and keep the United States from withdrawing into isolationism.

We realized that Eisenhower's continued statements that he wanted to stay entirely out of politics complicated the picture. They came from his sincere wish to return to civilian life, whether to go back to Columbia which held his university

7

presidency open for him, or to settle into the life of a gentleman farmer at Gettysburg, teach in a small college, perhaps write, but keep himself available for consultations in Washington on matters of defense.

Our group decided that because of my earlier work with Eisenhower, I should go to Paris to encourage him to run as a Republican, and to assure him of our support if he would consider running.

We studied the Gallup and other polls state-by-state, and concluded that Taft, now proudly wearing the title "Mr. Republican," might already hold so many commitments from Republican county and state chairmen around the country that it would be too late to prevent his first-ballot nomination in Chicago next July, even if we could get Eisenhower to indicate a willingness to run at an early date.

In those pre-television days, preferential presidential primaries contributed little to the candidate's ultimate party nomination. Many considered them only showcases for the radio and newsprint media, even though they could give a candidate his early public exposure, test his poise under pressure, and gain him name recognition while he won votes of questionable value.

Only a handful of states actually held primaries, and the end results of delegate selection varied widely. Some states did not even bind the delegates to a first-ballot convention vote for the candidate to whom they pledged support during the primary race. Some required delegates to vote for the candidate on the first ballot, but afterward the delegates could race off in any direction they chose. Others came to the convention bound to the candidate they supported in the primary until he released them.

If a single candidate garnered all the delegates in all the state primaries and held them when the convention voting started, his total would come to less than twenty percent of what he needed to be nominated.

"Nominating convention" meant exactly that; and over eighty percent of the delegates came from the "regular," "professional" party organizations in the precincts, wards, counties, and states. Instead of spending untold millions during years of pre-convention campaigning as happens today, the 1952 candidates of both parties and their supporters worked the county and state party organizations to get pledges of votes at the parties' conventions in July and August.

This gave the conventions great drama; they were real contests not decided until the final roll call when one candidate gathered enough votes to win the nomination. Television brought about the present-day emphasis on the primaries, with the comparative decline of the nominating role of the political organizations.

The year 1952 gave us our first TV convention, with gavel-to-gavel coverage and the pundit commentators in their crude boxes above the milling mobs of delegates.

That was the background of my December 12, 1951, meeting with Eisenhower.

I think the rest of our conference can best be reported by an eighteen-page letter I sent Eisenhower on December 15, handwritten on Hotel de Crillon stationery. I found the original in the Eisenhower Library in Abilene after his death.

Dear General:—

It was grand to see you! Your remarkable accomplishment in one year in Western Europe is thrilling to note and an inspiration to observe.

I am writing this forthright letter to you because I believe it is desirable that you have this specific information as 1952 begins. Of course no reply is expected nor appropriate.

9

First of all, it is my intention upon my return to America to state to the press that I consider from my personal observations before and now that you have performed a near-miracle in the one year progress you have made in developing the morale and the defense of Western Europe. I will say further that the American people owe you another debt of gratitude for this additional chapter in your unparalelled [sic] career of service.

I will decline to answer all questions about our discussions on the grounds that it was a personal visit, similar to others I have had in times past with other leading personalities such as Churchill, MacArthur, Atlee [sic], Hoover, and that I have never felt that it was right to report such personal discussions.

In response to their questions of my own intent I will say that I will confer with my key friends and announce my decision before the 1st of the year.

In meeting with my friends and in meeting with Tom Dewey and Cabot Lodge or others of their group, I will likewise state that I do not consider that I should attempt to report to them on our personal conversations.

I believed it best that they receive their own information from him. I learned later that U.S. Senator Henry Cabot Lodge of Massachusetts had paid Eisenhower a visit similar to mine the preceding September, urging him to run for president as a Republican. Lodge, the grandson and namesake of Woodrow Wilson's bitter nemesis in the fight for U.S. entry into the old League of Nations, himself served two Senate terms (1937-44, 1947-52), his second reelection loss coming in November, 1952, to John F. Kennedy. My letter continued:

But I will tell them on a confidential basis my analysis of the total situation and my own intended course of action.

I will say that I am convinced, from everything I have noted for years, that you will not become a "seeker" after the Republican nomination for the Presidency, that you will not enter personally into a prolonged contest versus Taft for that nomination, that to do so would be contrary to the very quality of service to country without seeking which people have much admired in you, that the further question of whether or not you would respond to an authoritative draft to be the nominee could only be conclusively answered if and when the circumstances of such an authoritative or agreed draft took place.

I will also say to them that in my judgment, based on my overall observations, you would not lay aside your present large responsibility of leadership unless there was a direct and clear call to greater responsibility or unless the present European-American task had been discharged in its major aspects, that under the present circumstances in Europe and the present adverse attitude of Taft, neither of these two conditions can be anticipated within the next ninety days and the situation thereafter is problematized.

During our conversation, I did get an indirect encouraging statement from the General. He believed that NATO's progress would permit him to return to the United States in early or mid-1952. He wanted to make this move, and would urge the other member nations and President Truman to name General Alfred Gruenther, his deputy commander, Supreme NATO Commander. This hope to "come home," he said, stemmed from personal reasons, not political ones, perhaps a twinge of homesickness. Certainly he did not want to stay at the NATO post too long. In any position of leadership,

11

new faces must be presented from time to time, with new styles and approaches to the tasks remaining.

I will say further that in my judgment Taft is making headway as the sole affirmative "seeking" candidate, and that unless he is met and countered promptly he quite likely will be the Republican nominee, that in my judgment he would have the poorest chance of beating President Truman, that I feel that Truman's defeat is important for the sake of the country, and that while I would support Taft versus Truman if nominated as the better of the two, I fear that he (Taft) would not be a good president, especially not in foreign policy matters.

I will tell them that under this estimate of the situation I will give my approval to my friends entering my candidacy in the various states and I will actively campaign on the basis of the constructive measures of foreign and domestic policy in which I sincerely believe.

I will make it clear that in beginning such a campaign it will be an all out campaign, that I do not believe it could be effective on any other basis, that I have not made and will not make any commitment to withdraw from the race under any given circumstances, that I will not pose as a standard bearer for anyone else, nor permit myself to be labelled as a stalking horse, but will campaign on my own feet for my own beliefs, and that this in my judgment is the right and wise course for all concerned.

Presumably this decision of mine will result in a head-on clash with Taft in Wisconsin, and perhaps also in Illinois and Ohio and other states, as I am convinced he cannot be permitted to be completely secure in his best territory while he concentrates on adding new territory. Thus I will have to try to keep him partially busy in his territory while I work hard to defeat him in the key battlegrounds such as the Wisconsin April 1st primary. He may also enter Minnesota as he has won over the National Committeeman, Roy Dunn, of my home state.

During our conference, one of the strongest points I tried to make covered Senator Taft's lead with party "professionals" and my fear that he could sew up the nomination long before convention time. I wanted to be sure that Eisenhower, in his removed seat in Europe and something of a novice in political maneuvering, appreciated Taft's threat:

> In that event the Minnesota primary battle on March 18th will also be important.

> I will say to them that this course of action by me and by my supporters can have one of three major alternative results:

> 1. It may be found that my strength is inadequate to overcome Taft's lead and he may move on through to the nomination with bandwagon psychology.
> 2. I may dent his support and slow him down and develop a preconvention stalemate along with Earl Warren, and native sons, and with support reserved for you in New York, Kansas and other states, in which event an overwhelming draft of you, or someone else who had not been in the heat of the struggle may take place.

> If this alternative develops and you then decide to accept the draft I am confident that you will be elected and will be a superb president and I will be very happy with this result.

> 3. I may decisively defeat Taft in the key states and move on to build sufficient strength for my own nomination.

I considered the possibility remote that I could defeat Taft, and feared that I might not even slow him down enough to deprive him of a first-ballot nomination. I hoped that I could make Eisenhower see the need for some early hint that he would accept the Republican nomination if offered. I certainly did not expect an all-out declaration of availability, but when I returned home, I hoped to encourage enough "favorite sons" to hold the votes of their own states to throw the convention into an initial deadlock so that Eisenhower might win on later ballots:

> As these events unfold I will maintain a liason [sic] to Tom Dewey and Cabot Lodge. <u>I will also be available at any time to personally discuss any phase of the developments with you if your circumstances change so that you wish to talk again with me.</u>
>
> I will at all times make clear my high regard for you and for your accomplishment for the country and also my own freedom from any private commitments.
>
> In view of the peculiarities of the laws of various states, some of which do not require the consent of the proposed nominee, and the requirements of the overall campaign tactics, it may develop that both our names are in the same primary. I hope that this does not occur, but it may nevertheless do so. I would anticipate that your name would lead any such primary and would intend to continue to express my high regard for you during such primary.
>
> The issues which I intend to stress are inflation and sound money, integrity and honesty in government, mutual respect between economic, social, and racial groups in our country, and an effective affirmative dynamic foreign policy.
>
> It will be my intention to write to you again when significant developments occur.

In the meantime may I close with a word of enthusiastic commendation and admiration for your superb leadership and for your solid contribution to the future of our country and to the cause of freedom!

Sincerely,

/s/Harold E. Stassen

Eisenhower's personal diary, also at Abilene, contains this entry of December 21, 1951:

With reference to the Stassen visit, I intended to summarize the account he gave to me. He has done that himself in the form of a note which I have just received. It is contained in my correspondence files under his name.

The letter shows how my analysis turned into a soliloquy. The General continued to doodle, looking up only when I stopped speaking. I do not remember exactly how he phrased his noncommittal response as we both stood, but it left me with mixed feelings about the interview. His future plans remained a riddle, and I sensed that he sincerely did not want to enter the presidential fray.

I do remember my words as I reached the door. I turned and called back: "General, I said at the beginning that I did not intend to ask you any questions, and I haven't. But I would like your permission to ask just one."

He looked hard at me, and I continued before he could speak. "That Guildhall speech you made in London in 1945—was that genuine Eisenhower? Did you actually write it yourself, or did you have help? What is the real story in the development of that speech?" He smiled, the famous grin spreading ear-to-ear, and walked up and down behind his desk, as though suddenly released from confinement. This is the substance of his answer:

That speech is genuine me. When I knew they would give me that great honor, I also knew that they would want a speech. It would be my first formal address of any consequence, outside of my reports or statements as ETO commander. I took a yellow, lined tablet and began working on the speech. I'd take it to bed with me and fall asleep working on it. I wasn't exactly a raw recruit at writing speeches, having written many for my War Department superiors to deliver over at least two decades; but I wanted this one to be a full cut above anything else I'd ever done. I worked and reworked the thing for weeks, and finally gave it to some of my staff to check for grammar and sentence structure, and particularly to see if it could be cut any place to shorten it, without doing damage to what I really wanted to say. By the time I got ready to deliver it in Guildhall, I knew the damned thing by heart.

Let me add that I think the Guildhall speech ranks as one of the great English language feats. It will never achieve the honored status of Lincoln's Gettysburg address, but it stands in that select category. I include it as Appendix 1.

A car with a GI driver picked up my wife Esther and me in front of the Crillon at 7:15 to take us to dine with the Eisenhowers. A light rain slowed traffic to a bumper-to-bumper creep. We wondered how all the cars could sprout in only six short years since the war and where the gas came from to run them. It took an hour to reach the Villa St. Pierre in Marnes-la-Coquette, where Mamie Eisenhower personally met us at the door, her own smile as broad and warm as her husband's.

Esther recalls that Mamie wore a chic, black silk dress, with one or two pieces of simple jewelry to highlight it. She led us into the Louis XIV drawing room where we shook hands with the General, in civilian clothes, and she introduced us to Averell and Mrs. Harriman. We both knew Averell from University functions in New York, but not his wife.

On the way in, Esther noticed a painting on the right wall and asked: "Isn't that one of yours?"

Mamie answered for her husband. "Yes. He just finished it a couple of months ago, and it's already my favorite." I chatted with Mamie and the Harrimans while Esther and the General returned to the painting, an oil landscape of the Bavarian Alps. She remembers that Eisenhower talked about his problems in getting the proper shadings of the light as it slanted across staggered rows of mountains of varying heights. Esther, an accomplished artist with many exhibitions to her credit including one at the Smithsonian, sympathized, adding that she often found it necessary to return to her landscape scenes at the same time of day to get a better feel for the shading, but it did not always work. Different cloud formations could come in to change the lighting.

At dinner, Esther sat on the General's right, with Averell Harriman on her right, I across the table at Mamie's right and Mrs. Harriman between the General and me. We remember the evening as a total delight: one couple of active Democrats, another of Republicans, and one undeclared. We worked over the great issues of the day, carefully avoiding the slightest hint of partisan politics.

Esther and I talked guardedly during the ride back to Paris. She and I can reconstruct accurately our conversation when we reached our room at the Crillon and began to prepare for bed. "I think Averell Harriman is here to urge General Eisenhower to run for president as a Democrat," Esther said.

"I agree, but what makes you say so?"

"Because he told me that he has a personal conference scheduled with Eisenhower for tomorrow, and the way he questioned me at dinner. He wanted to know why we were here, and why you spent time with Eisenhower earlier in the day. He tried to be casual, but he was trying to get information from me. I'm sure that's what he's trying to do."

"What did you tell him about my conference with Eisenhower?"

"I said that we were on a European trip, and that you wanted to line up Eisenhower to give the commencement address at Pennsylvania next June."

I smiled. No man ever had a more perceptive, helpful wife, one whose intuitions almost always proved true.

"What else did Harriman say?"

She smiled. "Averell asked me if I knew whether Eisenhower was a Republican or a Democrat. I said I could not remember him ever making anything that could be termed a partisan statement." Esther then showed her skill by turning the question back to Harriman. We knew that during Eisenhower's presidency at Columbia, he prevailed upon Harriman to give the historic Harriman House up the Hudson to Columbia. It served as a retreat for seminars and conferences for select audiences, as well as faculty study groups. They called some of these events "American Assembly Sessions."

"I asked Averell," she continued, "if he ever heard Eisenhower make a partisan political statement at any of the meetings at the Harriman House. He parried and said that he did not attend those sessions, except to welcome the first one. He claimed he was always too busy with other matters to attend anything else at the House."

Years later, I learned that the following morning Averell Harriman did try to persuade Eisenhower to run for President in '52 as a Democrat, and reported his December 13 conference to President Truman, who wrote (in longhand) his unprecedented letter of December 18, 1951, asking the General to declare his political intentions:

THE WHITE HOUSE
WASHINGTON   Dec. 18th 1951.

Dear Ike:—The columnists, the slick magazines and all the political people, who like to speculate are saying many things about what is to happen in 1952.

As I told you in 1948 and at our luncheon in 1951, do what you think best for the country. My own position is in the balance. If I do what I want to do, I'll go back to Missouri and <u>maybe</u> run for the Senate. If you decide to finish the European job, (and I don't know who else can), I must keep the isolationists out of the White House. I wish you would let me know what you intend to do. It will be between us and no one else.

I have the utmost confidence in your judgement [sic] and your patriotism.

My best to you and Mrs. Ike for a happy holiday season.

Most sincerely,

/s/Harry Truman

General of the Army,
Dwight D. Eisenhower,
Paris, France.

Eisenhower waited until New Year's Day, 1952, to work out his reply. Like Truman, he made no definite commitments and kept his options open:

January 1, 1952

Dear Mr. President:

Your letter of December 18 was delayed in transit, not reaching me until the 28th. At that moment I was intensively engaged in an effort to spur our European friends into developing an acceptable plan for a European Army as well as, eventually, some form of European political Union. All this explains the time required for my answer to reach you. I am deeply touched by the confidence in me you express, even more by that implied in the writing of such a letter by the President of the United States. It breathes your anxious concern for our country's future.

Part of my answer must almost paraphrase your own language where you say, "If I do what I want to do . . ." There has never been any change in my personal desires and aspirations, publicly and privately expressed, over the past six years or so. I'd like to live a semi-retired life with my family, given over mainly to the study of, and a bit of writing on, present day trends and problems with a little dirt farming thrown in on the side. But just as you have decided that circumstances may not permit you to do exactly as you please, so I've found that fervent desire may sometimes have to give way to a conviction of duty. For example—I'm again on military duty and in a foreign country!

Now, I do not feel that I have any duty to seek a political nomination, in spite of the fact that many have urged to the contrary. Because of this belief I shall not do so. Moreover, to engage in this kind of activity while on my present military assignment would encourage partisan thinking in our country toward a project of the utmost importance to the nation as a whole. (Incidentally it would be in direct violation of Army Regulations.) So I shall keep still in all this struggle for personal position in a political party. Of course, a number of people know of my belief that any group of American citizens has a right to fight, politically, for any set of principles in which its members believe and to attempt to draft a leader to head the fight!

Because of these beliefs and because particularly of my determination to remain silent you know, far better than I, that the possibility that I will ever be drawn into political activity is so remote as to be negligible. This policy of complete abstention will be meticulously observed by me unless and until extraordinary circumstances would place a mandate upon me that, by common consent, would be deemed a duty of transcendent importance.

This answer is as full and frank as I am able to devise and I would be very regretful if you thought it otherwise. But when one attempts to discuss such important abstractions as a sense of duty applied to unforseen [sic] circumstances of the future neither brevity nor arbitrary pronouncement seems wholly applicable.

This note brings to you and yours, from Mamie and me, our best wishes for a happy and prosperous 1952. To you personally, my continued esteem and regard.

Respectfully,

/s/ DWIGHT D. EISENHOWER

[original handwritten]

Truman's associates reported that the President, beaten at his own wily game, fumed at this standoff he could not control even though he ranked as Eisenhower's commander-in-chief. Eisenhower, for his part, simply sat back to await developments, this a strange posture for the Supreme Allied Commander of World War II, a man who intuitively preferred forceful action.

Chapter 2
The Republican Nomination

On my return from Europe, five of my key political supporters, Warren Burger, Ambassador Amos Peaslee, Congressman Elmer Ryan, businessman Dan Gainey, and Bernard Shanley, met me at the McAlpin Hotel in New York. At that time, Burger maintained his substantial law practice in Minnesota, Shanley his in New Jersey. Both men supported me vigorously in my bid for the nomination in '48; both maintained influential contacts in national Republican circles; and both participated in the earlier meeting I called at Amos Peaslee's New Jersey estate where we planned my visit with Eisenhower.

I told them I thought the General *would* accept the Republican nomination, but we faced two major hurdles.

In the first place, I doubted that Eisenhower appreciated the momentum of the bandwagon already rolling for Senator Taft. Eisenhower's laid-back posture of doing nothing affirmative to win the nomination could prove disastrous. Gallup polls showed that Taft already held commitments from a majority of Republican chairmen and workers all across the country.

Secondly, because of Eisenhower's active military status and his commitments to NATO, he would not be able to make any partisan political statements until after his return to the States and his retirement from the army, no earlier than June, 1952. This meant that for all practical purposes, Taft's speeches and statements on domestic and foreign policy would go unchallenged. Merely entering the General's name in the state primaries would not automatically win him the nomination, even though the American people loved and respected him.

We agonized in my hotel room for several hours over our staggering challenge—we must devise a strategy to slow Taft's bandwagon and prevent his first-ballot nomination at the Republican convention in Chicago in July.

We decided that I should become Taft's main challenger in the primaries, but to do this effectively, I would need to be an actual candidate, or no one would listen to my arguments. At the same time, I dared not launch a totally negative, anti-Taft attack. For the past five national elections, Republicans gained the label of being "against everything," the "negative thinkers." I must speak affirmatively.

Nor, as I told Eisenhower in Paris, could I sound an effective voice if it appeared that I served only as his stalking horse until he could be released from his military service. I would say nothing unfavorable about Eisenhower. When questioned, I would respond that yes, I thought he would make a fine President; but I needed to keep my efforts completely independent of those who openly supported the General.

We devised the special strategy whereby I would file as a candidate in New Hampshire, but would not enter a slate of delegates. This would give me bona fide entree into the state to speak, but since I did not seek a slate of pledged delegates, this would not sap strength from the Eisenhower slate that we anticipated Governor Sherman Adams would enter and head.

I would not enter New Hampshire as an unknown outsider, but would come with substantial clout. I won delegates away from the Dewey steamroller in 1948. A number of my supporters, including former governors Spaulding and Blood,

24

urged me to let them rally a full slate of delegates in the belief that I could do even better in 1952. They considered Taft a far more likely winner in March than Eisenhower, but a disaster in November.

The preceding month, Governor Thomas Dewey, loser as the Republican candidate against Roosevelt in '44 and Truman in '48, called a meeting of professionals in his suite in the Roosevelt Hotel. Dewey, Senator Henry Cabot Lodge of Massachusetts, and Herbert Brownell, a prominent New York lawyer and braintruster in Dewey's political activities for the past two decades, established themselves as coordinators for the Eisenhower campaign for President, with Lodge as its chairman.

Knowing that I must remain totally independent to be an effective debater against Taft, I named Burger and Shanley as my liaison contacts with the Dewey-Lodge-Brownell committee so they could understand our strategy and see that our plans meshed.

Events began to move feverishly after the first of the year. On January 7, General Lucius Clay and Cabot Lodge announced that General Eisenhower voted Republican in 1948 during his brief retirement from the army while president of Columbia. Senator Taft entered his name and a slate of delegates in the New Hampshire primary to be held March 11. Governor Sherman Adams did the same for Eisenhower, exactly as we anticipated.

On January 29, 1952, I entered the New Hampshire presidential primary, then the first to be held, *but did not file a slate of delegates.*

Another factor influenced my New Hampshire strategy. In 1948, I stumped the state on behalf of the reelection of Republican Senator Styles Bridges, a good friend whom I admired. The Taft people now hounded Bridges to declare his support for Taft, a fellow senator, and felt confident they

25

would get it. I hoped that my entry would help prompt Bridges to stay neutral, which he did. Although I do not claim the entire credit for keeping him inactive, observers told me afterward that Bridges wavered until he learned of my filing.

Shortly after my entrance into New Hampshire, I received a call at my office at the University of Pennsylvania from Cabot Lodge, concerned that my entry into New Hampshire would weaken Eisenhower's chances by drawing off independent and liberal voters, which could give the primary victory to Taft. I explained in considerable detail the rationale of my strategy, and reminded Cabot that Burger and Shanley presented it to the Dewey-Lodge-Brownell committee in advance.

Lodge replied that after reviewing the situation as of that day, the committee thought it best that I withdraw and openly pledge my support for Eisenhower. I repeated my position that I could not really debate Taft on the major issues without being a bona fide candidate on my own; but Cabot never really appreciated the distinction of my being in New Hampshire as a candidate, but a candidate without a slate of delegates.

Our conversation ended without rancor, but I did not feel comfortable with Lodge's reaction. Accordingly, I wrote to him:

February 22, 1952

Hon. Henry Cabot Lodge, Jr.
United States Senator
Senate Office Building
Washington, D. C.

Dear Cabot:

Supplementing our telephone conversation upon your call last week, I am writing to confirm the reasons for the entry of my name in the Presidential Preference Primary in New Hampshire, and the non-entry of a delegate slate.

It is, and has been, my appraisal since mid-December, that General Eisenhower did not intend to sign any primary election forms and did not intend to personally engage in any way in a pre-convention campaign versus Senator Taft. It has been, and is, my judgment that under these circumstances, if I stayed out of the race Senator Taft would win the nomination through immediately solidifying Wisconsin, Illinois, Ohio, and many other states and building up his early commitments as the only active candidate in the field. I consider that he (Taft) has the poorest chance of defeating President Truman, and I sincerely differ with him on foreign policy. Thus, while I will support him if he is the nominee, I cannot in good conscience resign to his leadership unless he is nominated.

Having decided to run, I consider that I can run only as a genuine candidate for the nomination, without commitments to any other candidates.

Having decided to run, the Wisconsin Primary on April 1st with a statewide test versus Senator Taft's slate of thirty delegates became a crucial contest. All preceding events then must be evaluated in relationship to that primary.

If I remained entirely out of the New Hampshire Primary there would be three especially undesirable factors that would prevail in so far as the Wisconsin Primary is concerned.

1. I would have great difficulty in shaking off the "stalking horse" charge since I had been in the New Hampshire Primary in 1948 and I am now entered in all the difficult Midwest Primaries versus Senator Taft.

2. A small number of New Hampshire voters would nevertheless write in my name and the unfriendly

section of the press could then claim that I only had blank number of supporters in the entire state. This would further weaken me for April 1st in Wisconsin.

3. My name would tend to be dropped from national stories, cartoons, and comment in the period leading up to the New Hampshire Primary. I have a difficult enough time in this respect in any event.

On the other hand, I felt that if I entered a delegate slate it would assist the Taft delegates and handicap the Eisenhower slate of my friend, Governor Adams. This I did not wish to do. Consequently, even though my position is weakened by not having a delegate slate to help in my local New Hampshire campaign, I decided to take the present course. It was not an easy decision. No really desirable alternative appeared, and my own key friends were divided in their judgment.

I write you thus frankly so that you will have the definite basis of my decision, since after all we are all part of the same ultimate Republican effort intent on the defeat of the Truman administration and the more we understand each other in the meantime, the better it will be.

I am sending a copy of this letter to Tom Dewey and Lucius Clay.

Sincerely,

/s/Harold E. Stassen

HES/L

cc: Hon. Thomas E. Dewey
General Lucius D. Clay

bcc: General Dwight D. Eisenhower

Years later in the Eisenhower Library at Abilene, I found the blind copy of this February 22 letter that I sent to the General. His handwriting in the upper right-hand corner reads "McCann has seen. DDE" (Kevin McCann served as Eisenhower's aide on public affairs.)

I crisscrossed New Hampshire the next several weeks debating Taft, advancing the affirmative premise that World War II changed the world and the United States' position in it.

As Charles Brereton described it in *First in the Nation: New Hampshire and the Premier Presidential Primary* (page 15):

> The former three-term governor of Minnesota, Harold Stassen, . . . was stumping the state; he soon began playing the role of inquisitor of Taft's foreign policy record, which included his 1949 votes against the North Atlantic Treaty Organization and the rebuilding of postwar Europe.(Portsmouth, N.H.: Peter E. Randall, 1987)

I did not call Taft a *total* isolationist, but he certainly dragged his feet in accepting the reality of the international situation. He opposed the NATO concept and did not want any American troops stationed on European soil or committed to the defense of Europe against Communist attack. He did not believe the Marshall Plan would rehabilitate Europe, looked with great suspicion on Europe's post-war leaders, and shunned any hint of a program to reach out to the USSR in an effort to warm the Cold War.

On domestic policy, labor and labor unions considered him their archenemy. During the original debates on the Taft-Hartley Act, he fought hard to include the right of employers to use the injunction to prevent and break strikes. I testified against the injunction provisions from my background of the ten-year-old Labor Peace Act in Minnesota that I put through in my first term as governor. The injunction provision did not end up in the final Taft-Hartley Act.

Taft also advocated an immediate tax reduction and the overnight lifting of all price and wage controls imposed during the Korean War, a move that I argued the economy could not stand without a disastrous period of runaway inflation.

In early March, Taft's lead in the polls prompted Cabot Lodge to issue a hedging, protective statement to the press: "A Taft win in New Hampshire would not be a complete disaster for the Eisenhower candidacy. After all, the General's other important duties which prevented him from personally campaigning in the state would make a big difference."

Taft decided that an intense final drive throughout the state would doom Eisenhower's candidacy nationwide, once and for all. He began a final twenty-eight city tour. With the blessings of the Penn trustees, I dropped everything and matched him city-for-city, speech-for-speech. For the first time, Taft lashed out at Eisenhower, as the Manchester *Union Leader* reported:

> [H]e inquired if General Eisenhower would be willing to "make an all-out attack upon the administration, of which he has been a part, for the disastrous results (of its foreign policy), the loss of China and the 100,000 American casualties in Korea?" Turning to corruption in government, Taft asked if General "Ike", in view of his close association with the present and previous Democratic administrations, and the constant advancement "he has received from them," would feel inclined to "present that issue in the perspective and with the force it deserves."

I avoided personal attacks on Taft, even though I thought his bitterness toward Eisenhower a serious political mistake. My main theme continued to be that World War II changed the entire world. No matter how we wished it, we could not return to the precepts of the '20s and '30s, either at home or abroad.

The March 11 result proved gratifying. Eisenhower received 46,671 popular votes to Taft's 35,838. Eisenhower won every delegate; Taft did not win a single one.

Minnesota's primary came March 18. Of course, I entered a slate of delegates in my home state, but opposition developed. Roy Dunn, Republican National Committeeman, declared for Taft and entered a slate of Taft delegates.

Eisenhower did not appear on the ballot as a candidate; but Bradshaw Mintener began a well-financed write-in campaign for him, without filing a slate of delegates. I did not oppose the write-in in any way. I received pressure from both inside and outside the state to withdraw and declare my support for Eisenhower, but I held firm in my belief that I could best help him by formally remaining in the race as an independent candidate and debating Taft.

I received all of Minnesota's twenty-eight delegates with my 120,000 votes, but over 108,000 voters spelled "Eisenhower" a dozen different ways, demonstrating his popularity with the public even though he was on active military duty 6,000 miles away. This Minnesota vote was a substantial psychological boost to his candidacy.

The Wisconsin primary came next on April 1, and for reasons that I still do not understand, the Dewey-Lodge-Brownell committee urged California Governor Earl Warren, Dewey's running mate for Vice President in 1948, to enter. Through Burger and Shanley, I suggested that the better strategy would be to let me take on Taft alone in this state abutting Minnesota; but Warren entered. The result proved a disappointing six delegates for Warren and twenty-four for Taft.

The primary battles see-sawed back and forth, Taft winning Nebraska, Illinois, Ohio and West Virginia; Eisenhower taking Oregon and New Jersey; Taft maintaining a strong delegate lead.

During these weeks, I maintained contact with Republican leaders around the country, urging them to stand fast for their favorite sons in Chicago, principally Governors Earl Warren of California, Theodore McKeldin of Maryland, and John Fine of Pennsylvania.

On April 11, the White House announced that General Eisenhower, at his own request, would be relieved of his duties as NATO Commander June 1, returned home, and retired without pay. Coincidentally this would be the same day as the primary in South Dakota, the last before the convention. This gave me an opportunity to write to General Eisenhower at SHAPE on April 14, bring him up to date on my activities, apprise him of the delegate situation, and caution him on Taft's strength. (See Appendix 2.)

Cabot Lodge told Bernard Shanley and Warren Burger that he thought it best for me to stay out of South Dakota so that Eisenhower could finish the primary circuit with a strong victory. Burger and Shanley protested, saying that some of my staunchest supporters lived in South Dakota, also Minnesota's next-door neighbor. South Dakota remained strongly isolationist; its people held to a rugged individualism that loathed "big government." They would consider Taft a stronger link to their heritage than Eisenhower, even with the General's Kansas background, and it would be a strategic error to assume that Eisenhower could win simply on his name alone, without anyone to challenge Taft on the issues.

I stayed out of South Dakota, despite my analysis of the situation. Taft swept the state and all its delegates. As convention time approached, it looked like Taft might well win a first-ballot nomination.

With political conventions today little more than TV spectaculars, it is hard to remember the drama and excitement of traditional conventions in those days. Unless an incumbent President sought renomination, the choice of the candidate remained up for grabs until the voting started, and deadlocked conventions requiring a half-dozen or more ballots happened frequently. For a great segment of the American public, the conventions offered as much entertainment as the World Series. Radio newsmen and print journalists speculated on who would be the nominee, and professional gamblers gave odds. For two weeks in summer every four years, the center of the world became the Republican and Democratic conventions.

When the 1952 Republican convention opened in the Chicago Stockyards Arena July 8, it looked like another of those fierce battles that could end in deadlock and possibly require several ballots to resolve, provided Senator Taft could not win on the first.

With 1206 delegates to be seated, it would take 604 to win. Our best count showed Taft with 530 delegates (458 firmly seated and 72 contested and temporarily seated). Eisenhower's count stood at 427: 406 uncontested and 21 contested. Taft needed fewer than 100 delegates to reach the magic 604.

We recognized that the final result might well turn on the votes in the Credentials Committee that would recommend the seating of the contested delegates, the principal disputes being the Texas, Louisiana and Georgia delegations.

I named Warren Burger as Minnesota's representative on the Credentials Committee; and his fine work with the California, Washington, New Jersey, and Maryland delegations resulted in a fair split of those contested delegations, which kept Taft from virtually cinching the nomination.

The fight within the Texas delegation illustrates the problems and the final solution. In early party caucuses in Texas, Eisenhower won slates of delegates, but regular party professionals called the results illegal on the grounds that Democrats had invaded the Republican precincts. In effect, they said, Democrats elected the delegates to the Republican convention.

Before the convention opened, the National Committee voted to give Taft twenty-two Texas delegates and Eisenhower sixteen. Lodge, acting on Burger's suggestion, rejected this result. He hoped to get a change in convention rules when the convention itself took up the matter of seating its delegates.

The first major order of business the convention faced, of course, concerned the delegate contests. Governor Arthur Langlie of Washington introduced what came to be called the "Fair Play Amendment," which provided that the convention as a whole (not just the National Committee) must vote on all contested delegations, but *no contested delegate could vote on any of the contests unless put on the temporary roll by a vote of more than two-thirds of the National Committee.*

The Taft forces saw the amendment as a vehicle to take votes away from Taft and vigorously opposed it. The Eisenhower supporters rallied the "favorite-sons" and all non-committed delegates and the amendment passed by over a hundred votes. The result gave Eisenhower the Georgia delegates, eleven from Louisiana, and all of the Texas delegates pledged to Eisenhower in the caucuses. More important, the vote on this "Fair Play Amendment" really decided the nomination. When the Georgia delegation question came before the convention, Warren Burger made the closing address to the convention on the motion that decided in favor of the Eisenhower delegates.

I arrived at my suite in the Blackstone Hotel July 5, the Saturday before the convention opened. I kept in constant contact with Burger, Bernard Shanley, and Dan Gainey who would serve with Burger as my convention floor managers, as well as Senator Ed Thye who headed the Minnesota delegation and hundreds of other leading Republicans from all over the country. By the time the balloting started, we knew surprisingly well what delegates intended to do on the first ballot, the strength of their pledges, and what they might do if a second ballot became necessary. As it turned out, our head count proved eerily accurate.

In today's TV spectaculars, the roll call by states bores most viewers, and they change channels or walk away. In 1952, the entire country sat spellbound as Katherine Howard, the tall, angular GOP secretary from Massachusetts, called "Alabama!"

In my room at the Blackstone, I kept a running count of the voting. When she received the Massachusetts report, I telephoned Bernard Shanley, who answered a special phone installed at his seat on the Stockyards balcony. From his perch high above the smoke-filled area below, he could see the Minnesota delegation and be seen by them. I told him that the delegate count to that point matched our predictions exactly, that while Taft then led Eisenhower 196-166, Minnesota's delegation could cinch Eisenhower's nomination on the first ballot.

By prearrangement Shanley flashed Burger our "thumbs up" sign so that Burger and Thye could signal Chairman Joseph Martin for recognition after the roll call ended, but before Martin announced the first ballot tally to the delegates. Burger made this arrangement with Martin before the balloting started.

When Katherine Howard reached "Minnesota," Senator Thye announced "Nineteen votes for Harold Stassen, nine votes for General Eisenhower."

The vote split in my own Minnesota delegation arose because several delegates became impatient to climb aboard the Eisenhower bandwagon early, too eager to wait for us to execute our plan for the dramatic ending by giving Minnesota recognition for putting Eisenhower over the top. In politics the name of the game is to board the right train early.

The roll call finished, the vote stood at 595 for Eisenhower, 500 for Taft. Eisenhower needed only nine more votes to win on the first ballot. Media commentators told the public to get ready for the second ballot. Pages 399-400 of the official convention report tell the rest of the story:

> THE PERMANENT CHAIRMAN.—The Convention will come to order.
>
> The Chair has been asked to recognize the delegate from Minnesota.
>
> SENATOR EDWARD J. THYE of Minnesota.—Mr. Chairman, Minnesota wishes to change its vote to Eisenhower. (Applause, loud and prolonged.)
>
> THE PERMANENT CHAIRMAN.—The Convention will please come to order.
>
> What is the vote from Minnesota?
>
> SENATOR THYE of Minnesota.—Minnesota casts its 28 votes for Eisenhower. (Applause and demonstration.) *(Official Report of the Proceedings of the Twenty-fifth Republican National Convention* [Washington, D.C.: Republican National Committee, 1952])

The delegates exploded!

I rushed upstairs to Eisenhower's suite to congratulate him, but learned that he dashed down the hall to Mamie's room where she lay confined to bed from an adverse reaction to antibiotics prescribed for an infected tooth.

Eisenhower walked back into the room a moment after I arrived. We shook hands, and I remember him saying, "Thanks for your help." Turning around hesitantly, as though not quite knowing what to do next, he announced, "I'm going over to see Taft!"

This brought a series of negative responses from several people around him: "That will violate protocol!" "It's the proper thing for the loser to make a courtesy call to congratulate the winner!" "General, you are the nominee. Taft should come to you!"

Eisenhower turned to me and said, "What do you think?"

I replied: "Follow your instincts and go!"

In *Mandate for Change* (pages 44-45), Eisenhower tells what happened next:

> I telephoned Senator Taft and asked for an opportunity to come across the street to call upon him. Although his voice indicated surprise, he agreed and I started on my way—a trip that proved to be far more difficult physically than I imagined. As I left my apartment, reporters, photographers, and crowds of the curious began to impede my progress, the press begging for a statement. Police officers detailed to me by the city of Chicago found it almost impossible to get me outside the hotel; but once in the street our real troubles began. I am quite sure that it took ten minutes to get across the street. Progress through the lobby and halls of Senator Taft's hotel was equally difficult, with the atmosphere of the crowds noticeably sorrowful and even resentful. I understood their attitude—I sympathized with it. All of them had worked for weeks and months with one purpose in view—to nominate Robert Taft. They wore great Taft buttons and ribbons. A not inconsiderable number of ladies were openly weeping.

Finally we reached the elevator and I was escorted to
the senator's quarters.

The first thing the senator asked after I had reached
his hotel room was whether his sons could be present. I
agreed readily. In the course of the talk I said, "This is
no time for conversation on matters of any substance;
you're tired and so am I. I just want to say that I want to
be your friend and hope you will be mine. I hope we
can work together."

Senator Taft's reply was cordial and matter-of-fact.
"My only problem for the moment," he said, "is that
for the twenty minutes it took you to get over here I
have been bombarded by requests from photographers
for a picture. Would you be willing to have one taken?"
We stepped into the hall to face the flash bulbs and our
short chat was over.

I returned to my hotel under circumstances much
easier than those of my former crossing. (Garden City,
N.Y.: Doubleday & Company, Inc., 1963)

Meanwhile, on the convention floor, other delegations
shifted their votes to Eisenhower, and Senator John Bricker
appeared on the platform. Bricker, an immaculate dresser
with flowing white hair and a ruddy complexion, looked the
part of a Hollywood casting office's stereotype statesman. He
ran as Dewey's Vice President on the '44 ticket after first
backing Senator Taft for the nomination, and managed Taft's
campaign in this latest 1952 venture. Chairman Martin introduced Bricker:

The Chair will recognize the Senator from Ohio,
Senator John W. Bricker, first. (Applause.)

SENATOR JOHN W. BRICKER of Ohio.—Mr.
Chairman, members of the Convention, guests, and
people of America: Senator Taft has communicated
with me, and first of all, I want to express for him his
appreciation for the support you have given him.

From what I am about to tell you, I think that you will realize the import: General Eisenhower and Senator Taft have already met. (Applause.) Senator Taft has pledged his unlimited and active support to elect General Dwight Eisenhower as President. (Applause.)

General Eisenhower most graciously responded that he could not be elected without the wholehearted support of Senator Taft and his friends, and that he could not carry out his program, when elected President—as he will be—without the support of Senator Taft. (Applause.)

It is dangerous to try to encapsulate any person's greatest personality trait in a word or two, but I think you can do it with Eisenhower. "Reaching out" is the key to his success as military leader, party builder, President, and international statesman dedicated to peace. His "reaching out" twice to Taft at exactly the right moments made his election in November possible.

Chief Justice Warren Burger's memorandum of September 1966 details my role and that of the Minnesota delegation in helping secure General Eisenhower's nomination. He graciously gave his approval for me to print it as Appendix 3.

Chapter 3
The Campaign

Before we broke from Chicago, Eisenhower to Colorado to fish and relax, me to the University of Pennsylvania, he told me he wanted me to play a key role in the campaign, to "be on the team." "Team" would become an important word during my next six years of close association with him.

I heard nothing directly from the General for over a month, but followed his activities as reported in the press. He spent a week on a ranch owned by his friend Aksel Nielsen where he listened by radio to Adlai Stevenson's acceptance of the Democratic nomination. Eisenhower's friend, George Allen, observed about Stevenson, "He's too slick an orator; he'll be easy to beat!"

He set up headquarters in the Brown Palace Hotel in Denver, with Governor Sherman Adams of New Hampshire as campaign manager.

In mid-August, the press gave great coverage to the arrival of a delegation of Republican leaders headed by Arthur Summerfield, now Chairman of the Republican National Committee; Sinclair Weeks and Douglas Stuart, RNC finance directors; Robert Humphreys, a public relations specialist; and several other staff members.

Congressman Leonard Hall and Senator Everett Dirksen represented the Republican Congressional Campaign Committees. Senator Richard Nixon's campaign manager, Murray Chotiner, came, as did Cabot Lodge. Walter Williams and Mary Lord attended on behalf of the "Citizens for Eisenhower" groups.

In politics, those who are on-site with continuous access to the person with power always end up with the key roles. As an absentee, I assumed that I would hear nothing more about activity in the campaign.

Although formal campaigns usually did not begin until around Labor Day, the Democrats and some of the press tried to put Eisenhower on the defensive early, painting him as an amateur in government, a "pawn in the hands of the mossbacks of the Republican Committee," "out of touch with Asia where the Korean War dragged on," "indecisive," "unable to stand up to the McCarthys and the Jenners within his own party," "a real novice in politics who could not hold his own in that strange rough and tumble field."

Others clamored for him to start his formal campaign immediately. They accused him of following the Dewey format of sweetness-and-light that led to defeat in '48. Some went so far as to call him a clone of Dewey.

On August 24, Eisenhower moved his headquarters to New York's Commodore Hotel, where Adams and his assistants took over the entire ninth floor.

A couple of days later, I received a worried call from Mamie Eisenhower saying that the schedule Ike's managers proposed would kill him. He came home at the end of each day totally exhausted and she feared not only for his health but maybe his life. Could I possibly do something about it?

I told her I would come to New York the next day if she could be sure that I could see the General. She suggested that his schedule called for him to be home at 4:00. Why didn't I come to their Morningside Heights house at Columbia and be there when Ike arrived?

I drove up from Philadelphia, arriving around 3:45, and Mamie invited me into the living room. She looked tired and drawn, not the bouncy, vivacious lady we dined with at the Villa St. Pierre eight months earlier. Esther once told me, "Mamie really worships her husband," and I read deep concern in her face and voice. Four o'clock came, and no Ike; then 4:30; 5:00 and her anxiety deepened. We tried small talk to relieve the awkwardness of silence. Finally at 5:30 we heard him on the porch talking and waving to a crowd of well-wishers in front of the house.

As the door closed, Eisenhower sank down on the carpeted stairs inside the reception room. He described his ride around the city in an open convertible, with stops to shake hands and short informal speeches.

I told him of Mamie's worries, and her efforts to enlist my help. I added that Willkie's loss in '40 to FDR came partly from his physical exhaustion before his campaign formally opened in September. The key weeks of a national campaign are always the last two in October. By that time, Willkie lost his voice, his temper, and his drive, and knocked himself out of the race before his campaign formally began.

Eisenhower agreed with Mamie and me and said he did not know the ropes of campaigning, but he did not want to hold back, especially in view of what "those papers and radio people are saying." He also knew he could not stand many more days like the one he'd just finished.

I told him I would go see Sherman Adams the next day.

Mamie invited me to stay for food, but I declined. I could tell she wanted only to get her husband fed and to bed as quickly as possible. I sympathized with Ike and Mamie, with the formal two-month campaign still ahead of them, both insecure and really not knowing what to expect, as I left quickly to get a room at the Commodore so that I could see Adams the next morning.

When I talked to Adams, he promised to be more mindful of Eisenhower's energy level, and I returned to Philadelphia.

Two days later, I received a call from Eisenhower to thank me for my visit to Morningside Heights, saying he felt more rested. He asked me to come up for a meeting the next afternoon at the Commodore. I told him I could shift my schedule and would be happy to see him.

As I walked into the living room of his Commodore suite, I saw Herbert Brownell. A Nebraskan originally, the Yale Law School graduate met Thomas Dewey, the Crime Buster of Manhattan, some twenty years earlier, and joined the political organization that made Dewey governor of New York. Brownell also helped Dewey win the Republican nomination in '44 and '48. When Dewey decided he would not make a third try for the presidency but instead would support Eisenhower, Brownell came along eagerly.

Of medium height, trim, and always well-dressed, Brownell never spoke much above a low, soft tone, but his word choice and logical arguments were always delivered so firmly and persuasively that he did not need to modulate his voice.

Eisenhower then introduced me to C.D. Jackson, a top executive of *Time-Life,* Inc. I knew him by name but not in person. Jackson first met Eisenhower in Europe during the war, and Eisenhower arranged for him to come "on loan" from *Time* for the campaign.

Both Brownell and Jackson knew American politics up one side and down the other. Someone once called Brownell "The Republican's Jim Farley," referring to the political genius who engineered Roosevelt's elections in '32 and '36. Brownell and Jackson reveled in plotting strategy, guessing public reaction, and anticipating what countermoves the opposition would try. Both possessed sophisticated senses of humor. In addition, Jackson brought with him the skills of an experienced writer.

Characteristically, Eisenhower came right to the point.

"Those National Committee people," he began, and proceeded to describe, with mounting anger, the campaign plans presented earlier in Denver. The plans detailed exactly where he would go every day until the election, who he would see at each stop, television and radio appearances, press conferences, motorcades and whistle-stopping train excursions, posters and other campaign literature, airport quickie speeches, and the most minute details of the next two months of his life. Mamie was to be at his side practically every minute.

They gave him an entire program already finished; they did not ask him for a single suggestion. He felt the National Committee members treated him like he "didn't have a brain in [his] head." A lot of their notions he didn't believe in at all, some he did, but their attitude that he would play as their trained seal infuriated him most. They hoped only to use his name for their own personal goals. He knew how to work with people and get things done, and it wasn't by shoving the other fellow around without asking him whether he wanted to go or not.

"I'll work with everybody to win this election," he went on, "but I plan to do it my own way. That's where you fellows come in."

He outlined a program whereby the three of us should state the broad strategies of the campaign, and then deal tactically with the specific issues. We would supervise all the speech writing. We needed to talk to as many people as we could with different points of view and pay particular attention to what his brother Milton and his long-time friend, deputy European commander General Lucius Clay said. "They've both got good common sense, with no axe to grind. They'll call it like they see it," Eisenhower said.

If the three of us could not reach a consensus on any subject, we should come to him together, not singly, so it wouldn't look like any one of us might be trying to go behind the others' backs.

I raised the question of whether Sherman Adams approved this arrangement. "Of course," Eisenhower replied testily. Adams would run the staff and the campaign trains. He'd give input on strategy and the speeches when he thought it important, but the three of us would set the substantive tone and decide the course of the campaign. Although Adams, of course, would maintain close liaison with the Republican National Committee and the Congressional Campaign Committees, the presidential campaign would be Eisenhower's. "It's got to be that way, or I can't do it."

Once Eisenhower decided to cover a subject, he warmed to it:

> They think I'm some kind of moron about government because I've been a soldier all my life. Why, I've worked on defense budgets and appeared before committees on defense, appropriations and foreign affairs of both houses of Congress more than all of them combined.
>
> I've worked closely with Roosevelt and Truman and all the heads of government of all the countries in the free world—and that includes Churchill, Attlee, and de Gaulle.
>
> I don't brag about it, but for some reason, I got interested in ancient history when I was in high school—read all I could find on the Greeks and the Romans, especially about Carthage and Hannibal and the Punic wars. Sure, I've always been interested in battles and military leaders; but I've read history for the love of it. I think I'm in a position to have some of my own thoughts about what this campaign should be, particularly since I'm somewhat involved in it.

Now, it doesn't take any mathematical genius to figure out that the Republican party is a minority party; so if we're going to win, we've got to reach out to the independents and the Democrats who are dissatisfied with what's accumulated in Washington over the last twenty years. Why, if all the Republicans voted for me in November, with all the Democrats voting for Stevenson, I wouldn't have a prayer of winning.

What I want you fellows to help me do is plot out the parameters of the campaign. Decide what it'll take to reach out and pull in as many independents and Democrats as we'll need to win in November. I don't mean that we want to be insincere and make promises that violate what we believe in; but we've got to remember that I must appeal to the mainstream of Americans, not just the "Last Century Mossbacks" on the National Committee, and for that matter, a great many of the Republicans running for the House and Senate. We've got to help them; but we've got to set our own larger and wider goals, and keep to them.

For the next three hours, we debated strategy and tactics, each of us taking copious notes on our ruled yellow pads.

We decided that in the post-World War II world, foreign and domestic policy merged, but for the campaign we needed to treat them separately.

All America agreed that the stalemate in Korea must be ended honorably. We would treat this definitively, but carefully, later on.

Truman's policies of "Communist containment" stagnated. Within Republican ranks, the conservative Taft Old Guard still stood anti-NATO and wanted to pull all U.S. troops out of Europe. As Eisenhower continued to point out, we needed the support of every last Republican we could round up; we did not dare alienate Taft or this group who only reluctantly admitted that the U.S. might even possibly belong in Europe or play an international role of any kind.

Our strategy, therefore, would be not to mention NATO by name. We would talk about Europe in general, our need to remain active there, our future trade potential with a continent in recovery made possible by the Marshall Plan. We would also build up the important role of the United Nations and our need to support it vigorously.

Perhaps even more important, we needed a new approach to the Soviets. Eisenhower used his favorite phrase of "reaching out" to them. He held no illusions regarding Russia's paranoia about protecting itself from another invasion, which included its policy of expansion to hold western borders that it could defend strategically, even though this required the political annexation and domination of the Eastern bloc countries: Poland, East Germany, Czechoslovakia, Romania, Bulgaria, and Hungary.

The Republican Party platform, engineered by John Foster Dulles, called for the "liberation" of these satellites. We all decided that the use of "liberation" alone would do nothing but continue the hostile rhetoric between Washington and Moscow started by Truman. Eisenhower suggested the inclusion of the important words "through peaceful means" after "liberation" in any speeches on the subject.

One further note on foreign policy: For years, Republican orators called the Democrats the "War Party" because they "led us into both World Wars, the first under Wilson, the last under Roosevelt." We considered it a trite, exhausted, harmful phrase that could do nothing but offend the thinking independents and dissatisfied Democrats we needed to attract in November. Eisenhower would never use the allegation and we would encourage all other Republicans to cast it from their vocabularies.

Domestic issues presented more serious challenges. We could agree wholeheartedly with the Taft people on:

(1) The growing, oppressive, debilitating size of the Federal bureaucracy and the need to reduce it;

(2) The stifling threat to a broad-based, healthy economy posed by the top-heavy military-industrial complex;

(3) The unconscionable scandals and corruption that sprang from the temptations of the billions of available federal dollars; and

(4) The need to seek out Communists and disloyal government employees.

We split with the Taft people on four basic issues:

(1) They wanted to stand pat on the Taft-Hartley Act, which caused organized labor to accuse the Republican party of "union busting." We thought the Act needed revision;

(2) They wanted to slash taxes immediately, take off all wage and price controls put on because of the Korean War, and return to a pre-war laissez-faire approach to business and the economy. We believed that tax reductions and the elimination of wage and price controls must be introduced gradually;

(3) They wanted to repeal Social Security and Unemployment Insurance and other social programs put in by the New Deal. We wanted to keep the ones that made sense over the long haul;

(4) They wanted to root out Communism in government through any and all means, including the reckless, unproved charges of the William Jenners and Joe McCarthys. We wanted to do it on a sound, legal basis with proper regard for the Bill of Rights.

Already Stevenson and the Democrats had attempted to hang the cloak of Taft, Jenner, and McCarthy on Eisenhower and we knew that if they succeeded, it would end up as the campaign shroud. We needed the Old Guard, but could not let it appear that they controlled the candidate or his campaign.

I hurried back to Philadelphia and got the approval of my Trustees at the University to jump into the campaign with both feet. I might add that neither Brownell, Jackson, nor I received as much as one dime for pay or expenses from any of the Eisenhower committees or the Republican National Committee. Ours was a labor of love for a cause in which we believed wholeheartedly.

The schedule of his first whistle-stop trip showed Eisenhower's control of the campaign. All the "pros" on the National Committee told him not to waste his time on the South. It would continue Democratic; therefore, he should devote all his money and energies to sections of the country he could win. I recall the substance of his thundering:

> If I am to reach out to all the country, how in God's name can I justify ignoring a great big part of it? I was born in Texas. I've been based in the South. I know the Southern people. I respect them, and enjoy being with them. I'm going into the South.

When the first campaign train pulled out of New York September 2, it headed for Atlanta, then Jacksonville, Miami, Tampa, Birmingham, and Little Rock. He would later make forays into other southern cities: Richmond, Charlotte, Columbia, Memphis, Knoxville, Shreveport, Tulsa, Oklahoma City, and New Orleans. On November 4, he carried Florida, Oklahoma, Tennessee, Texas, and Virginia. His instincts paid off again.

Brownell, Jackson, and I worked in the sixth-floor Commodore Hotel office Sherman Adams set up for Emmet John Hughes, a *Time* magazine writer brought over by Jackson to become the chief speech writer. Later, from time to time, others would join us: Major General Wilton ("Jerry") Persons, a long-time friend of Eisenhower who would later be White House Liaison with Congress; Robert Cutler, Boston banker; Gabriel Hauge, brilliant young economist; and Milton Eisenhower. These larger gatherings took place in the living room of the Eisenhower's Morningside Heights home. When in town, Eisenhower sat in on the strategy sessions at both locations, but until the end of the campaign, Brownell, Jackson, and I remained in charge of the speechwriting.

Hughes' work presented several problems. To begin with, he admitted that 1952 would be the first time he actually voted in any election. He arrived primarily apolitical, but confessed to sympathies toward New Deal social programs. He came to us disenchanted with the "mess in Washington," a popular phrase thrown around by many people of all political hues.

Hughes' writing showed brilliance in phrase-making, but tended toward the elaborate. It read well, but often did not "speak" well. Some of his phrases came out complex and obscure, which upset Eisenhower. He once told us, "I'm basically a Kansas farm boy, and damn it, I'm going to talk that way. I want to say what I mean in a way that people can understand what I mean." Hughes once included "status quo" in a speech. Eisenhower used it, but later fumed: "You're trying to make me sound like a pinhead intellectual, and by God, I'm not. Don't give me that again."

Brownell, Jackson, and I edited Hughes' texts. He tried to follow our instructions for content, but his writing style kept segments of the speeches from developing rhythm, which made Eisenhower uncomfortable in delivering them.

One speech precipitated a crisis, caused Eisenhower's lead in the polls to nose-dive dangerously, and demoralized his headquarters team at the Commodore and across the country.

Senator William Jenner of Indiana and Joseph McCarthy of Wisconsin ran for reelection in 1952. Both alleged that the government was full of Communists. McCarthy said in West Virginia, "I have in my possession a list of 205 card-carrying members of the Communist party now working in the State Department." He later reduced his claim, but could never come up with any hard proof. Jenner made similar reckless charges and helped create a poisonous atmosphere of hate and suspicion, but totally without solid evidence.

At one point, Jenner called General George Catlett Marshall, Truman's special ambassador to China in 1946 and later Secretary of State, "a living lie," and "a front man for traitors." The Democrats and media embellished this to mean, "Jenner called Marshall a *traitor!*" McCarthy lumped Marshall with a group whom he called "either half-loyal or disloyal."

Both Jenner and McCarthy linked Marshall to those who "lost China to Mao and the Communists." This gave the Democrats an opening to demand that Eisenhower defend Marshall. General Marshall served as Eisenhower's superior officer and Chief of Staff in Washington during World War II. The man most responsible for Eisenhower's meteoric rise in two years from lieutenant colonel to major general, he also recommended Eisenhower's eventual appointment as Supreme Commander of the European Theater of Operations.

Eisenhower defended Marshall's patriotism with statements in Denver, calling Marshall "a perfect example of patriotism and loyal service to the United States," but the Democrats continued to shout that Eisenhower must denounce Jenner and McCarthy, something he refused to do: "I'm not going to speak against anyone running on the Republican ticket." Stevenson pounded the theme that Jenner and McCarthy dictated the direction of Eisenhower's campaign.

Brownell, Jackson, and I thought the situation serious enough to devise a subtle strategy to let Eisenhower show exactly where he stood on the Marshall affair, but without a pointed, direct rebuff of either Jenner or McCarthy by name.

We told Hughes to draft an insert for an Eisenhower speech in which he would defend Marshall, which Hughes did in somewhat verbose, non-Eisenhower style:

> Freedom is not only a precious but also a complex privilege. It is essentially the most generous way of life known to man. . . . It places its faith in the ultimate ability of the people to think clearly, to choose wisely, to act compassionately.

> So full and generous a way of life must never be allowed to become narrow and stingy. The most awful poverty for people in this way of life would be a poverty of ideas. Their food for thought can never be rationed, nor their diet dictated by either an intellectual elite or self-appointed censors . . .

> To defend freedom, in short, is—first of all—to *respect* freedom. This respect demands, in turn, respect for the integrity of fellow citizens who enjoy their right to disagree. The right to question a man's judgment carries with it no automatic right to question his honor.

> Let me be quite specific. I know that charges of disloyalty have, in the past, been leveled against General George C. Marshall. I have been privileged for thirty-five years to know General Marshall personally. I know him, as a man and as a soldier, to be dedicated with singular selflessness and the profoundest patriotism to the service of America. And this episode is a sobering lesson in the way freedom must *not* defend itself.

Brownell, Jackson, and I argued against Eisenhower going into Indiana and Wisconsin, since we anticipated awkward incidents. Both senators could be expected to latch onto the presidential candidate with joint pictures, podium stances, and anything that would help them win in November. Adams and Summerfield overruled us. We then decided that the "Marshall insert" should be given October 3 in Milwaukee, in McCarthy's own state.

Since I cannot give a first-hand reconciliation of the conflicting reports, most detailed and dramatic, of what happened between the time we sent the Marshall insert to the campaign train and its non-delivery October 3, I will report only the basic facts on which all eyewitnesses agree: Someone leaked the Marshall insert and Wisconsin Governor Walter Kohler, National Committeeman Henry Ringling, and Senator McCarthy came to the Peoria, Illinois hotel the day before the Milwaukee speech. They also boarded the campaign train for the trip through Wisconsin. They argued that the Marshall insert would be an unnecessary rebuke to McCarthy in his home state, the exact thing Brownell, Jackson, and I hoped for. It must *not* be given, they continued. Hauge and Cutler aboard the train argued vehemently to keep in the insert. Sherman Adams waffled and finally sided with the Wisconsin contingent, and the Marshall insert went into the waste basket.

The media exploded across the country. Stevenson and the Democrats rode their advantage, saying that Eisenhower's "knuckling under" to the Jenners and McCarthys showed weakness and proved him incapable of being an effective President.

Adams' performance did not inspire confidence. First, he denied urging Eisenhower to omit the Marshall insert, but later questioning by reporters forced him to backtrack and admit his advice to delete the passage, surrounding the affair with an aura of deception and indecision.

The New York Times, which supported Eisenhower, said: "Yesterday could not have been a happy day for General Eisenhower. . . nor for his supporters." *Times* publisher Arthur Hays Sulzberger wired Adams: "Do I need to tell you that I am sick at heart?"

Emmet Hughes called me in Philadelphia to see if I could come to New York. When I got there, I found palpable gloom descended upon the headquarters staff.

"That did it," several argued. "The election went down the drain last night."

I called together as many workers as I could get to listen and told them not to despair. My disappointment exceeded theirs, but the unfortunate episode meant only that we must re-double our efforts for the final month ahead. Emmet Hughes gives this description of what I said in his book, *The Ordeal of Power* (page 43):

> The scent of irresolution in politics is never pleasant, and this time was no exception. Yet the most compassionate response to the dismal event came from one of those who, personally, was most dismayed. This was Harold Stassen, and I recall his tempered remarks. "It is easy to judge harshly," he cautioned, "sitting back here in New York and not knowing the pressures that go on inside that insane campaign train. You are trapped there. There are just a few people near you whom you trust. You don't have a chance to get out in the clean air and think things through. You have to decide fast. Time is always running out on you. And when all of them around you gang up, to insist you do this or that, it is just about impossible to fight back." (New York: Atheneum, 1963)

I thought the developments serious enough to warrant a letter to Eisenhower which I sent by special messenger to the campaign train. I expressed my empathy for his position in much the same language I used with the staff in New York, but I bore down hard on the rationale Brownell, Jackson, Hughes, and I worked out for the speech's delivery and its exact wording.

He took the time to dictate a response:

<u>Personal and
Confidential</u>
                            Aboard Eisenhower
                            Campaign Special.
                            October 5, 1952.

Dear Harold:

In principle I agree with the criticism you make on the revisions made in the Milwaukee talk. However, there were three things that finally persuaded me to eliminate the Marshall paragraph:

(a). My staff became practically a unit in recommending it.

(b). The balance between the hunt for Communism and the methods used in the hunt seemed fairly well preserved without the particular paragraph. This seemed especially true because I insisted on keeping in the sentence that said "The right to challenge a man's judgment does not convey the right to question his honor."

(c). A considerable amount of argument was presented to show that Senator McCarthy had never made the flat allegation that General Marshall was traitorous in design.

The following morning I saw that the local headlines emphasized the "Communist hunting" part of the talk at the expense of my insistence upon proper and ethical methods. Consequently at my first two whistle stops I referred to the Milwaukee talk and stated that I hoped that what I had to say about real Americanism in method would be understood as clearly as was my contention that we had to uproot subversion and disloyalty from the government.

From here on out I shall try—in every talk—to emphasize the liberal side of our program. Certainly I shall try to make it clear that I am no man's creature. Last evening at Fargo I repeated again that the Republicans stood firmly behind social security and its expansion and so on.

As always I value your advice. Thank you for the trouble you took to write.

With personal regards,

Sincerely,

DE

Governor Harold E. Stassen,
c/o Eisenhower Headquarters,
Commodore Hotel,
New York, New York.

[Longhand] P.S.   Also, Governor Kohler was so determined in his argument for-revision—that I felt it difficult to campaign through his state if I completely disregarded his advice.

Eisenhower's letter-writing always struck me as gifted. He dictated his letters without help, did his own editing when necessary, and ended up with an in-depth analysis of the episode the letter covered.

Years later, and I do not remember how the matter came up, he told me that although the Marshall affair turned out all right in the end, "I've never been happy that I let those guys talk me into taking the Marshall thing out of that Milwaukee speech."

Eisenhower carried Wisconsin by 100,000 votes, more than McCarthy received in his reelection to the Senate.

Chapter 4
Liaison to MacArthur

Fascinated, I watched Douglas MacArthur pace the carpeted floor of the living room of his suite in the Waldorf Towers. An aide once said, "The General cannot talk sitting down."

Biographer William Manchester calls him the "American Caesar." His regal bearing came with his birth; and he wore it naturally, more a part of the Victorian era in thought, tastes, and demeanor than of mid-century America.

I sat and watched as part of a special assignment Eisenhower gave me shortly after I became active in the campaign: "You've dealt with MacArthur before. I want you to be my personal liaison to him. Report directly to me on all your contacts. Don't go through Sherman Adams or anyone else. This will be between you and me and the General."

MacArthur continued to look twenty years younger than his then seventy-two years; and I could not find much changed in his appearance since I had last seen him seven years before on the deck of the *Missouri* as he accepted the Japanese surrender.

My mind flashed back to that historic day—September 2, 1945— when I stood as the junior naval officer among at least a hundred admirals and generals from the Allied nations. Above and around, sailors and war correspondents covered every inch of metal of the great ship—guns, turrets, hoods, stacks, decks—all straining to see and hear this final, dramatic chapter of the Pacific War.

The band played "The Star-Spangled Banner" and the chaplain gave a short invocation. MacArthur appeared suddenly, striding to center stage, flanked by Admirals Nimitz and Halsey. They peeled off to each side, while he continued to a place behind the table that held the surrender documents. MacArthur also arrived without a single ribbon or other decoration, wearing his scrambled-egg visor, khaki shirt open at the neck, five stars in circles on his collar tabs—his casual attire telling untold millions that he needed no ribbons or other regalia to show who stood in the center of the whole world, and who commanded it.

His pacing in the Waldorf began when I complimented him on the brilliance of the Inchon landing in Korea that at the time saved UN and U.S. forces from a stalemated war, much like the horrors of the trenches of World War I that MacArthur knew first-hand as brigadier general in command of the famed Rainbow Division.

He launched into a detailed description of the Inchon operation, his own brainchild, describing his problems in convincing the pussy-footers in the Pentagon to let him move before the Communist Chinese could mine the harbors and send reinforcements to the North Korean troops. He told me of his great fears that an intelligence leak would let the North Koreans blast the landing armada out of the water before the Marines could even get aboard their landing crafts, of the speed with which the operation became final, and of his great relief at seeing lights burning in Flying Fish Channel as the invasion force sailed in—lights that told him the North Koreans would be taken completely by surprise.

He marched up and down, ramrod straight, hair thinning but still so black that people wondered if he dyed it, the paunch that a correspondent once called the "military secret" almost entirely hidden by deep pleats around the front of his belt line.

MacArthur warmed to the telling and the pacing, describing how the Marines of the assault force took Walmido Fort, which guarded the channel and harbor, without a single casualty. He considered this perhaps the proudest operation of his long career since his graduation from West Point in 1903.

I could not help but think back to the first time I met him, in Brisbane, Australia, in 1943, when I went with Admiral Halsey to meet MacArthur for strategy talks on the Pacific War. The fiery admiral told me, "Harold, I want you to sit in on this conference, but don't open your damned mouth. When we get back to base, I want your detailed analysis of MacArthur and what he proposes."

At Brisbane, MacArthur also paced, lecturing in sonorous tones and Churchillian phrases on his philosophies of war generally. He held forth on flanking maneuvers, military supply lines, troop mobility, naval fire power to support Marine and Army amphibious landings, the need to provide for thousand of casualties as we island-hopped toward Japan, the ultimate assaults in the Philippines and the Japanese home islands, air bombing and strafing potentials, carrier strike forces—on and on it went.

Halsey, MacArthur's complete opposite, fidgeted and grew restless, until finally he could stand it no longer.

"But goddamn it, Doug," he exploded, "why can't we hit the --- ----- right there, right now?"

In the tomb-like silence of the Waldorf, MacArthur needed to talk; and I lent him not one ear but two, to establish complete rapport before moving into my real mission: to keep MacArthur from making any deprecating statements about Eisenhower, as the rumor mills told us he might.

In 1930, MacArthur became Army Chief of Staff, then the country's top military job. A young major, Dwight D. Eisenhower, served as his chief aide. In 1936, when MacArthur moved to the Philippines to create a Philippine Defense Force, he took Eisenhower with him as chief of staff.

As the rumormongers told it, when asked his opinion of Eisenhower, MacArthur replied, "The best clerk I ever had." About MacArthur, Eisenhower reputedly said, "I never learned much from him in the way of tactics and strategy, but he was a great dramatics teacher for nine years."

When we talked in the Waldorf that September of 1952, we knew that MacArthur statements carried considerable weight with a broad segment of the voting public. He could even cost Eisenhower the election if he chose to make some demeaning remark.

Not only that, we feared that MacArthur might come out with some substantive statement, formally or casually, about what we should do in Korea. The press would then quiz candidate Eisenhower on whether he agreed with MacArthur. This would force Eisenhower into a no-win posture by injecting a side issue into the campaign. The opposition would have enjoyed the chance to compare Eisenhower's views with those of his former superior, who many claimed knew more about the Far East generally and Korea specifically than anyone else.

We hoped to avoid this diversion. Prevention fell on my shoulders. Eisenhower rightly suspected that MacArthur would feel that no one whom he ever commanded as a junior officer could possess the ability to function well as President of the United States.

MacArthur's unique position in the public's eye grew from his 1951 dismissal by Truman and recall from his command of United Nations forces in Korea. Technically, the Korean conflict bore the label of United Nations "police action." In reality, it became a bloody war with an estimated

1,000,000 casualties all told: 33,629 Americans dead; 47,000 South Koreans killed, wounded, or dead from injury or disease; untold numbers of North Korean and Chinese Communists killed and wounded; and innocent men, women, and children as civilian victims. The "war" destroyed forty-three percent of Korea's industrial capacity, thirty-three percent of its homes, and eighty percent of the city of Seoul.

The Korean War came as yet another chapter in Korea's violent history. The twentieth century started with Japan's brutal military occupation of Korea in 1905 after its victory over the Russians in the Russian-Japanese War. The Japanese tried to erase Korea as a nation, forcing the Koreans to adopt Japanese names, worship in Shinto temples, and attend Japanese schools, which excluded the teaching of the Korean language and the country's history. The invaders seized Korean lands and sold them cheaply to Japanese colonizers, forced the natives to exist on substandard nutrition while expropriating Korea's rice crops for Japan's own use, drafted Koreans into Japanese armies to fight against the Chinese and Allied forces in World War II, and used Koreans as slave laborers in factories, mines, and on military bases.

Then in the middle of the century, Roosevelt at Yalta and Truman at Potsdam invited the Russians into the Pacific War. Russia entered two days *after* the first atomic bomb devastated Hiroshima and immediately occupied Manchuria and the northern half of Korea, stopping at the 38th parallel. We occupied the south, up to that division line.

Korea's status continued in debate with various proposals for its future, including a five-year trusteeship to be administered jointly by the United States, the Soviet Union, Great Britain, and China. The United Nations ratified this plan in September, 1946.

The Soviets set up a Communist puppet government north of the 38th parallel and pulled out Russian troops in

1948, but left a Moscow-trained army of 135,000 Korean troops, with armor and heavy artillery. The United States withdrew our troops from the south the following year, leaving an "army" of 98,000 equipped only with small arms and trained as a local constabulary force to keep the peace internally.

On June 25, 1950, acting on Russia's orders, North Korea marched across the 38th parallel, heading for Seoul, the capital of South Korea. On June 26, the UN Security Council passed a resolution condemning the invasion and calling on all member nations to assist South Korea, the Russians unable to veto the resolution because of their boycott of the UN over its failure to seat Mao's Chinese Communist government.

On June 27, Truman ordered United States air and naval forces to support South Korea. Seoul fell to the North Koreans the next day. On June 30, Truman ordered U.S. ground forces stationed in Japan to Korea under the command of MacArthur, who then served as our proconsul of our occupation of Japan. Some sixteen UN member nations later sent contingents to Korea, but the United States supplied the great majority of air, ground, and naval forces, plus virtually all the money required to sustain the "police action."

Events followed rapidly and unpleasantly:

Early August—North Korean armies bottled up UN forces inside a precarious defense perimeter in the southeast corner of Korea.

September 15—MacArthur counterattacked with his surprise amphibious landing half-way up the west coast at Inchon, trapping the North Korean armies in the south, many fleeing in panic.

September 27—U.S. Joint Chiefs of Staff ordered MacArthur to destroy the North Korean armies.

October 1—UN returned to 38th parallel.

October 7—UN General Assembly approved a resolution calling for the reunification of Korea.

October 20—UN forces occupied Pyongyang, capital of North Korea.

October 26—UN troops reached the Yalu River, on the border between North Korea and China.

Early November—An estimated 1,200,000 troops of the Peoples Republic of China invaded North Korea.

November/December—UN troops were beaten back.

January 4, 1951—Seoul fell again, this time to the Red Chinese.

February/March—UN forces once more slugged their way back to the 38th parallel and stopped.

March 20—MacArthur learned that the State Department, the Pentagon, and Truman planned to propose a truce with the opposing forces in place at the 38th parallel.

March 20—MacArthur issued an ultimatum to the Chinese, belittling their soldiers and industrial capacity and telling them that they would be annihilated if they did not surrender immediately.

March 22—The State Department issued an apology to UN members, saying that MacArthur did not speak for the United States, but MacArthur's ultimatum scuttled Truman's planned cease-fire appeal.

March 23—House of Representatives Republican leader Joseph Martin made public a letter from

MacArthur that concurred with a Martin speech made on March 8 in which Martin said, "If we are not in Korea to win, then this Truman administration should be indicted for the murder of thousands of American boys."

March 24-April 11—Truman, Congressional leaders, the State Department, and the Pentagon agonized over the Truman-MacArthur stand-off. Our UN Allies expressed fear of a broadening war that could bring in Russia as China's ally.

April 11—Truman issued a curt, abrupt order relieving MacArthur of both his UN command in Korea and his proconsulship of Japan, and called him home.

Truman's arbitrary, vindictive, humiliating firing of MacArthur gripped the nation. Organized labor, preachers in the pulpit, politicians of all ranks and all party lines, state legislatures, city councils, all took MacArthur's side. A Gallup poll found that sixty-nine percent of Americans backed MacArthur. Before the White House communications center stopped counting, 78,000 letters, wires, and telephone calls poured in favoring MacArthur by a margin of twenty to one.

Senator Joseph McCarthy called the firing "treason in the White House." William Jenner alleged, "This country is in the hands of a secret coterie which is directed by agents of the Soviet Union." Richard Nixon proclaimed, "The happiest group in the country will be the Communists and their stooges."

The audience booed Truman at an appearance in Griffith Stadium in Washington, the first President to receive this treatment since Herbert Hoover almost twenty years earlier. Bumper stickers and newspaper ads appeared that called for not only Truman's impeachment, but also those of Dean Acheson, Secretary of State, and the Joint Chiefs of Staff.

MacArthur came home to a hero's welcome: 100,000 greeted him in Honolulu; 500,000 in San Francisco; another half-million in Washington; and several million in New York. New York rates its official parades by the amount of litter the sanitation workers clean up afterwards. The score: Four times as much for MacArthur as for Eisenhower's parade in 1945, some estimating MacArthur's gala as the largest in the city's ticker-tape history.

The Republican and Democratic leadership in Congress invited MacArthur to address a joint session. Perhaps no speech since FDR's first inaugural held the nation so completely spellbound. His congressional listeners interrupted the thirty-four-minute speech thirty times with applause. When he ended with "Old soldiers never die, they just fade away," everyone stood, clapped hands, wiped tears from their eyes, and whooped and hollered.

Congressmen and senators crowded around to touch him as he fought his way out of the well of the House of Representatives.

Congressman Dewey Short of Missouri exclaimed for the media, "We heard God speak here today, God in the flesh, the voice of God!" Herbert Hoover called MacArthur "a reincarnation of St. Paul." Others combined praise of MacArthur with damnation for the "traitors in the State Department who are in bed with the Communists."

Harry Truman labeled it "one hundred percent bullshit!"

A groundswell for MacArthur-for-President grew spontaneously and perhaps MacArthur did see himself as the nation's savior, but the country's emotional binge abated and his popularity declined. Still, the conservatives of the Republican party saw him as a dark horse with which to stop Eisenhower, if they could not gain the nomination for Taft. One line of speculation still holds that Taft planned to name

MacArthur his vice presidential running mate if he got the nomination.

MacArthur kept enough of a following to be invited to keynote the Republican convention, the one that nominated Dwight Eisenhower. Now I sat in the General's suite on Eisenhower's behalf, watching him pace and listening for close to an hour before getting around to my real mission.

Eisenhower and I worked out a straightforward strategy for my dealing with MacArthur.

First, I would establish rapport by listening, certainly not an unpleasant chore with MacArthur. In fact, I welcomed the opportunity.

Second, I would tell him right out that Eisenhower wanted me to serve as liaison between the two men. I would be happy to be the "company runner," to carry any messages one of them wanted to get to the other without the risk of leaks or confusing signals. We all appreciated the folly of snafus in messages.

Third, I would tell MacArthur that if Eisenhower won the election, I knew in my own mind that he would want to seek MacArthur's opinion on how to end the Korean War before he took office. This meeting or any hint of it before the election, however, would be premature and introduce distracting speculations.

Fourth, I would tell MacArthur that we did not want the campaign to get off on tangents that might reopen the Truman-MacArthur controversy. There would be time enough after November to talk about substantive plans for Korea. We sincerely hoped that General MacArthur would be on his guard against enterprising editors or nosey reporters who might try to draw from him some embarrassing statement or create diversionary issues which could damage the Republicans' chances of victory.

Fifth, I would express my strong confidence in the campaign, but remind him that we both knew Truman would throw the full weight of his office behind Stevenson in an effort to salvage Truman's bankrupt foreign policies generally, and more specifically those in Asia.

An hour into my visit to the Waldorf Towers, my chance came to present my entire plea. When I reached the fifth point, MacArthur stopped pacing, turned 180 degrees, paused for effect, and spoke in his richest tone: "We do not want a candidate backed by President Truman to be elected. You may assure Eisenhower that I will accept no speaking engagements until after the election."

I listened a while longer, said my goodbyes, and walked down Lexington Avenue to the Commodore, confident of the successful start of my liaison mission.

Chapter 5
"I Shall Go to Korea"

The campaign sagged, the post-convention euphoria long gone.

Senator Karl Mundt of South Dakota, co-chairman of the Republican speakers' bureau, devised a clever formula: $K_1 C_2$. The "K" stood for the Korean War which other Republican campaigners blamed on the Democrats; or at least, they blamed the Democrats for its current stalemate. The two "C's" stood for Corruption and Communism. Interestingly enough, polls showed the American voter far more interested in Corruption than in Communism.

Mundt's theme never really became the national text, and it partially backfired when the Nixon Secret Fund surfaced on September 18.

An enterprising New York reporter broke the story that during Nixon's tenure in the Senate, seventy-six Californians contributed $18,235 to an expense fund that Nixon used to help him meet the expenses of his office. Even though they closed out the fund when Nixon became Eisenhower's running mate, the Democrats thought the fund's earlier existence gave them a weapon to take some of the luster off Eisenhower's promises to clean up "the mess in Washington."

They talked of Nixon's own financial "mess," and called the fund's contributors Nixon's "Millionaires Club." They wondered how his voting record paralleled the economic wishes of those who helped "buy a Senator."

I cannot offer any firsthand knowledge of the solution to this episode; but Nixon's famous "Checkers" TV speech stifled cries for him to take himself off the ticket, and assured Eisenhower that Nixon would not be a detriment to the campaign. The "Checkers" label came from the name of a dog Nixon said his two little girls received as a gift from an admirer. They loved the dog, and Nixon did not intend to give it back, no matter what anyone said.

"Pure corn," the Democrats yelled as they saw their target slip away.

The biggest challenge, however, proved to be Senator Taft. Right after the convention, he retired to the family's remote retreat at Murray Bay in Canada and sat on his hands.

The Republican Old Guard also sat silently, waiting, as one writer put it, for Taft to "sound the bugle" and call the troops to arms; but the call did not come. Some speculated that Eisenhower's chances of winning Taft's support stood at zero. Ike did not talk like a Republican—more like a clone of Dewey and the despised "eastern establishment." Eisenhower did not represent "Mr. Republican's" idea of the party spokesman.

Eisenhower's early speech to the American Legion convention in New York fell flat compared to Stevenson's. Much of the media presented the Democrat as a deep thinker, with evenness of personality, wit, graciousness, elegance, good common sense—a man perfectly fitted by character and political experience as governor of Illinois to be president. His oratorical flourishes before the Legionnaires received twenty-five interruptions by applause, Eisenhower's speech only ten.

The Scripps-Howard newspaper chain, one of Eisenhower's earliest and most vigorous boosters, ran a box on page one of all its nineteen papers: "Ike is running like a dry creek." Sadly, he acts like just another "me-too candidate." If he isn't ready to come out swinging and hit hard, "he might as well concede defeat."

Ninety-three members of the faculty and staff of Columbia (Eisenhower remained their University president) signed a manifesto, printed as a full-page ad in *The New York Times*, saying that no military man should ever become president.

The reports back from the first campaign train frustrated us. The crowds cheered Eisenhower and Mamie wildly, then melted away when he began his attacks on the Democrats and Washington, as though satisfied with a quick glimpse of this historic figure. Hauge and Cutler aboard the train told us that Ike's speaking performances improved tremendously as, to use Eisenhower's words, "I got the hang of the damned thing," but they could not explain crowd reactions.

Brownell, Jackson, and I decided to concentrate on speech handouts for the local press at each whistle stop and hope that those who saw Eisenhower in person would go home and read what he said.

Two months went by after the convention, and still Taft pouted. We needed to rally him and the Old Guard to win, but do it in such a way that we did not turn off the disenchanted Democrats who must cross party lines. We also needed to attract the independents.

"I've got to see Taft again," Eisenhower announced at one of our strategy meetings at the Commodore. "I know the liberals will scream, but I'll take my chances with them. We can't pull the party together this way."

Senator Fred Seaton of Nebraska, who served as Sherman Adams' administrative deputy at the Commodore headquarters, immediately wired Taft an invitation. He and Eisenhower met for two hours at Morningside Heights on September 12.

The media looked forward to what might be the biggest story since July. Taft emerged with a long press handout prepared in advance—what some writers labeled "the Republican manifesto" and "the Republican orthodox ultimatum." He prefaced it with the statement that he and Eisenhower stood "in full agreement" on all items of domestic policy: reduction in size and activity of the federal government; immediate removal of all price and wage controls; drastic limitations on federal spending; lower taxes; and a crusade for "liberty against creeping socialism."

Taft committed Eisenhower to his own profoundly isolationist statements of foreign policy, saying that "our differences are only differences of degree."

Eisenhower fumed when he read the media reports that called the meeting "the surrender of Morningside Heights." Stevenson pounded: "Taft lost the nomination, but won the nominee." Oregon Republican Senator Wayne Morse withdrew his support of Eisenhower with a stinging public rebuke.

Stevenson's standing in the polls began a steady climb upward. We feared this trend, especially as the results showed over twenty percent of the voters "undecided." Some polls showed the candidates running neck-and-neck. *Broadcasting-Television* magazine gave Stevenson the edge by fifty-six to forty-four percent.

Harry Truman jumped into the fray with arms flailing. "This fellow [Eisenhower] don't know any more about politics than a pig knows about Sunday."

We entered the last two weeks of the campaign with the election up for grabs. The Nixon Fund took some of the steam out of our attack on corruption. The wild swings of Jenner, McCarthy, and their ilk against Communism in high places lost us votes.

I knew when Eisenhower named Brownell, Jackson, and me as his coordinating committee on speeches that we would eventually need to hit hard at the "K" of the Korean War. We struggled to find the right thing to say about it.

I'm fascinated by the different versions of the genesis of the Korean speech, several eyewitness reports differing 180 degrees; but that's the way of human reporting and the vagaries of the fact-finding process, whether in the jury room, or by historians, biographers, or diary keepers. It's like the old adage, "Success has a thousand fathers, but failure is an orphan."

In my effort to "set the record straight," as the trite phrase tells it, I'll begin by saying that I don't know where the idea for the "I Shall Go to Korea" speech came from, nor do I think anyone else can say with certainty. I've read a dozen accounts claiming credit for it, some absurdly fictional. All I know for sure is that Brownell, Jackson, and I considered every suggestion that came in on what to say about Korea and we did not label each source. From time to time, Milton Eisenhower and Lucius Clay sat in on our discussions, and General Eisenhower, too. We considered a number of positions on Korea:

1) The Super Hawks insisted that we use atomic bombs against North Korea and Red China to break the stalemate and save American and Allied lives, those of the Asians not worth considering. Give the "Commies" a deadline to either lay down their arms or face Hiroshima's fate;

2) At the opposite extreme, a large body of opinion held that we should withdraw from Korea immediately, ours a no-win posture in a place we never belonged. It made no difference that we would lose face before the entire Asian world and weaken our position in Europe. The tragic loss of life, American and others, must be stopped at all costs;

3) We should restore MacArthur as Supreme Commander and give him carte blanche to end the war—something he had promised to do before Truman fired him;

4) We should inform the United Nations that America tired of carrying most of the load. We'd turn Korea back to the UN General Assembly and see what they would do with it, particularly in view of the biting criticisms coming our way from our allies, England and France;

5) We should withdraw and leave the South Korean troops to defend themselves, but urge Chiang's Nationalist Chinese on Formosa to join the South Koreans in a war against Communism;

6) We should negotiate a truce immediately, leaving the hostile armies facing each other at the 38th parallel, exactly where they stood before the fighting began two-and-one-half years before; and

7) We could even claim that we possessed a secret plan to end the war, which we could not divulge until after Eisenhower reached the White House.

I do not exaggerate when I say that we carefully examined every suggestion, no matter how wild or by whom submitted. We knew the whole country ached under the burden of the war. We knew we must set forth a strong position on it, but we dared not advocate a program that might tie Eisenhower's hands after the election.

We shied away from labeling it "Truman's War" or damning the United Nations for entering it. This would weaken Eisenhower's plan to strengthen the UN as he reached out to grasp a formula for world peace. As a matter of future policy, we approved a Hughes-drafted release on UN Day approving the UN's entrance into Korea in 1950.

We finally hit on the format of including a simple statement in a speech. Eisenhower would say, "I will go to Korea" after the election.

Nothing more!

No promises of a quick solution with anything resembling a deadline. Nothing to encumber him later. No cop-out to the UN. Nothing to be construed as anti-MacArthur, pro-MacArthur, anti-Truman, or pro-Truman in the MacArthur saga which could open up that no-win debate.

"I will go!" Say it and stop.

We worked over three or four drafts of a speech by Emmet Hughes for Eisenhower to give in Detroit on October 24 in a half-hour radio and television speech to receive national coverage.

We realized that this could be the key speech of the entire campaign, and when we finally agreed upon its content, we did not want it tampered with. We did not want a repeat of the debacle of the Marshall non-speech in Milwaukee. Brownell and I urged Jackson, in whom Eisenhower showed great confidence, to hand-deliver the speech to Eisenhower aboard the campaign train. We wanted Jackson to explain our consensus on substance, style, and word choice, then get Eisenhower's approval and stay with him until he delivered the speech in Detroit to guard against any chance of the speech going awry.

Brownell could not go because of a court appearance on the 24th; Jackson said that his commitments in New York that same day would prevent him from riding the campaign train to Detroit. Jackson suggested that he and I both go see Eisenhower in Buffalo on October 23 where he would speak after a seven-city whistle stop. We would hand the speech to Eisenhower and make our arguments for its delivery exactly as written. Jackson would then return to New York and I would stay with Eisenhower on the train to guard against any deletions, additions, substitutions, amendments, or word changes.

With advance notice to the campaign team on the train, Jackson and I flew into Buffalo and found Eisenhower stretched out on a bed in his hotel, resting from the day's seven speeches and getting ready for the eighth later in the evening.

He looked up and said, "Is something very wrong—to bring both you fellows out here?"

"No, General," Jackson answered, "We think something's very right."

Jackson nodded to me to present our pitch for delivering the speech, but I suddenly felt the need vanish for a preliminary argument.

"You've already seen the draft for the Detroit speech tomorrow night which is on Korea. Here is an insert we—Herb, C.D., and I—think should go in it."

I handed him the insert paragraphs and stepped back, tomb-like silence taking over the room as he reached for his glasses and read the short paragraphs once, and then a second time. Jackson and I stood motionless awaiting his reaction, both ready to present our strongest arguments in the event he reacted negatively. He slowly removed his glasses with his left hand, laid them at his side on the bed, put the speech down on the other side, and looked off toward the window. Jackson looked at me and I at him, both trying to decide who should speak and what to say.

Eisenhower saved us the trouble, and I can paraphrase his words with no fear of inaccuracy in substance:

> I've been planning to go to Korea all along if I'm elected. You can't measure a war, its men, its generals, its company-grade and field-grade officers by reading paper reports.
>
> You've got to get out there on the front lines, talk to the troops, get the feel of the thing yourself. I found this out the hard way, first in North Africa, and I confirmed it in France and Germany.
>
> I've already made up my mind to go to Korea and see for myself what the hell the situation out there is. My

only question has been when I should make the announcement, before or after the election. If you say we should do it now, we'll do it now!

I don't want to talk to just the military people. I want to get to know the Korean political leaders. We've got to reach out to them and help them rebuild their wrecked country. It won't do a damned bit of good to stop the war right now if they and we don't have some pretty specific long-range plans for their future. If we don't, the whole thing will be a foolish waste; and it might start all over again if they can't get strong enough to defend themselves—or want to defend themselves.

That is undoubtedly the easiest argument I ever won, the one I never gave.

Jackson and I next huddled with Jim Hagerty about the most dramatic way to handle the insert page, the main Korea speech already duplicated and ready to be passed out to the reporters late the next day. We decided that to be 1000% secure against leaks that might dull some of the dramatic edge, Hagerty would hand out the insert page separately, just before the speech's delivery the next night, and keep it absolutely secret until then.

Jackson flew back to New York, while Eisenhower and I boarded the eight-car campaign train that pulled out of Buffalo at 11:00 p.m. en route to Detroit. I spent all the next day in Eisenhower's private car, the last one, as we whistle-stopped across parts of New York, Pennsylvania, and Ohio to reach Detroit.

Mamie and I visited on and off at intervals during the day. She said that, surprisingly, she now liked campaigning and would miss the great camaraderie of "all our gang" at the finish. She marveled at her transformation in just four months from a person who never once did a single thing or uttered a word with the slightest political meaning, into a "campaigner" who felt as strongly about the need for her husband to win the election as did he and all those around him.

I talked at length with Sherman Adams, Bobby Cutler and Gabe Hauge, never once hinting the real purpose of my mission aboard the train and my choice seat in the General's private car.

Years later, Sherman Adams wrote that California's senior Republican senator, William F. Knowland, boarded the train with his own speech "in his pocket that he wanted to substitute for Hughes' speech." Adams dismisses the Knowland episode flippantly with, "But Eisenhower never gave in to the self-appointed editors and the speech remained pretty much as Hughes had written it."

I never heard of the Knowland effort until Adams wrote about it, but I do know that no one ever presented the Knowland offering or any other speech on Korea to Eisenhower before he reached the rostrum that evening in the overflowing Masonic Auditorium.

I milled around in the rear of the hall as I often did to gauge the crowd's reaction. They sat with interest and interrupted several times with applause. I tensed as Eisenhower began the paragraphs of the insert that I now knew by heart:

> The first task of a new Administration will be to review and re-examine every course of action open to us with one goal in view: To bring the Korean war to an early and honorable end. That is my pledge to the American people.

> For this task a wholly new Administration is necessary. The reason for this is simple. The old Administration cannot be expected to repair what it failed to prevent.

> Where will a new Administration begin?

It will begin with its President taking a simple, firm resolution. That resolution will be: To forego the diversions of politics and to concentrate on the job of ending the Korean war—until that job is honorably done.

That job requires a personal trip to Korea.

I shall make that trip. Only in that way could I learn how best to serve the American people in the cause of peace.

I shall go to Korea.

I could literally feel an electric jolt run through the crowd as it exploded in whoops and yells that drowned out the handclapping, the reaction so violent and sustained that it totally startled Eisenhower.

I made no effort to get to the podium to congratulate the General or say goodbyes. Rather I caught a taxi to the airport for my flight back to New York. I always carried a portable radio with me when I traveled to let me get local news reports. When we brainstormed the speech, Brownell, Jackson, and I tried to work out scenarios of Stevenson's potential responses. The most telling seemed to be: "General Eisenhower has a good idea, and if I become president and commander-in-chief, I will send him to Korea. I will also consult with General MacArthur and other generals with more Far East experience than General Eisenhower."

As I waited in the Detroit airport, a news report quoted a quickie interview that night with Stevenson. When asked his reaction to the Eisenhower proposal, the master of the quip replied: "Eisenhower is proposing to catch a bus to the wrong location. The Korean War will be settled in Moscow."

Truman and the other Democratic leaders recognized immediately the mortal nature of the speech's blow, and struck back wildly and negatively:

Truman: "Anybody who poses and talks like a superman is a fraud."

"Eisenhower uses the 'Big Lie' technique of Joseph McCarthy."

"Eisenhower is thoroughly dishonest about Korea."

Wilson Wyatt [Stevenson's campaign manager]:   Eisenhower's visit to Korea "could touch off World War III."

Stephen Mitchell [Democratic National Committee Chairman]:   "I think it is a grandstand play to get votes . . . a desperation move."

Stevenson: The Detroit speech is Eisenhower's "last desperate bid" for votes . . . He changed the course of the campaign and now plays "politics with peace." . . . The speech did not come from General Eisenhower but from the brain of "a speechwriter from a slick magazine."

The next night in Boston, Stevenson added to his advance text.

The General has announced his intention to go to Korea. But the root of the Korean problem does not lie in Korea. It lies in Moscow.

If the purpose of the General's trip is to settle the Korean war by a larger military challenge, then the sooner we all know about it the better.

You can always gauge the power of your hit by the reflexive reactions of your target. We thought the speech a real bullseye, as did a veteran political reporter who left the campaign train the day after Detroit with the observation, "The campaign ended last night! There's nothing of real interest left."

Smarting badly, Stevenson further revised his Boston speech as *The New York Times* reported:

MacArthur Plan Issue

One of the purposes of Governor Stevenson's statement tonight was an attempt to make General Eisenhower say whether he had now adopted the line of General of the Army Douglas MacArthur, which called for expanding the war in the Far East, with the prospect of even higher casualties, or whether he agreed with the Truman Administration that all efforts should be made to confine the present conflict and to settle it, if possible, by negotiation.

The Democratic nominee made the addition to a speech in which he declared again that General Eisenhower was a captive of the Republican "Old Guard" that has voted for policies "which would encourage Soviet aggression and against policies which would check it."

We knew a public statement on Korea by MacArthur at this time could hurt us badly, but we felt confident it would not come because of Eisenhower's anticipatory reaching out to his old boss through my liaison contacts.

Brownell, Jackson, and I decided that we should hit the "I Shall Go!" theme one more time while the Democrats floundered. Working with Emmet Hughes, we built it into a Pittsburgh speech on October 27, which I again hand-delivered to the General to be sure no one doctored the wording:

Throughout this campaign I have talked at length about our nation's security against Communist aggression. I can summarize my conviction about one very important aspect of this quite simply. It is this: so long

83

as a single American soldier faces enemy fire in Korea, the honorable ending of the Korean war and the securing of honorable peace in the world must be the first—the urgent and unshakable—purpose of a new administration.

I repeat to you the pledge I made to all the American people last week: This will be the first great labor of our new administration. To advance it—to appraise on the spot methods for solving that particular problem with speed and with honor—I shall go to Korea.

The American people—since I first made that pledge—have learned that the Administration forces do not like the idea of my making such a trip and undertaking such an effort. The people have learned this with some astonishment and much bewilderment.

This has been my rudest lesson in partisan politics. I had thought that all Americans shared one simple feeling of mine.

That feeling is this: If a journey to Korea and a close study of our military and political problems there can save the life of a single American soldier and bring peace of mind to a single American family, I must make that journey.

My good friends, I shall make that journey.

The next day, I hand-delivered full-draft copies of both the Detroit and Pittsburgh speeches to General MacArthur, brought him Eisenhower's personal good wishes, and said that Eisenhower wanted him to see the full texts. I asked him about the *Times* reports of Stevenson's Boston speech and his attempts to reopen the Truman-MacArthur controversy.

"I read it," he replied in a defiant tone barely concealing his anger. "You may reassure Eisenhower again that the Truman candidate will not receive any help from me!"

We talked—perhaps I should say, I listened—for another half-hour. The General finally asked the question I knew needled him: "Will Eisenhower want to see me before or after his trip to Korea?"

I replied that while I could not commit General Eisenhower, my best guess would be that he would want his conference with MacArthur after his trip, when he could come back with his own first-hand appraisal of the situation and their meeting would be far more meaningful. This satisfied MacArthur and we said our goodbyes.

November 4th finally arrived. Eisenhower received 33,936,252 votes to Stevenson's 27,314,992, a spread of almost eleven percent. With it came 442 electoral votes to Stevenson's 89. Equally important, the Republicans captured the House of Representatives by a slim margin, the Senate evenly divided which meant that the Republicans could organize it with the Vice President's tie-breaking vote.

Eisenhower's intuitive ability to reach out to all factions of the divided Republican party, to the dissatisfied Democrats, and to the great body of independents, actually gave renewed life to the two-party system in America at a time when it faced virtual extinction.

Chapter 6
Transition Without Trap

Even after the election, Truman and Dean Acheson continued their efforts to trap Eisenhower into committing himself to their bankrupt foreign policies, especially in Korea.

Back in mid-August, before Eisenhower left Denver, he received a public telegram from Truman inviting him to lunch at the White House with Truman's full cabinet. General Bedell Smith, then CIA Director and Eisenhower's chief deputy during World War II, would also be there to brief the Republican nominee on foreign affairs.

Eisenhower declined the invitation on the grounds that he needed to "remain free to analyze publicly the policies and acts of the present administration whenever it appears to me to be proper and in the country's interests."

Truman's vitriol rose and he shot back a patronizing handwritten reply:

August 16, 1952.

THE WHITE HOUSE
WASHINGTON

Dear Ike:—I am sorry if I caused you embarrassment.

What I've always had in mind was and is a continuing foreign policy. You know that is a fact, because you had a part in outlining it.

Partisan politics should stop at the boundaries the the [sic] United States. I am extremely sorry that you have allowed a bunch of screwballs to come between us.

You have made a bad mistake and I'm hoping it won't injure this great Republic.

There has never been one like it and I want to see it continue regardless of the man who occupies the most important position in the history of the world.

May God guide you and give you light.

From a man who has always been your friend and who always wanted to be!

Sincerely,

/s/Harry Truman

Hon. Dwight D. Eisenhower,
Denver, Colorado.

Eisenhower's handwritten response to Truman went out three days later:

August 19

Dear Mr. President:

My sincere thanks for the courtesy of your note of the 16th. I assure you that your invitation caused me no personal embarrassment. My feeling merely was that, having entered this political campaign, I would have become involved in the necessity of making laborious explanations to the public, if I had met with the President and Cabinet. Since there was no hint of National Emergency conveyed by the telegram of invitation, and since I belong, no longer, to any of the public services, I thought it wiser to decline.

I repeat my gratefulness for the invitation and for the offer to send me weekly CIA reports. Through these I shall keep familiar with the foreign situation. Further, I assure you of my support of real bi-partisanship in foreign problems. With renewed assurances of my respect and esteem,

Sincerely

/s/DWIGHT D. EISENHOWER

Three days after the election, I became aware of the renewed efforts to trap Eisenhower as I sat in my University of Pennsylvania office, working on a report for my trustees.

My secretary came in cautiously. She knew I did not want to be disturbed, but a man on the phone insisted that he must speak to me. He would not give his name and declined to leave a number where we might return his call.

I asked, "Does he sound like a nut?"

"No," she replied. "He sounds completely rational. His voice is refined and controlled. He is courteous and respectful. I would guess him to be maybe in his forties or fifties."

I valued her judgment and told her I would talk to the man.

"You do not know me," the voice said when I picked up the phone. "I am a foreign service officer, and I have some information for you which I think extremely important."

I cut in at once to tell him that since I held no governmental post, I could not receive classified information.

"My information is not classified," he persisted, "But I think it important enough for the country for you to pass it on to President-elect Eisenhower."

"All right," I said, "but may I ask you a couple of questions first?"

He agreed, and my mind raced to dredge up a few questions to which a bona fide foreign service officer would know the answers—answers that I knew, but that members of the general public would probably not know.

I started with the first one that came to mind. "Who is our ambassador to Brazil?"

He told me.

"How long has he held that post?"

I could confirm the correctness of his answer since I knew the ambassador personally and remembered exactly when he received his assignment.

I asked similar questions about our ambassador to Czechoslovakia and back came the correct answers.

I tested him twice more, and he came through.

"All right," I proceeded, "what is it that you wish to tell me?"

"I happen to know that there will be a major effort by President Truman and Dean Acheson to trap the President-elect into a commitment in support of certain foreign policy matters advocated by Truman and Acheson. I think the policies are wrong for the country, especially what is happening in Korea. That is really a bad situation, badly mishandled. I think that General Eisenhower should be on his guard against this effort by Truman and his advisors."

I thanked the caller, told him I could guarantee that the President-elect would receive his advice, and that if he needed to contact me again, we would use the Navy method for identifying dispatches as our code.

"It's now 10:43 a.m. in the eleventh month on the seventh day of the month, in 1952," I said. "If you want to talk to me again identify yourself to my secretary with the code 10:43-11-7-52. I'll leave word for her to put you right through to me."

I've often wondered about the identity of my anonymous informant. His information proved to be 100% correct. He never called back.

I knew that Eisenhower, bone-tired from the rigors of the campaign, vacationed at the Augusta Country Club in Georgia at the course famed golfer Bobby Jones designed. He would not want to be disturbed. Still, the news from Korea continued grim, with mounting casualties: Americans, UN soldiers, the ROKs (Republic of Korea soldiers), and the Communists of China as well as of North Korea.

The UN General Assembly, then in session, anguished over what to do about Korea, our British and French allies especially uncertain about their roles. Sometimes they looked ready to desert us. I knew that the Democrats would use every tactic possible to wring some sort of commitment favorable to them from Eisenhower, and it might come from a reporter's off-hand question to the General in an unguarded moment.

I decided that I dared not sit on the information from the nameless caller. I must report it to Eisenhower immediately in a letter, which I gave to one of my executive assistants to hand-deliver to the General in Augusta:

HAROLD E. STASSEN
8212 St. Martins Lane
Philadelphia 18

November 8, 1952

President-Elect Dwight D. Eisenhower
Augusta National Golf Club
Augusta, Georgia

CONFIDENTIAL

Dear Mr. President:

I have received confidential information from a reliable source that President Truman intends to persuade

you to agree with him in support of the present
Truman policy on prisoner repatriation in Korea.

Among other problems, a bitter stalemate over prisoner
exchanges in Korea thwarted hopes for negotiation. South
Korea held at least 25,000 North Koreans, and North Korea
wanted them back. South Korean President Syngman Rhee
swore that the Koreans—he did not call them
"North"—absolutely would not be returned to their oppressors in the northern half of their one country. The UN vacil-
lated and our Allies waffled.

He will urge that the United Nations situation
requires prompt action on your part because the
Assembly is in session and four proposed resolutions
on this subject have been presented.

I respectfully submit that it would be a great mistake
to make this agreement with him.

It would be your first foreign policy decision and it
would be taken without the essential advance consultation abroad and at home.

It would be contrary to your Detroit speech in which
you stated that you intended to carefully consider all
phases of the Korean situation, consult with friendly
nations of Asia and with cooperating United Nations,
and establish a new policy designed to bring the
Korean War to an early and successful end without a
World War. It would link your first foreign policy decision to the discredited Truman administration, when
all of America now looks for a fresh appraisal and a
change in policy.

It would reduce the possible range on your future
policy decisions and do so at a time when you do not
yet have complete information in the hands of your
own people, nor the authority to implement your own
policies.

By contrast, I feel very deeply that your tremendous prestige can be a precious immediate asset for progress toward a peaceful world, provided Truman's clumsy moves are carefully sidestepped and your own policies are established and unfolded through the use of your own great prestige and superb skill.

I thought long and hard about stopping my letter right there, but then realized Eisenhower's position in Augusta without staff or other advisors. I knew him well enough to be sure that he would not think affirmative suggestions presumptuous, so I continued:

Specifically I respectfully recommend that the following steps be taken before you enunciate or agree to any fragment of a Korean policy.

1. Your own trip to Korea be taken for first hand information and evaluation of our own forces, of the South Korean potential, the Formosan factor, the psychological warfare possibilities, and other items.

2. Your consultation with Nehru either by meeting him on Okinawa after your visit to Korea, or by sending a personal emissary to consult with him in India, or by conferring with his Ambassador in Washington.

3. Consultation with Winston Churchill and [French Premier] Pinay through their representatives.

4. Conference with the leaders of both parties of the forthcoming Congress.

In my judgment the Kremlin communistic program for the period immediately ahead involves the avoidance of belligerent and violent action on their part and concentration upon Cold War activity, seeking to divide the rest of the world from America; stirring up uneasiness toward you because of your military background, and fomenting distrust because of the capitalistic and imperialistic atmosphere which Europeans relate to the Republican Party.

By consulting with Nehru before you make a foreign policy decision on the Korean question, you will move dramatically counter to this communistic line. It will have a beneficial result in the attitude of all of the brown and black and yellow people toward America and toward you. The personal conference in Okinawa would obviously be the best, if Nehru is agreeable. But the other alternative of sending a special emissary to him or of conferring with his Ambassador in Washington would also be very beneficial.

India's prime minister tried hard to establish himself as the "neutral" power broker between the Communists and the free world. He brought down the wrath of American conservatives who argued that no one could be really "neutral" in the raging philosophical battles. If a leader would not actively align himself against the Communists, he must be considered for them.

Likewise the consultation with other European countries and consultation through emissaries or Ambassadors with the Arab Moslem group and with Israel will have further desirable effects.

The bipartisan congressional conference at home is obvious in its merit.

At the risk of sounding redundant, I wanted to emphasize the the critical nature of Eisenhower's first foreign policy pronouncement and make certain that it contained no taint of carry-over from Truman-Acheson. I also knew that Eisenhower respected my ideas about the UN, as we talked earlier and often about my experiences in San Francisco at its founding and my optimism over what it could become if all free nations gave it wholehearted support.

In summary your first foreign policy decision can be a great asset in establishing the foundation for a peaceful world, and, on the contrary, these foundations would be injured if your first foreign policy move was an agreement with a discredited retiring President who has seriously blundered in his conduct of foreign policy.

The claim that the United Nations session requires immediate action is not valid. I am confident that if it became known that you would prefer to have the Assembly recess until February so that you could consult with them after your administration was established and after you had visited Korea, they would recess.

Or, in the alternative, any advisory resolution which they passed now would not have any serious effect when evaluated over against the importance of your own opening foreign policy move.

It is my further information that Truman may make some attempt to get a minimum commitment out of you for foreign economic aid for the next budget and put on a rush act in behalf of the European nations.

It would also be a mistake to do this. Some of the forgoing [sic] reasons apply, and in addition there is a great need for straightening out the world raw material situation. This should be done concurrent with the working out of next year's foreign economic and military aid. America has been bidding some raw material up out of sight in competition with its own grants of aid held by other nations. A long-term sound raw material policy worked out with the nations that we are aiding can do much to stabilize our own and other economies and avoid sharp inflation or deflation in the key nations.

Likewide [sic] a discussion of further moves toward European unity, convertibility of currency and lessening of trade restrictions between them, should be carried on in conjunction with the agreements for the new American foreign economic aid program.

Once more I debated about going further with the letter; but again, the thought of Eisenhower's lack of staff in Atlanta propelled me to suggest the contents of the press release.

I suggest that the insistence on the desirability of advance consultation before commitments, could be the basis of a general refusal to commit—if Truman does make the attempts which my information indicates. The most desirable type of an announcement after your conference with him appears to be along these lines.

That you have conferred for the purpose of assisting in the orderly change to the new administration which the people had voted in—that you appreciated the courtesies of the President in assisting in arrangements for that orderly change—that your own policies in foreign and domestic affairs were quite well known from your past actions and your public pronouncements—that so far as your further statements of policy were concerned, you would make them in due course on further occasions and particularly in your inaugural and Congressional messages.

By the way, please remind our friend Robinson that he lost his big bet with me about MacArthur as the latter did not come anywhere near polling 150,000 [primary] votes in the seven states.

Best wishes as always,

Sincerely,

/s/Harold E. Stassen

I sent the letter down to Augusta with my assistant who caught the President-elect just as he finished a round of golf. He expressed surprise at receiving a letter from me, thanked the messenger, and went into the club house.

Naturally, I wondered how he would react. The first paragraph of his response reassured me about his continued level-headed approach to his new status as President-elect.

<u>Confidential</u>   Augusta, Georgia.

November 10, 1952.

Dear Harold:

I was delighted to have your letter of November eighth. I most particularly agree with the first parts of it—those parts that are cautionary with respect to the making of premature decisions or giving premature concurrence to some existing policy. To allow myself to be tied up too closely with existing arrangements would, of course, seriously limit flexibility in later treatment of some of these problems.

With respect to the positive steps that you suggest, I think there is some danger that attempts of this kind might create resentment among nations or individuals who would feel they had an equal right to consultation, but who would be omitted because of time limitations.

The Korean trip can be defended because of its unique character—a spot where a quarter of a million Americans are in action. Consequently, the trip would be a completely American affair undertaken to protect and advance American interests. While, during such a trip, I would be quite ready to meet and talk with allied personnel, the essential purpose of serving American interests would still be preserved. On the other hand, a visit with Nehru would, it seems to me, imply a readiness to meet with the heads of the Formosa government, the Philippines, and even the governments of Indonesia, Australia, New Zealand and so on. On the other side of the globe, conferences with Winston and with Pinay would undoubtedly be resented unless similar ones were held with De Gasperi and others.

Having said this, I still agree with your conclusion that we should spare no pains to dispel the mistaken notion that American [sic] intends to be indifferent to the best interests of other free states.

The idea of an emissary—who could, of course, devote his entire time to visiting governments around the world—does not seem to me to be as risky as the direct contact could be.

In any event, I shall thoroughly consider the entire letter and will have two or three others give me their views on it. This is the hastiest kind of a reply. Although I have already warned my representatives in Washington to agree to nothing that sounds like policy, I shall give them an added caution not to be enticed into anything through the medium of the Budget or any other indirect way.

We are returning to New York early next week to be there for a minimum of a week's time. I hope you will find it possible to come to see me during that time—I should like to have a long talk with you.

With warm regards,

Sincerely,

/s/ Dwight David Eisenhower

Governor Harold E. Stassen,
8212 St. Martins Lane,
Philadelphia, Pennsylvania.

Truman and Acheson attempted to spring their trap at a November 18 meeting in the Oval Office that Eisenhower attended with Henry Cabot Lodge and Joseph Dodge, the next Director of the Budget. I cannot add anything about this meeting not already covered in a dozen books. Writing later, Acheson and Lodge both described Eisenhower's attitude as cool but courteous, and cooperative in tone. But Eisenhower spurned offers by both Truman and Acheson to make any commitments whatsoever on any matters of policy, foreign or domestic.

I find Eisenhower's letter to me revealing. It shows his skill as a letter writer who could organize his thoughts and get them on paper cogently and clearly, without staff or help of any kind. It also shows his quick, deep grasp of foreign relations and his ability to take a long-term, careful look at goals and potential repercussions.

A quick postscript on my liaison mission to MacArthur is that he did not inject himself into the election campaign, but on December 5, a month after the election, he spoke to the National Association of Manufacturers, telling them, "While it is well known that my own views have not been sought in any way, yet I am confident that there is a clear and definite solution to the Korean conflict" that would not involve broadening the war. He would not make a "public disclosure" of his plan, but would present it to the proper person or persons when asked.

Eisenhower learned of MacArthur's statements while aboard the *Helena* on the way home from his successful inspection trip to Korea. His advisors traveling with him were future cabinet members John Foster Dulles (State), George Humphrey (Treasury), Douglas McKay (Interior), Herbert Brownell (Justice), Charles Wilson (Defense), press secretary Jim Hagerty, personal aide General Jerry Persons, trusted comrade and advisor General Lucius Clay, and speech writer

Emmet Hughes. Some urged Eisenhower to ignore the MacArthur speech because a response of any kind could do nothing but reopen the Truman-MacArthur controversy, present Eisenhower with a no-win posture, and possibly restrict his further dealings with the "Korean problem."

In his characteristic posture of reaching out, Eisenhower overruled them and cabled MacArthur December 7:

> Have just received aboard the *USS Helena* excerpts of your speech before NAM and am gratified by your continued interest in the Korean War which so vitally affects the United States and our Allies. Naturally I and my associates in the new administration, particularly the Secretaries of State and Defense, are vitally concerned about Korea and the Far East. We are now in the process of outlining a future program to be based upon the best interest of our country and the free world. It will aim, of course, at ultimate peace in that section of the world. I appreciate your announced readiness to discuss these matters with me and assure you that I am looking forward to [an] informal meeting in which my associates and I may obtain the full benefits of your thinking and experience. With personal regards. Eisenhower.

MacArthur answered:

> Dear Ike:
>
> I have just received your message. I am grateful for your interest in my views concerning solution of the problems involved in the Korean War and the Far East. This is especially so because, despite my intimate personal and professional connection and well known concern therewith, this is the first time that the slightest official interest in my counsel has been evidenced since my return. A failure of policy there might doom indefinitely the progress of civilization. A successful solution on the other hand might well become the key

100

to peace in the world. You know, without my saying, that my service is, as it always has been, entirely at the disposition of our country. My best to you, Ike, as always.

MacArthur

The drama of the meeting of the two generals December 17 in Dulles' New York brownstone still intrigues me—Eisenhower, the best clerk MacArthur ever had, now President-elect of the United States, and MacArthur, the best dramatics teacher Eisenhower ever had, now in his declining years. John Foster Dulles sat in as the only eyewitness to the epic encounter.

MacArthur handed Eisenhower a typed memorandum outlining a fourteen-point program not only for winning the Korean War, but on United States foreign policy generally. It called for an ultimatum to the Soviets as well as to North Korea and China, with the threat of atomic annihilation if the Communists did not permit the unification of both Koreas, both Germanys, and a general retreat within their own borders.

In MacArthur's *Reminiscences* (page 412), he describes the reactions:

> While Eisenhower was studying the memorandum I asked Dulles his own reaction. He said:

> "Your premature relief has resulted tragically for the free world. I regard it as the greatest mistake Truman ever made. Your present plan is a bold and imaginative one and could well succeed. I believe, however, that Eisenhower should first consolidate his position as President before attempting so ambitious and comprehensive a program. It might take him a year to do so."

I replied that Eisenhower would be at the peak of his power and prestige the day he was sworn in as President; that every day after his inauguration his power with the people would diminish, the first three months arithmetically, the second three geometrically, and the final six months astronomically; that by the end of a year he would be just the leader of his party fighting for the programs of his administration; that the plan represented action, to wait inaction; that he was the one American the Soviet esteemed highly; that if he did not act at once he could never do so, that it would then become too late. (New York: McGraw-Hill, 1964)

MacArthur's headlines afterward came few and far between. The ballad he recited at the close of his speech to the Joint Session of the Congress finally worked its will—the old soldier did, in fact, "fade away."

Chapter 7
Eisenhower Enlists Me

Esther and I talked over the possible import of Eisen-hower's call for me to meet him the next afternoon at his Morningside Heights home on the Columbia campus. What should I say if he invited me to become a part of his new administration in Washington?

We both felt strongly that we really did not want to leave the University of Pennsylvania. When I accepted its presi-dency in 1948, we thought that a ten-year tenure would be about right and adjusted our long-range plans accordingly. Now, in late November, 1952, we found ourselves not even to the halfway mark.

We could point to major accomplishments: the damper on the rantings of the anti-Communist extremists who threatened the free speech rights and academic freedom of several faculty members; balanced budgets to brighten the financial picture; increased endowments; Depression-delayed building maintenance corrected; a new building (Dietrich Hall) to house the historic Wharton School of Finance, the first of its kind in the United States; the new medical clinic in Donner Hall to enhance the prestige of its already famous Medical School, the first Northern school to reach out to Southern students after the Civil War; the appointment of retired U.S. Supreme Court Justice Owen Roberts to head the law school on a temporary basis; effective search committees that enticed nationally known scholars and deans, helping the

University regain its luster as one of the great Ivy League schools; the appointment of the first female trustee in the school's history, the first black students in the medical school, the first black member of the faculty, and the first black player on the football team.

Still, much remained to be done.

On the personal side of the ledger our son, Glen, performed well at the Penn Charter School and loved to come down to the University research laboratories and library. Our daughter, Kathleen, progressed beautifully at Springside School, conveniently located near our home. We did not want to uproot them.

We both dreaded the thought of moving and decided that even if Eisenhower should offer me a cabinet post, I would turn it down.

When I arrived at the Eisenhowers' home, Mamie ushered me into the living room, explaining that her husband would be a few minutes late. She reported ten "glorious" days at Augusta that refreshed them both, but she worried about Ike's upcoming trip to Korea. It would drain him physically and it did involve risks. A compensating factor would be his chance to visit their son John, an army major, on the front lines.

Eisenhower bounced in, looking as fresh and vibrant as in the days when we met as university presidents. He kissed Mamie before shaking hands with me.

He came right to the point. I paraphrase his words:

> Harold, I want you to be an important part of my administration, play a unique role. I'm not going to give you a regular cabinet post, as that would be too limiting for what I have in mind.
>
> Sherman Adams will be my chief of staff for administrative matters. He'll run the day-to-day affairs. Of course, he'll have input into policy matters, but that won't be his primary job.

I need someone I can trust who has practical experience in the political world. I think I know government. God knows I've spent my whole life in one phase of it. I've been directly involved with both the legislative and executive branches on such things as military plans, budgets. Of course, I worked intimately with Roosevelt and Churchill and the other civilian leaders of our Allies during the war.

But I have not had any direct experience working with the professional politicians who actually run the political parties and the government as a whole.

I interrupted to say that the batting averages of the so-called "professional" politicians over the past two decades didn't really hold up too well, particularly the Republicans, and I did not think he should discount his abilities as a political leader. The important ingredient of political leadership rested on the trust of the people and his overwhelming election victory should reassure him that the people stood behind him. He thanked me and continued:

It's been my experience that you get to where you want to go most of the time through compromise. That word has a bad sound to a lot of people. I don't mean you give in or give up the basic substance of your program or compromise on your principles. You stay flexible and let yourself maneuver on tactics.

I had a bit of experience with compromise during the War. God, what a job to keep the great prima donnas, Montgomery and de Gaulle, working with us instead of pulling against us; and Winston had his own ideas of strategy—even battlefield tactics—which took some listening, and counter-talking and compromise to overcome.

Years later, I read one of Eisenhower's similar statements on compromise in an October 16, 1952, letter to his lifelong friend, Swede Hazlett: "I am convinced that leadership in the political as well as in other spheres consists largely in making progress through compromise—but that does not mean compromise with basic principles."

The President-elect went on:

> I want you to start out as Director of Mutual Security, the post Averell Harriman holds under Truman. I don't know yet exactly what it now includes, but I'll want you to be in charge of all foreign operations—foreign aid, foreign relief, military and defense assistance programs, distribution of arms, technical and educational assistance—everything except covert operations which, of course, the CIA will still handle. The separate intelligence services will continue to handle their own needs.
>
> You'll have cabinet rank.

The potential scope of this assignment stunned me, and my adrenalin began to flow as I tried to think through the challenge.

> We've got some basic things to establish. In the first place, we've got to get the whole world involved in a global economy that will let the United States prosper, and keep us from pulling back into an economic shell behind a hostile tariff wall that could cause us and the world a repeat of the Great Depression, which we must avoid.
>
> Just mark my word, you'll see that a pulling back within national borders, like the Communist bloc is now doing, will be their economic downfall. Their economies will shrink instead of grow, and you'll see hardship, poverty, shortage, and starvation.

I interrupted from time to time with little more than a "Yes," "I agree," or simply a nod, because I did agree fully with everything he said.

> You know how I feel about NATO. We've got to keep the Communists from expanding over the rest of Europe. But we've got to go beyond bare containment. We've got to reach out to the Soviets and try to break through this Cold War stalemate. This is where your foreign operations post can be every bit as important as Foster Dulles' work at State.
>
> In today's world, foreign operations are so closely interwoven with domestic affairs that I don't think you can really separate them. I'll want you to sit in on the economic committees or the private sector groups, or whatever we end up calling them.

These economic committees eventually evolved into, among other things, the Council of Economic Advisors.

> To do the job that needs to be done in this assignment that I have in mind for you, I'll want you to also sit on the National Security Council and on C.D. Jackson's Psychological Strategy Board.

The Psychological Strategy Board eventually became the Operations Coordinating Board, composed of the Deputy Secretary of Defense, the Under Secretary of State, the Director of the CIA, C.D. Jackson from the White House staff, and me as Director of Mutual Security.

> I want to get back to this matter of compromise. In both parties we have widely opposite views. Across the country and in the Democratic party, we find the Reactionary Right and the Radical Left. I've got to compromise these views into the broad middle road if I am to lead effectively and get our programs across.

I'll expect help particularly from you and Cabot Lodge. I think your views pretty well mirror mine; but I want to listen to all sides. As you know, I'm bringing diverse philosophies into the cabinet; and this upsets a lot of the Taft people but I think we've got to do it.

My mind raced back to Esther's and my agreement the night before about staying in Philadelphia, and I realized that I already wavered. Eisenhower presumed my acceptance.

I'll want you to be a special consultant that I can bounce things off of. From time to time, I'll want you to sit quietly and listen in on conferences and later give me your reactions.

This "sit quietly" later became his code for me to do just that in meetings to which he sent me. The active participants, I'm sure, sometimes resented my presence. They knew my real reason for being there—to evaluate what they said, report back to Eisenhower, and discuss it with him.

I thanked the President-elect for his confidence, and told him that I wanted his administration to succeed, emphasized that for the good of the country, it must succeed; but I also told him that I would need to talk through with Esther this drastic change for my family.

Esther and I decided to make the personal sacrifices the move to Washington required: a fifty percent cut in salary, the surrender of our beautiful campus home, and the trying arrangements for our children. I mention this not to sound like a martyr, but to emphasize that all the members of the Eisenhower team accepted their assignments in the spirit of public service.

The pre-inaugural cabinet meeting January 12, in a room off the Commodore's mezzanine, proved prophetic of cabinet divisions to come.

The President-elect presided from the center of the closed horseshoe table arrangement. As one faced him, attendees sat in the following configuration:

Eisenhower

Richard Nixon (VP)	John Foster Dulles (State)
George Humphrey (Treasury)	Charles Wilson (Defense)
Herbert Brownell (Atty. Gen.)	Arthur Summerfield (Post Office)
Douglas McKay (Interior)	Ezra Taft Benson (Agriculture)
Sinclair Weeks (Commerce)	Martin Durkin (Labor)
Sherman Adams (Chief-of-Staff)	Henry Cabot Lodge, Jr. (UN Ambassador)
Oveta Culp Hobby (Federal Security)	Harold Stassen (Mutual Security)
Joseph Dodge (Budget)	Gen. Wilton Persons (Legislative Counsel)
Gabriel Hauge (Economic Counsel)	Emmet Hughes (Speeches)
Robert Cutler (Cabinet and NSC)	Thomas Stephens (Appointments Counsel)
James Hagerty (Press Secretary)	

The President-elect called on Benson, one of the twelve ruling apostles of the Mormon Church, to open the session with a prayer. Eisenhower then welcomed us and repeated a substantial amount of his discussion with me at Morningside Heights. He moved to what he said would be a key consideration for his administration. I paraphrase it, since minutes of cabinet and National Security Council are "minute" summaries only of the person writing up the proceedings the following day. They do not pretend to be verbatim transcripts of the meetings:

I want you—and all my key advisers—to speak up on all subjects, even though they are not within your own department or agency. I don't want a group of specialists who can tell me how many angels can dance on the head of a pin, but don't know what an angel is or why they might want to dance, period.

I want every member of this administration to feel a sense of responsibility for letting us reach our broad goals, and these are to reduce the size and power and cost of Big Government. This will let a market economy work and if we keep our economy strong, we can keep our national security at a safe level. This will help us in our efforts to find the right formula for a lasting world peace.

Naturally, you are responsible for your own department, but I want you to be more than advocates of your own department. We've got this problem over in Defense with the Joint Chiefs of Staff. The navy chief thinks he's got to present the navy's side of the thing, and the army and air force chiefs do the same for their services. They won't step back and look at the whole picture.

I find it of interest that ten months later the President, obviously not completely pleased with performances to date, felt compelled to emphasize this concept of management. The October 14, 1953 minutes of the National Security Council, declassified from "Eyes Only—Top Secret" in 1984, read:

1.   CONCEPT OF THE NATIONAL SECURITY COUNCIL AND ITS ADVISORY AND SUBORDINATE GROUPS

The President announced at the opening of the Council meeting that he wished to go over with the members of the Council his own conception of the National Security Council. Two conceptions of the functions of this body, he said, were prevalent. One is that each member represents his department or agency and is present primarily to defend the position of that department or agency. The other conception is that while you members have the staff support of your agency, you come to this table as an individual in your own right, not merely to represent a department. Your background helps us all to reach a corporate decision and not merely a compromise of varying departmental positions. What we are seeking is the best solution of our problems by the corporate mind represented here.

This second conception, said the President, must apply if the National Security Council is really going to work. This concept applies also to advisory and supporting bodies such as the NSC Planning Board and the Joint Chiefs of Staff. To my mind, said the President, there are in each of the three military services at least six individuals who would be competent to direct that service as a chief of staff. But the job of the Joint Chiefs of Staffs [sic] is both distinct and much more difficult. It is the task of the Joint Chiefs not merely to support the three services, but to bring their consolidated wisdom and their corporate experience as statesmen to solve the problems of the national security. Hence, said the President, I hope that all who come here will give the best they've got. I am convinced that a great many meetings in Washington are nothing but meetings designed to achieve acceptable compromises. I don't want that view to prevail here. "We want your brains and hearts, with your background."

The National Security Council:

> Noted a statement by the President of his conception of the NSC as being a corporate body composed of individuals advising the President in their own right, rather than as representatives of their respective departments and agencies. Their function should be to seek, with their background of experience, the most

statesmanlike solution to the problems of
national security, rather than to reach solutions
which represent merely a compromise of
departmental positions. The same concept is
equally applicable to advisory and subordinate
groups, such as the Joint Chiefs of Staff and the
NSC Planning Board.

The President-elect continued his briefing at the Commodore
meeting:

If all of you see the overall goals, and know what the
other people are trying to do, we'll all have a better
chance of coming up with creative ideas that will help
us win the battles.

The minutes, of course, seldom show direct quotes, but I
think this is where he first made his oft-repeated statement:
"Let's keep in mind that if we're going to make a big mistake,
let's not make it in one hell of a hurry."

He continued that unless some grave crisis forced an
immediate decision, he planned to move deliberately, slowly,
and to call people back for additional debates. We would hold
night sessions if necessary.

I know this will give the wiseacres the chance to say
that we are afraid to make decisions, or take bold
action. Well, let them say it. I'll take my chances on
that kind of reaction.

The President-elect then went around the table, asking for
suggestions on his inaugural speech, a draft of which had been
passed out in advance.

George Humphrey, powerful Chairman of the M.A.
Hanna company, a great conglomerate of the day, said the
chief emphasis should be on the immediate removal of all
price and wage controls and all other restrictions put on as a

result of the Korean War to control inflation and assure the flow of priorities. This would signal a clear break with the Truman administration and announce to the world that we were moving back into a market economy that would give business room to expand.

I looked up and down the table. No one else spoke or seemed ready to speak. I got Eisenhower's permission to talk, and said that if we removed all controls immediately—particularly since we did not know what would happen in the Korean War—the result would be an inflationary surge that could be disastrous. Materials in scarce supply would be bought up by major companies. Profiteering would result. The public would lose confidence in our leadership and fear that we were headed back to the days of the Great Depression.

We must move cautiously, I continued, only after the President-elect took office and got the facts from his own advisers. We would probably find then that the removal of price controls should be taken gradually, spread out over a period of months, and probably staggered among various products—maybe wages approached the same way—to prevent a precipitous loss of confidence.

Cabot Lodge backed my position, adding that before removing controls, we should consult with Congressional leaders and try to gain bipartisan support.

George Humphrey restated his position, with Charles Wilson and Sinclair Weeks supporting him.

Eisenhower looked around the table again, then said, "I think that Harold and Cabot are right. We'll stay away from that subject in the inaugural message and take it up gradually after we are in office."

The official minutes of the meeting show their skeletal nature:

8. Most of the discussion on Tuesday morning had to do with price and wage controls. Mssrs. Humphrey and

Wilson were the strongest proponents of a quick and definitive end to such controls. Mr. Humphrey later softened his stand on the timing of such action—towards a slight delay if necessary.

The possibility of having stand-by controls was discussed. Humphrey advocated that there not be any, but that the administration should merely indicate its willingness to go to Congress for new controls should they become necessary as the result, for instance, of a further outbreak of war.

General Eisenhower, Senator Lodge, and Gov. Stassen maintained a position of moderation in regard to timing and extent of decontrol. They did not want to move too quickly, or to strip the admin. of all powers.

When the session adjourned, I went to George Humphrey and told him that I realized the matter of controls fell mainly within his bailiwick at Treasury. Since the subject did not appear on the pre-meeting agenda, I could not anticipate its coming up as a main item of debate and I could not discuss it with him beforehand. I obviously held a point of view different from his, and I tried to follow the President-elect's admonition to speak out on any subject, no matter who held primary jurisdiction over it.

My comments did not mollify Humphrey, who said that he thought me completely wrong on this item of economic policy, that I gave the President-elect some bad advice, and that Eisenhower made a serious blunder in following my line of thinking.

I immediately went to Eisenhower's suite on the ninth floor. I asked if he thought me out of line to speak up on the controls issue. He answered:

That's exactly what I want you to do. I know you're worried about making George Humphrey mad, but I don't intend to run any Ladies Aid Society. I want differences of opinion. I don't know that I'd say I want controversy; I guess I don't. But I sure as hell meant it when I said I wanted you all to speak up on all subjects.

You did exactly what I wanted you to do. So did Cabot. I want both of you to keep doing it, and let me worry about any ruffled feathers.

Chapter 8
Able Communicator: Speech Editor, Letter Writer, and Speaker

The impression survives that Eisenhower spoke only in Casey Stengelese, unable to hone in on a subject, with rambling, unending sentences and imprecise syntax. Actually, he tailored his communications to his needs of the moment, and used his different styles with great skill.

We stood around the coffin-shaped table in the cabinet room, our places dictated by protocol, all eyes on the President as he entered.

He sat, then we sat.

He announced that his poll of the members on opening the cabinet meetings with prayer brought complete differences of opinion. Some opted for no prayer at all; others wanted a formal prayer. His compromise decision: We would begin each meeting with a short period of silent prayer so that each in his or her own way could ask God for guidance. We bowed our heads, perhaps for thirty seconds—which always seemed longer—until he said, "Thank you," and looked up.

The cabinet minutes for that first post-inaugural session, January 23, 1953, state no more than vague summaries:

2. State of the Union Message.

The President urged Cabinet Members to submit specific recommendations to Congress which they want incorporated in the Message. He was concerned

117

lest the Message not have sufficient substance to warrant assembling Congress in joint session. Negative statements in the Message will be appropriate, for instance, that certain actions will not be recommended.

The White House minutes under the heading "Notes on State of the Union Message 2/2/53" add to the story in retrospect:

> Following his session with the President on January 22, [Emmet] Hughes had prepared a third draft (dated January 23) which was intended specifically for presentation at the Cabinet Meeting, but the President decided not to take time for it until it was in better form.

I remember distinctly what happened, and what the President said:

> I had hoped that we'd spend most of our time this morning going over the State of the Union message; but the Third Draft we now have is not in good enough shape to spend time on. The way it reads, I wouldn't even feel comfortable to waste the Congress' time by asking them to hear me in special session. It doesn't represent what I believe in, and what I want to say.

I could not help but feel Emmet Hughes' discomfort as he sat in one of the chairs toward the door, at the end of the room.

The President looked down the table to his left toward me where I sat next to Henry Cabot Lodge, and said: "Harold, I want you to prepare a new draft of the message. It will probably be better to start all over from the beginning. Have it ready by the morning of the 26th." Looking around the room, he concluded, "I want all of you to treat this message as your top priority, and send Harold your comments by the end of the day. We've got less than three days to whip this new draft into shape."

When the session ended and the President left the room, I buttonholed Dulles, Wilson, Humphrey, McKay, Brownell, and as many others as I could stop, and told them to please get their suggestions to me by four that afternoon. I would be working on the message that night. I told them to emphasize the needs of their own departments, but reminded them of Eisenhower's admonition at the Commodore that he wanted them to comment on all facets of the administration's program, not just limit themselves to their own bailiwicks.

Before I left the office late in the afternoon, I collected their suggestions which arrived by special messengers. Driving home, I tried to think up a dramatic way to open the message, but it did not come immediately. I knew from my own years of public speaking that you need an attention-getting opening statement to grab an audience. If you do not get them in the first paragraph, you stand little chance of ever capturing their attention.

I realized, too, that this assignment carried special considerations: I would not be the one delivering the speech, so I must keep in mind not only the President's substantive beliefs, but also his own special style and speaking rhythm. Many speechwriters fail to take these two key elements into account, and the speech falls flat in its delivery.

After a quick dinner during which I sat so engrossed in my thoughts that I could scarcely converse with Esther, I moved into my study and closed the door. I turned to my files of all the Eisenhower speeches during the campaign, his statements before the nomination, his speeches while serving as President of Columbia, even the Guildhall speech, which I still think a masterpiece. I knew they gave a good measure of the man and his philosophies. Naturally, I examined carefully Hughes' Draft #3 to be sure that I did not repeat its shortcomings.

I also reread my December 30, 1952 memo to Hughes following my review of Draft #1:

> Pursuant to C. D. Jackson's request I am forwarding to you my preliminary reactions to Draft #1 of the Message to Congress.
>
> I feel that it needs more "lift" and more "warmth." It seems too matter of fact, and does not bring out the humanitarian quality in President Eisenhower's approach to the people.

In my memo, I ran through this Draft page-by-page, making specific suggestions which I thought would better capture the President's thinking, then concluded:

> I suggest consideration of an indication of confidence that the best years are ahead for both America and for the other free countries notwithstanding the obstacles and difficulties of debts, Communism, trade barriers, confusion, etc., etc., which are present as the administration begins its task. Some glimpse of what can be accomplished by cooperation of the free peoples of the world in economic, cultural, and military matters should be given.
>
> I further suggest inclusion somewhere of an expression of determination to improve the lot of those who are in need, either struggling with small pensions or handicapped in some way.
>
> A tribute to heroism of Korean forces is indicated. "I saw etc."
>
> I suggest consideration of a request for specific Congressional action to end discrimination in the nation's capital with its special importance as the place where

representatives of many countries of all races and religions come to do business with our nation.

At midnight, Esther brought me a pot of black coffee and a toasted cheese sandwich. I began to dictate random thoughts into my machine. I would play them back, write out in longhand what I thought worth saving, and repeat the process. I worked through the night; and by daylight, I felt my draft worth taking to my secretaries.

I grabbed a quick bite, rushed to my office, and parceled out my legal-sized yellow pages to three secretaries. By mid-morning, we ended with a working draft adequate to go by special messenger to all cabinet members. I wrote appropriate notes to each of them, pointing out the location of segments that directly affected his or her department, and asked them to please get their comments back to me by early afternoon.

At the end of a long day that began some thirty-six hours earlier, I gathered up all comments and headed for home. I fell asleep before I could make it to the dinner table, but woke around 10:00 p.m., ate something, and turned again to the draft, knowing that I needed to polish it for final typing the next day.

By the end of January 25, on schedule, my secretaries handed me copies of the final draft. I called Ann Whitman, the President's personal secretary, to see when the President would like to see it.

When I reached the Oval Office the morning of the 26th, Ann told me the President wanted us to work on the speech in his study in the family living quarters on the second floor where we would not be interrupted. I went up immediately, found him at his desk, and handed him the draft.

He took it in his right hand, made two or three up and down motions as though assaying its weight, turned to the last page, and blurted out: "It's too heavy. It's too damn long!"

I can paraphrase my response:

> It's really not as long as it looks. In the first place, it's
> triple spaced and some of the pages are not full.

This did not pacify him. I knew he hated long speeches,
although his writers gave them to him, knowing that he would
edit them down to what he considered usable length.

I continued my argument:

> This is your one, proper, constitutional opportunity
> to tell the whole country of the changes you think
> should take place during your presidency. You will be
> speaking not only to the Congress, but to the people of
> the country and world. This is your golden opportu-
> nity, and you should take advantage of it.

> I've tried to shape this speech into language it will be
> appropriate for you to use. I've gone back over your
> speeches of the last eight years, starting with Guildhall.
> You'll never have this same opportunity again; so I
> don't think that length should be the prime
> consideration.

"All right," he said, looking at me over his glasses and
reaching for his pen. "Let's go through it together."

We spent two hours on it, paragraph by paragraph, while
he commented:

"What's this in here for?"

"What do you mean by that?"

"I don't think that's the way I want to say it."

"That needs to be changed."

"Why don't we shorten that?"

"I don't think that belongs in it at all."

"I'm not ready to say that now—maybe later, but not
now."

At the end, he took off his glasses, laid the speech down, looked at me and said: "This is more like the kind of message it will be worthwhile for me to deliver to the Congress. It's a good job, but I'll be making some changes in it. I always do; but I like it."

He always did make changes. During the years I worked closely with him I can't recall him ever delivering a speech exactly as he received it. His fine editorial hand went to work automatically. I've always thought back to what he told me of how the Guildhall speech came into being, as I stood in the door of his NATO office a little over a year before: "That speech is genuine me!"

Certainly, he began with the drafts of the speech writers; but by delivery time, the speech evolved into "genuine Eisenhower."

The White House minutes of February 2 continue:

> The fourth draft (dated January 26) was prepared on the basis of efforts by Mr. Stassen who, in conjunction with Mr. Hauge and at the direction of the President, conferred with Members of the Cabinet and secured new material concerning agriculture, natural resources, labor, and social security.
>
> The fifth draft (January 27) resulted from the President's editing of the fourth.
>
> The sixth draft (dated January 29) was the product of extensive editing by the President in sessions with Hughes on January 28 and 29. This draft is merely a clean copy of the fifth draft on which the President had penciled extensive changes in his own handwriting.
>
> The seventh draft (January 30) contained a new section on agriculture, prepared by Dr. Milton Eisenhower, new material on loyalty and on social security, and other changes of wording. Dr. Eisenhower has commented that not until the completion of this draft

did the President seem to be fairly well satisfied with the message.

The eighth draft (February 1) differed from the preceding one only by virtue of slight changes in the sections on the budget and on wage-price controls. This draft was made available to the press in mimeographed form.

Finally, there is the reading copy which the President had in front of him when he delivered the message before the Joint Session of Congress on February 2. A few very minor changes of wording were made for the reading copy and final delivery.

I include portions of the speech as delivered alongside my Draft #4 in Appendix 4. The important observations are not the similarities of ideas and verbatim wording, but rather the differences that show the infusion of Eisenhower's own personal style and emphasis.

The State of the Union message, with the Eisenhower imprint clearly showing, accomplished everything we hoped for it and more, as the Associated Press reported:

WASHINGTON, Feb. 2 (AP)—President Eisenhower's State of the Union Message today appeared to have gone far to restore any prestige he might have lost by the rough spots encountered in his first days in office.

He also apparently made a hit with television viewers and radio listeners in his first appearance before Congress as President.

Two veterans at judging political trends in Congress—Senators Robert A. Taft, Republican of Ohio, and Walter F. George, Democrat of Georgia—agreed that the President had gone a long way toward washing up the controversies of his first two weeks in office. These have centered on his Defense Department appointments, Government reorganization and taxes.

All have contributed to make some of his supporters wonder whether the Administration was getting off to a bad start.

But in fifty-seven minutes of intensive speaking at today's joint session, the President seemed to have asserted the leadership role assumed by his sweeping victory in November.

Four boxes of Ann Whitman's drafts of letters reside in the Library at Abilene. They show the care—I'm sure pride is an accurate word—he took in this form of communication. I place examples of his editing and rewriting in Appendix 5.

While at the Abilene library in 1989, I found a wonderful letter to Milton Eisenhower dated January 6, 1954, almost exactly one year after this pre-inaugural cabinet meeting. It tells a lot about Eisenhower's general philosophy of government, and continues to demonstrate his genius as a letter writer. I include it in Appendix 5.

He dictated his letters to Milton, Swede Hazlett, Al Gruenther, and other close friends to secretary Ann Whitman, one of the ablest persons I ever worked with. She typed them, he read them hurriedly, and signed many of them with practically no editing or rewriting.

Sometimes a pressing demand on his time stopped the letter in mid-page. When he got back to it maybe two weeks later, he moved to finish it as though never interrupted. The letters seemed to give him a needed chance to unburden himself informally to close friends—to "let go" as he once told Hazlett—even though the letters now read as polished literary pieces.

Eisenhower spoke in four distinct styles: (1) his crisp, almost clipped formal parlance when he presided over cabinet meetings or participated in National Security Council sessions; (2) his "command tone" for any occasion that

125

required it; (3) his informal, relaxed, private conversation with friends; and (4) his Stengelese when he did not want to answer questions from the press directly.

My conversations with Eisenhower stemmed from our working relationship of mutual respect, coupled with a certain degree of circumspection. You might call it a relaxed formality in which we enjoyed each other's company, but we never reached a plane of undue familiarity.

Eisenhower contrived his Stengelese to serve his purposes. When I came back from my first encounter with Senator McCarthy's subcommitee and reported to Eisenhower, he told me:

> The press, sure as hell, will be after you to elaborate on what you said about our efforts to keep those Greek ships from carrying strategic cargoes to ports for transshipment to the Commies.
>
> Don't ever tell a reporter, "No comment!" The minute he hears that, his nose will start twitching, and he thinks you're trying to hide something. He'll go sniffing around to find out what you are hiding; and sure as hell, he'll find someone who will leak him an "inside story."
>
> Well, that won't be the thing at all that he asked about in the first place, or he'll get a one-sided, erroneous leak that misrepresents the real picture.
>
> What you do is talk in circles. Don't lie, or say you don't know. Just talk on. If they accuse you of not being responsive, give 'em something else that will let 'em get some sort of story, but keep you from having to disclose what "no comment" would protect.

A couple of excerpts from press conferences demonstrate his technique.

In May 1954, reporters asked about polls that showed the Republicans would likely lose both houses in Congress in

November. Naturally, the President did not want to be drawn into an appraisal of either the polls or Republican prospects:

> Q (Robert J. Donovan, New York Herald Tribune) Sir, from what you now hear and know, what do you think the Republican chances are in November?
>
> (Laughter.)
>
> THE PRESIDENT: There seems to be a very great interest in casting every public figure in the terms of a prophet, and certainly it is something I know very little about.
>
> I will tell you: I have believed from the beginning that the American people want to see a well-thought-out comprehensive program dealing with our principal affairs abroad, and our principal affairs at home put before the Legislature and enacted into law. That program we have labored very earnestly to produce, and we have laid it before the Congress.
>
> Now, no one has ever thought that in every detail it would be enacted, but I do believe that if the results are achieved in Congress, that I still believe are going to be achieved, which is that the great bulk of that program is enacted into law, that the supporters of that kind of action are going to be favorably considered by the voters.
>
> Now, I am just not going to predict any more accurately than that, but I believe thoroughly that the American people want a constructive program that is concerned with the future of America.

At the March 24, 1954 press conference, a downturn in the economy with a rise in unemployment generated lots of questions about how the Administration evaluated the situation and what he proposed to do about it.

Q (John Herling, Editors' Syndicate) And if unemployment continued to rise as at that time then things would require—then action other than has been pursued would be called for.

Now, unemployment has risen, sir, and I wonder whether there is an Administration policy that has been projected at this time?

THE PRESIDENT: I don't recall the exact words. I implied and indicated that March would normally be a rather significant month, that is, a month when normally, seasonally, there is an upturn, and I don't believe I said that instantly there would be programs set. I said there would be a new examination of the problem, and would cause—it would cause real concern.

It is difficult to talk about this question without taking a little bit more time than just a "yes" or "no,"ladies and gentlemen.

Coming out of a war economy, and going back into a peacetime economy, has traditionally caused, in every country, very, very marked fluctuations in—sometimes marked by great inflation, lowered productivity, all that sort of thing.

What has been the task that has really been going on for quite a while, but especially since last July, has been trying to make this transition, with a cutback on all kinds of war production, ammunition and everything else being used in Korea, in such a way as to cause the least damage.

Now, there has been, of course, a continuous rise in unemployment since that time. The figures for March are, of course, not all in, and they won't be in until some time in early April.

A contributing cause here, they tell me, although I am not so sure of the effect of this one, is that Easter, being late, that the ladies have not been buying as rapidly as they normally do this time of year, and that all kinds of qualifying conditions enter into this thing.

Now, the only thing that I am sure of, up to this moment—and we study this every single day of our lives, there is a conference in my office on this subject every single day—there is nothing that has developed that will call for a slam-bang emergency program being applied at this moment, and that doesn't mean that we are not watching everything.

Many things have been done. There is easier credit, there is cheaper money, there is things of that kind; there are housing and building programs before the Congress which should be helpful.

There is every kind of thing constantly under consideration that we can think of that would be helpful, but we just don't believe this is the time to move on an emergency basis, because if we do, we could easily distort the picture very badly.

Joseph C. Harsch, widely-read political columnist of *The Christian Science Monitor*, once asked:

Mr. President, sir, in your letter to Secretary Wilson about the new military budget you referred to the need for mobile forces and you said: "We should provide for meeting lesser hostile acts in situations not broadened by the intervention of a major aggressor's forces." Could you enlarge for us your concept of what these mobile forces would be like, the means for giving them mobility, their equipment and their weapons?

Eisenhower did not want to get into technical details that he considered classified, so he used his Stengelese for several minutes.

As the reporters left the conference, one asked Harsch what the President said in response to his question. Harsch replied, "I don't have the vaguest idea. I'll have to get back to the office and try to figure it out from my notes!"

Chapter 9
Eisenhower Reaches Out to the World

"Foster—Harold—sit down," the President said, his tone firm but not brusque, his words actually a command but softened not to sound that way. "I want you fellows to go on a special mission for me, and I want you to go together since your jobs in foreign policy are closely interlinked. And I want it done right away."

The calendar read January 27, 1953, three days before Eisenhower's first State of the Union speech, the speech that would spell out the foreign policy priorities of the new resident of the White House.

But to understand anything at all about the foreign policy of the Eisenhower administration, you must understand John Foster Dulles.

His biographical summary in the international field covers several pages, he and his entire family always conscious of his preordained life of diplomacy.

His great uncle, John Welsh, served as Rutherford B. Hayes' ambassador to the Court of St. James. His mother's father, John W. Foster, became Benjamin Harrison's Secretary of State. His uncle, Robert Lansing, followed William Jennings Bryan in 1915 as Woodrow Wilson's Secretary of State, and held the post during the tempestuous years of World War I, the Versailles Peace Conference, and Wilson's lost fight for the United States entry into the League of Nations.

The son of a Presbyterian minister, Dulles chose legal and diplomatic careers, but worked actively as a Presbyterian layman, becoming Chairman of the Federated Council of Protestant Churches, and heading the Commission for a Just and Durable Peace of the National Council of Churches of Christ in America. Perhaps his parsonage upbringing explained his need to sermonize and give moral lectures.

His first diplomatic exposure came as a nineteen-year-old student at Princeton. He accompanied his grandfather to the Netherlands in 1907, where the former Secretary of State served as a member of the secretariat of the Second Hague Peace Conference.

A year later, after graduation with honors from Princeton, Dulles moved to the Sorbonne in Paris, then to law school at George Washington University, graduating in 1911. He joined the prestigious New York firm of Sullivan and Cromwell, which specialized in international affairs, and became its managing partner in 1927.

His assignments in the diplomatic world seem without end: Special Representative of President Wilson and the State Department in Panama and Central America in 1917; Army major in intelligence during World War I; assistant to the Chairman of the War Trade Board, 1918; counsel to the American Committee to Negotiate Peace in 1918-19; member of the Reparations Committee and Supreme Economic Council in 1919; legal advisor to the Polish Plan of Financial Stability, 1927; American representative to the Berlin Debt Conference in 1933. On and on it goes, ad infinitum.

During Governor Thomas Dewey's run for the presidency in 1944, Dulles served as his foreign policy advisor. He performed a similar role for three Secretaries of State—Byrnes, Marshall, and Acheson—at meetings of the Council of Foreign Ministers in 1945, 1947, and 1949. He became a delegate to the UN General Assembly in 1946, 1947, and 1948. In

1950, he helped negotiate the Japanese Peace Treaty as a State Department Consultant with the rank of Ambassador.

He drafted the foreign policy plank of the 1952 Republican platform, and from time immemorial, everyone knew that John Foster Dulles would claim his rightful heirship to the post of Secretary of State the minute any Republican won the White House. He became Eisenhower's first cabinet appointee. Several writers report, with slight variations in wording, that Dulles told Eisenhower: "With my understanding of the intricate relationships between the peoples of the world and your sensitivity to the political considerations involved, we will make the most successful team in history."

I first met Dulles in 1945 at the Charter conference of the United Nations in San Francisco where I worked as one of eight official United States delegates, first appointed by Roosevelt and reappointed by Truman after Roosevelt's death. He came as a member of the United States consulting secretariat, but not as a delegate. This meant that I, twenty years his junior by the calendar and with a minimum of experience in foreign affairs, outranked him in protocol; but he never gave the slightest hint that this disturbed him.

As we sat in the Oval Office that morning, barely seven days after the inauguration, Dulles approached his sixty-fifth birthday. Various writers described his face as "unremarkable," "brooding," "boring," or "blank," his plain-rimmed glasses making the face even more expressionless. Nor did his dull gray three-piece suits add the slightest speck of luster. You could pass him on the street, look right through him, and never once see him. Some wag coined the quip: "Dull, Duller, Dulles!"

He slouched when he sat or walked, and spoke in a flat voice, not quite but almost a monotone, confident that the mere logic of his words wiped out any need for variations in pitch or modulation, rhythm or stress. No one ever accused him of oratorical skill, either in private or from the podium. He read his speeches painfully, never once considering the reactions of his audience.

Perhaps his saving feature rested on the fact that he never repeated himself. He said something once, assuming that his listeners would grasp his meaning; and if they did not, they deserved to suffer their own misfortunes.

Someone once asked me if I would characterize Dulles as "self-righteous." I replied that I did not think one-word descriptions ever turned out to be much more than vague generalities, misleading more often than not. My best summary of Dulles is that he always *knew* he was absolutely right. Further, he *knew* that anyone who disagreed with him was, of logical necessity, absolutely wrong. And finally, he could not understand how anyone could dare question the fact that he was *always* absolutely right.

Still, and this is the incredible thing, he did not show arrogance or disdain or condescension toward a person who challenged his opinions. Always the perfect gentleman, he spoke evenly and exhibited the patience of the learned scholar trying to lead the errant pupil back to the path of righteousness. I didn't find much of a sense of humor, but always good taste, a reserved charm, and graciousness.

No one can doubt that Dulles brought great assets to his post, but a number of liabilities offset them.

He suffered a fixation that Colonel Edward House, Wilson's special adviser, confidant, and from time to time, diplomatic messenger, kept Uncle Robert Lansing from becoming a great Secretary of State. Lansing advised Wilson not to go to Paris for the Peace Conference and strongly recommended against Wilson's insistence that the League of Nations be created immediately. Lansing wanted the peace treaty disposed of first, negotiated at the foreign ministry level. The League, he argued, could follow in a more orderly,

deliberate manner. He also argued against a number of specified provisions in the League Charter that Wilson insisted
upon, but that ultimately doomed its ratification in the U.S.
Senate.

Dulles remained convinced that Colonel House, the inter-
loper in Lansing's and Wilson's foreign policy, "did in" Lansing; and Dulles determined that there would never be a
"Colonel House" in his tenure as Secretary to undermine his
own policies. This made it difficult for anyone, the President
included, to work intimately with him, or to shake him from
his fixed-in-cement views.

His second great liability rested in the belief that no military man could function effectively in the diplomatic arena.
This included Eisenhower, even with all his diplomatic experience during World War II and in NATO. A non-military
mind must always be on call to save the military thinker from
a diplomatic blunder.

Finally, Dulles' unbridled hatred of Communism gave
him a blind spot that made him stubbornly inflexible. This
deprived him of the ability to embrace wholeheartedly Eisenhower's concept of reaching out to the world in an aggressive
effort to break through the stalemate of the Cold War.

I wish I could report that someone made a verbatim transcript or tape recorded Eisenhower's briefing so that we could
study his words, but we are limited to my paraphrasing from
my notes and memory:

> As both of you know, we've had reports from around
> the world of a lot of skepticism of what kind of Presi-
> dent a military man can be.
>
> The term "military" man means something a lot
> different to the people in Europe than it does here.
> They think of Prussian General Staffs, and invading
> armies, and massive armaments. They think of mili-
> tary governments, with oppression, and a loss of civil

liberties. They think of concentration camps, and dictators.

I won't be able to reach out to the other nations of the world in our search for world peace until we assure those people that I'm not going to turn into some sort of ogre, ready to drop the atomic bomb if they don't snap to and do what I want them to do.

Then, we've got this matter of the first Republican President with a Republican Congress in twenty years. They think we're going to pull back into a pre-war isolationism; and the speeches of Taft, and Jenner, and McCarthy, and a lot of others sound like that's exactly what we intend to to.

The Europeans think the new Congress will rip out all foreign aid and Mutual Security programs, and leave Europe entirely on its own, at the mercy of the Communists.

So, I want both of you to go see the leaders of the countries in Europe and set them straight on these fears.

I made no effort to inject anything into his briefing, watching Dulles out of the corner of my eye. He sat completely impassive, not moving a facial muscle, as though he did not need to hear any words of advice from anyone.

I think you both know the main points of the message I want you to take as we try to reach out to our friends and neighbors, and also develop programs to break through the Iron Curtain.

The first is we aim to contain the Soviet expansion in Europe. Make it clear that we're in Europe to stay, that it's in our best interest to be there, no matter what some of the Republicans in the Senate say.

Foster, that's your job primarily. Be sure they know that we expect not only the Soviets but every other nation to respect each others' borders.

> We think we can coexist with the Communists, but
> we want to do more than that.

I think Dulles nodded, perhaps he made some audible response; but I make no attempt to remember it at this date, much less report it.

> Now, Harold, the second point of the message fits right into the first. That is that we are committed to develop a world economy built around a free exchange of people, goods, ideas, and ideologies. Your job is primarily in the economic field, so carry my message that a strong, open world economy is in our best interest, as well as theirs—and that's what we plan to work for. We want expanded world trade on a fair and reciprocal basis. I've already called for renewal of the Reciprocal Trade Act.
>
> The Communists will rue the day that they withdrew behind their economic Iron Curtain. Their economies can't expand. As a matter of fact, they will shrink, and the whole Communist world will sink back to the Middle Ages.
>
> You know what you're going to find in Europe—jealous nationalism. Fear of Germany and Italy, although Italy didn't amount to an awful lot on the broad European scene under Mussolini. Fear of the Communists. Each nation with its hand out trying to persuade you that it needs more than anyone else. Harold, that's where you have to wear your diplomat hat.

He finished the session with: "How quick can you get going?"

I looked at Dulles and he at me, Dulles making the reply: "In two or three days."

The President concluded:

137

Good! I want you in Europe when I give my State of the Union Message to the Congress. I'm pleased with the way it's shaping up; but no matter what I say, it will be interpreted a dozen different ways.

Harold, you know what's in it. I want you there so you can straighten out any distortions anyone puts on that State of the Union Message.

Three days later, January 30, Dulles and I breakfasted at the White House with the President. With considerable press coverage, he wished us well as we headed for his private plane at National Airport for the first leg of our trip, Ciampino Airport in Rome. I brought along Bob Matteson, my Deputy Director of the Mutual Security Agency; Dulles took three top aides at State.

We targeted the six nations we wanted to bring into a European Defense Community. Our routine gave us a briefing by our own ambassador in each country, the Head of our Mutual Security missions, and anyone else they thought could give us helpful information. Then we set off to deliver the President's message to the heads of state of the country, their top aides, diplomats, military advisers, and business leaders. I made a special effort to confer also with heads of labor unions in each of the countries.

Rome (January 31): Premier De Gasperi; cabinet ministers; our ambassador, Ellsworth Bunker; Admiral Robert Carney (Commander of Allied Forces in Southern Europe), the Head of our Mutual Security mission; and two dozen other Italians and Americans met us at the airport. Dulles and I issued this joint statement:

We are particularly interested in the progress which we can anticipate in relation to the European Defense Community. This courageous and far reaching project now nearing consummation was conceived by the Continental countries themselves. It has caught the imagination of the American people. Our Government and our Congress have now come to look on it as a vital part of the over-all program for closer cooperation among the nations of the Atlantic Pact community.

For thirteen hours we conferred. Dulles' emphasis on containment included primarily improving the status of Italy's armed forces, their future development, and their need of arms from the United States.

I led the economic discussions, the Italians concerned about U.S. tariff policies that could limit their sales of such items as shoes, clothing, perfumes, and other luxuries which could let them earn hard dollars. They also wanted relief from our "restrictive" immigration quotas, which they thought prevented the flow of Italians to the U.S., a means of reducing Italy's high unemployment rate.

Dulles pressed hard on the theme that the NATO pact must be much more than a military alliance among politically disunited countries, as the Communists propagandized it. The Communists predicted NATO would fall when the North Atlantic partners ripped themselves apart through internal bickering.

I emphasized the President's message of economic development on a global scale that would raise the standard of living for the entire world, while letting Italy and all the other European countries prosper as never before in history.

Paris (February 1): The French dragged their heels on the European Defense (Army) Treaty. Dulles relayed Eisenhower's impatience at the French Parliament's failure to ratify it, saying ratification would show the Soviets that the Europeans meant what they said about containing Communist expansion. He strongly hinted that

Eisenhower might consider a change in U.S. policies if ratification did not come quickly.

Dulles and I both praised the French for their "creative thinking" in proposing a European Coal and Steel Community. This did conform with Eisenhower's firm belief in the need for a united Europe and a global economy.

We next faced the complex problem of a multilateral approach to convertibility of currencies. The French argued that direct exchange between the pound and dollar would doom the European Payments Union, a key element in European economic integration. The French expected us somehow to solve their problem overnight.

London (February 3): We found the atmosphere charged and hostile, the press and Labor members of Parliament castigating Dulles as "a man not to be trusted," who is "not really a friend of Britain," and who "lacks understanding of Europe."

They damned our policies in China, Britain recognizing Mao's Communist government in Peking while we shunned it and stuck by Chiang in exile on Formosa.

They also accused us of being reckless about the possible expansion of the Korean War and criticized Eisenhower's insistence that Europe's only hope for future stability rested on unification, something England could not agree to at this stage. They accused both Dulles and me of knuckling under to the French, who insisted upon England's immediate full-scale membership in the European Community.

We lunched at 10 Downing Street with Prime Minister Churchill, Foreign Secretary Anthony Eden, the Chancellor of the Exchequer, and the Minister of Defense, and issued this noncommittal press statement:

The purpose of these exchanges was not to reach any fresh agreements, but to exchange views and establish a full understanding of the position of the two governments on the wide range of world problems in which they have a common interest.

There was full recognition of the importance of maintaining the efforts for defense through the North Atlantic Treaty Organization, and of the desirability of rapid progress in the setting up of the European Defense Community.

The discussions also covered the Far East, Southeast Asia and the Middle East.

Bonn (February 5): We wanted West Germany to rearm *as part of the European Defense (Army) Treaty*. From a perspective of military strategy, Eisenhower saw this as the only way to halt Soviet aggression if they decided to move westward. Russia dangled the promise of a reunified Germany if West Germany refused to rearm and enter the European Defense Community.

We also wanted to bind France and Germany to the same treaty organization, so there would be no chance of their fighting each other again, as in both World Wars of this century.

This tempted the West Germans and they dallied. Dulles argued that they could not rely on the Soviet promise of unification, supposed to take place at a four-power Foreign Ministers meeting some time in the future.

It fell to my lot to point out that if the West Germans did not accept the European Defense plan when the North American Council met April 23, we would drastically change our economic aid program.

The Hague (February 6): A horrendous flood altered every facet of our mission to the Netherlands, the Dutch government asking to be put back on our aid list, although they had crossed themselves off only the preceding week. Dulles and I flew over the flooded area of the Netherlands and Belgium. I assured the Premier of our sympathy, and told him that while I could make no specific commitments, I knew President Eisenhower would want us to help.

The industrious Dutch did not give us any worries over either their contributions to the military alliance or their economic development, once they recovered from the temporary setback of this Act of God.

Brussels (February 7) and Luxembourg (February 8): We found great progress toward European economic unity in the Coal and Steel Community. Dulles suggested that if the nations involved could do as well in the formation of a European Army as with their heavy industry pool, Soviet expansion would be greatly discouraged.

Dulles and I returned home the next day and made our reports to the President and to the National Security Council on February 11.

The President asked us to make a similar trip to the Near East and Asia, but other demands on our time delayed it. We finally made it May 11-30: Egypt, Israel, Syria, Iraq, Iran, India, Pakistan, Greece, Turkey, and Libya. The NSC minutes of June 2 summarize Dulles' report of our trip:

> Conclusions. To sum up, said Secretary Dulles, the prestige of the Western powers in the Middle East was in general very low. The United States suffered from being linked with British and French imperialism. Nevertheless, we still had a reserve of good will, as was shown by the security precautions taken to protect him and Mr. Stassen in the course of their journey, and by

the friendly demeanor of the ordinary people in these countries. Accordingly, Secretary Dulles believed we could regain our lost influence if we made a real effort. The great difficulty was the complete preoccupation of the Arab States with their own local problems and their lack of understanding and interest in the threat posed by the Soviet Union.

The general concept that Secretary Dulles brought back with him was that Pakistan could be made a strong loyal point. So, obviously, could Turkey. Syria and Iraq realized their danger, and could probably be induced to join with us. As for the countries further south, they were too lacking in realization of the international situation to offer any prospect of becoming dependable allies. Iran, continued Secretary Dulles, was the obvious weak spot in what could become a strong defensive arrangement of the northern tier of states: Turkey, Iraq, Syria, and Pakistan. But this arrangement was not hopeless if we could save Iran. Our immediate need, therefore, was to concentrate on changing the situation there. There was still much strong anti-Soviet sentiment in the country.

Our conference with Pandit Nehru in India deserves a special note. He saw himself as leader of a "neutral, unaligned" group of nations, not only in Asia but throughout the world, envisioning his role as ultimate arbiter between the free and Communist worlds. He maintained full diplomatic relations with Mao's government in Peking. We knew that he would relay anything of major importance affecting Communist China to Mao.

As we sat in Nehru's rather simple but immaculate office, sipping our tea, Secretary Dulles made this short statement:

> I am authorized to say for President Eisenhower that he fully intends to bring the Korean War to a close at the earliest possible moment. He will not tolerate any further military action in Korea by the Chinese, and

143

will move against them with every force he needs to stop further aggression by them. *And this includes the use of the atomic bomb.*

Nehru sat impassive while Dulles waited for his message to sink in, then moved to something else.

We knew that Nehru would hurry Eisenhower's message to Peking, which is exactly what he did.

My travels with Secretary Dulles disturbed me. His unabated hatred of Communism and the Soviet leaders compelled him to think primarily in terms of containment by force. Any other attitude, he thought, would be interpreted as a show of weakness and would invite aggressive moves. I studied hard but could find no basic differences between Dulles' fundamental approaches and the Truman policies that we considered bankrupt. Dulles' mindset left no room for Eisenhower's policy of reaching out in an effort to change directions.

I recognized the paradox: Dulles, the man of diplomacy, preaching force and threats of force, and Eisenhower, the military man, searching desperately for diplomatic breakthroughs; the diplomat ready to "go to the brink" to reach his goals, while the general of the armies sought peaceful solutions to prevent the need for brinksmanship.

Chapter 10
"You've Got to Restrain Greed"

"Harold," the President-elect had told me at the Commodore when I reported back in December '51 that I would accept the appointment as Director of the Mutual Security Administration, "you and Charlie Wilson run some special risks. Before you do anything else, I want you to protect yourselves—and the rest of us—against them. I've already talked to Charlie."

I listened, and can paraphrase his warnings:

> Any time you have as much money to pass around as you and Charlie have, there'll be greedy hands out, all trying to get some of it. That's human nature and we don't have a prayer in the world of changing it.

> The only way to handle it is to place enough restraints on greed to keep it from leading to corruption, and from corruption into fraud, and bribery and kickbacks, and God knows what else.

> Unless you get the restraints on greed in place from the beginning, greed develops its own power. It spreads like a disease; and before you know it, it takes over the whole program. It becomes so common that everybody accepts it; and pretty soon we'll get tarred with our own "mess in Washington," which is what we campaigned against and promised to clean up.

> We don't have the final figures on the new budget yet; but when it's put together, you and Charlie will control at least a third of it, probably more.

145

The Mutual Security Administration—later to become the Foreign Operations Administration—grew from the Marshall Plan, the European Recovery Program named for General George C. Marshall.

World War II devastated virtually all of Europe, disrupted its food supplies, its trade and transportation facilities, knocking the bottom from under its currencies and distorting every phase of its society, cultures and economies.

After VE Day, May 8, 1945, a great body of American opinion urged the Truman administration to move aggressively to try to keep World War III from happening. We all knew that the Soviets could appeal to Europe's debilitated, starving masses with promises of bright days under textbook Marxism-Leninism. They could infiltrate Europe's labor unions, subvert all its political parties, and enslave the entire continent. This would leave us, our former Allies, and the rest of what came to be called "the free world" with nothing but military options, including the awesome decision of whether to drop an atomic bomb on Russia's mainland.

Much of Asia also reeled from Japan's cruel destructions.

The world stood only a third of a century away from the end of World War I, the "war to end all wars" and the "war to make the world safe for democracy." Now a completely changed world suffered the more destructive ravages of World War II. The United States remained the only nation with strength enough to try to do something about the great abyss, but with limited experience as a world leader in international affairs.

Truman and his advisors fumbled for almost two years before announcing the Marshall Plan for Europe, but not without loud voices against it who wanted the U.S. to pull back behind its "safe" oceans. The same loud voices reasserted George Washington's admonition to avoid all foreign entanglements. What difference did it make to us that the

Communists controlled Europe's labor unions, subverted its governments, set up their own dictatorships, subjected its peoples? We could feel sorry for them; but God did not endow us with any special mission to police the world.

Even as we drafted the UN Charter in San Francisco in 1945 before the end of the War, strident voices said that World War III would be inevitable, just as World War II followed World War I. We wasted our time trying to form an organization of nations to keep the peace. We should let the rest of the world take care of itself while we built Fortress America into a new Garden of Eden.

That division of opinion between the interventionists and the isolationists still entered into the debates of both Democrats and Republicans during the 1952 campaign and would present a burden for the Eisenhower years. The isolationists fought mightily to pull us back from foreign involvements by reducing Mutual Security projects, and searched for ways to curtail all military expenditures.

The President-elect continued:

> The thing that concerns me is the size of all these figures.
>
> The army runs a pretty good campaign against theft and fraud. I remember, with humor, a fight I had with the quartermaster over some damned entrenching shovels when I was a captain way back during the First War.
>
> We'd ordered a box of the shovels, with carriers to put on the backpacks of the infantrymen. A great big box came. When we opened it, the shovels were there, but the carriers were the wrong kind. I immediately nailed the box shut and sent it back to Ordnance. I've forgotten how many months went by before I got a bill for $22.04—I'll never forget that exact amount—for the price of nineteen items—shovels and carriers—missing from the box we'd opened.

147

I hadn't followed Quartermaster regulations. I should have taken everything out of the box, made an inventory count, then sent this in the box when we returned it. Of course, we hadn't taken one damn thing out of the box. When we first looked in, we saw it wasn't what we could use, we nailed her up and sent it right back.

Well, after months of wrangling, I finally had to pay that $22.04 out of my own pocket. I tell you this to show that the quartermaster had such strict rules that they scared people into being honest. That's what you and Charlie have to do—set up such strict procedures that everyone is afraid to be dishonest. That's the only way you can restrain greed; and you've got to restrain greed.

When there are billions and billions of dollars, contracts, materials of all kinds—that much money to be tossed around—how can you possibly put the brakes on greed?

My trip to Europe with Dulles delayed my moves to develop "restraints on greed," to use Eisenhower's phrase, but as soon as I got back, I went to see J. Edgar Hoover. The FBI at that time enjoyed perhaps its highest peak of national respect. I knew Hoover personally from my days as Minnesota governor when the FBI helped us with racketeering cases involving some of our dishonest labor union leaders.

I told Hoover of the President's and my concerns over the possibility of greed and corruption in our foreign aid operations. I knew that some FBI agents retired in their early fifties, still vigorous and ready for new challenges, so I asked him for the names of three recently retired agents whom he would recommend as capable of setting up an inspection arm within my agency to police greed and investigate any allegations of not only illegality, but even of the appearance of improper practice. I told him that the President insisted that everyone be "clean as a hound's tooth," and behave "like Caesar's wife."

Hoover gave me the three names I asked for. I chose Tom Naughtin and named him Director of Personnel in a complete reorganization of the agency. I also appointed an investigative accountant, John Murphy. By this time, the agency employed 4,000 people and administrated almost four billion dollars in aid programs in seventy-one countries—not huge amounts by today's standards, but astronomical and unheard-of then.

We recognized that our procedures to control greed and corruption needed to be two-pronged. First, we required monitoring at the supply end of those who entered into contracts with the Mutual Security Administration to supply goods and services, and second, we needed to watch those who dispensed them in the country of destination.

Our projects ran the gamut of human activity: fertilizer plants to improve food supplies; advice by agricultural experts on rotation of crops to increase yields and restore worn-out soil; hybrid seeds and new strains of grains; dams to control flooding, permit irrigation, and run electric power plants; well-drilling equipment and know-how to improve water supplies; doctors, medical technicians, vaccines, and drugs to control disease; locomotives to restore rail transport destroyed by saturation bombing; trucks to reactivate transportation fleets; economic advisors to help ruined economies regain their viability; hard dollars to back up weak currencies to create sound monetary systems and eliminate inefficient barter arrangements; contracts with fifty American universities to send faculty and professional teams to universities in fifty countries to help them restart and expand after stagnation during World War II.

Our greed control routines required at least two people to sign on and sign off of every delivery of goods or services on the theory that if a corruptor did enter the picture, he would need to infect two co-conspirators instead of only one. This would make his task more difficult and more risky, and, we hoped, deter him.

In the foreign country that received the goods or services, we required the extra step of on-site inspections to be certain the project went forward as planned, without diversions by embezzlement or misappropriation. Again, we required two people to sign on and sign off on every single delivery, with the additional step of continuous inspection.

In the beginning, some of the recipients complained: "Don't you trust us?" "You treat us like colonies of the United States!" "Do you think we are all a bunch of crooks?"

Our heads of mission replied, "These are standard, world-wide procedures under the Eisenhower administration. This is not a reflection on your honesty or good intentions, but a requirement that we make certain everywhere in the world that these grants and programs are proving effective."

I issued a strong directive to all our 4,000 employees, requiring each to read and initial it, emphasizing the President's concern about greed and corruption. I told them that we would not tolerate even the slightest appearance of irregularity.

On one occasion, a prominent Congressman tried to pad the costs on a contract for the delivery of special equipment to foreign aid countries. I ordered the contract canceled immediately before the payment of a single dollar. The word ran quickly throughout the Congress.

Everything we did emphasized Eisenhower's earlier admonition: "You and Charlie have to set up such strict procedures that everyone is afraid to be dishonest. That's the only way you can restrain greed."

In one of my last conversations with President Eisenhower after we both left office, we reminisced about his administration and our work together. I can quote him exactly on this statement: "One of the things I'm proudest about is that we did keep greed out. Everybody knew that I wouldn't stand for it, and that's the secret."

I'll make no effort to quote the President exactly, but will paraphrase another statement he made in that meeting:

> We had good luck in containing Communist expansion in Europe, yes. But mark my word, the most important thing we accomplished was in the economic field. That's where Communism is bound to fail. The system is designed against humanity and human instincts. The pathetic thing is that millions and millions will suffer, probably for a couple of generations, before everyone admits that the miserable system simply won't work.

We also wanted to make sure that as many people in the receiving countries as possible knew that the goods came from the United States. I called in an artist and asked him to give us a logo to go on every bag of food, every sack of grain, every can of powdered milk, every tractor, every box of electrical equipment, every carton of machine tools, and every other item that flowed into these seventy-one countries as part of our foreign aid program.

He returned with the design of a shield, its interior divided into three separate segments. The top third held a blue field supporting four white stars. In the middle, two strong hands clasped in "one of the oldest gestures of human comradeship and cooperation." Bold print below the handshake read: "United States of America." The bottom third contained thirteen red-and-white vertical stripes.

I called Ann Whitman and asked if I could bring the design over to the Oval Office for the President's comment.

"I like it," he said. "Use it!" And we did, beginning with seven-foot replicas on both sides of the hull of the freighter *Anchorage Victory* as she sailed from Baltimore harbor with wheat for starving millions in Pakistan.

This logo remains in use today.

Chapter 11
"Stalin Is Either Dead or Dying"

Nothing better illustrates Eisenhower's innate drive to reach out, and Dulles' equally strong compulsion to thwart it, than the reaction in the White House to Stalin's death.

I always prepared for the meetings of the National Security Council the afternoon before, carefully studying the black "Top Secret" briefing book with my representative on the NSC Planning Board, Brigadier General Robert Porter.

The March 4, 1953 agenda listed Iran as the major topic of discussion. Two years earlier, Premier Mohammed Mossadegh had nationalized the Iranian and British Oil company, and now threatened to give the Soviets easy access to a big chunk of the world's oil. The tensions of the entire region increased. What should we do about Mossadegh, as well as Shah Mohammad Reza Pahlavi's moves to displace the Muslim leader and assume more power?

The NSC agenda also called for consideration of crucial budget items, Congress threatening to slash Secretary Wilson's defense requests, as well as my foreign aid items.

I took my briefing book from the safe and left my office on the second floor of the Executive Office Building (EOB) ten minutes before the hour to make the short trip down the elevator, across the closed end of 16th Street, up the side stairs of the White House, and into the Cabinet Room. I knew from previous clockings that my route never took longer than four minutes, but I allowed extra time to keep from arriving late.

The President ran by a precise clock, his lifelong military routines controlling his personal and official habits, and he signaled his displeasure at anyone who came late.

Normally, the President opened the NSC meetings with a nod to Robert Cutler, NSC Secretary (the job from which Henry Kissinger would launch his career a decade later), and a simple, "Bobby!" Cutler would state the agenda, then yield to Allen Dulles for a short intelligence briefing on current developments related to our agenda topics.

The bare bones minutes of the March 4 NSC meeting, only partially declassified in 1984, show the break in routine:

1. STALIN'S ILLNESS
   (Program of Psychological Preparation for Stalin's Passing from Power (PSB D-24), dated November 1, 1952; Appendix A to NIE-64 (Part I))

   Mr. Cutler explained that the President had met early this morning with Mr. Allen Dulles, Mr. C.D. Jackson, Mr. Hagerty, and himself, and had prepared a Presidential statement on Stalin's illness which it was now desired that the Council discuss and approve.

"Stalin is either dead or dying," Cutler explained, citing Radio Moscow's announcement a little past midnight Washington time that Joseph Stalin "suffered a sudden brain hemorrhage." At 7:00 a.m. the President, C.D. Jackson, Cutler, Allen Dulles, and Jim Hagerty drafted a public message for the President to send to the Russian people. It said, in part:

   [T]he thoughts of America go out to all the peoples of the U.S.S.R.—the men and women, the boys and girls—in the villages, cities, farms and factories of their homeland.

They are the children of the same God who is the Father of all peoples everywhere. And like all peoples, Russia's millions share our longing for a friendly and peaceful world.

Regardless of the identity of government personalities, the prayer of us Americans continues to be that the Almighty will watch over the people of that vast country and bring them, in His wisdom, opportunity to live their lives in a world where all men and women and children dwell in peace and comradeship.

As I read through it, I thought back to the State of the Union Message and to the Guildhall speech in London and recognized the draft as "genuine Eisenhower," flowing from his deep belief in God and his lifelong reliance on daily prayer. The NSC minutes continue:

> After Mr. Cutler had read this statement and Mr. Jackson had briefly noted the reactions to the announcement of Stalin's illness in various quarters of the globe, the President stated that the meeting earlier in the morning had been prompted by a desire to see whether and how the announcement of Stalin's illness could best be exploited for psychological purposes. He believed that the moment was propitious for introducing the right word directly into the Soviet Union. The Russians would be so interested in the reaction of the rest of the world that it would be possible on this occasion to penetrate the Iron Curtain. The President stressed that this was a psychological and not a diplomatic move, and added that it was proposed to make the statement temperate in tone to offset possibly intemperate comment from the Hill, though such comments had thus far been cautious.

From time to time, the President used the words "psychological and not diplomatic" to shift the play from Foster Dulles and State to C.D. Jackson's Psychological Strategy

155

Board. Later known as the Operations Coordinating Board, it comprised Under Secretary of State Walter Bedell Smith; Under Secretary of Defense Roger Kyes; CIA Director Allen Dulles; me as Director of Mutual Security; and Jackson as Chairman. I could see the President's strategy unfold in these early discussions. He anticipated opposition from Foster Dulles, and subtly laid the groundwork to take the matter away from him, without saying so directly.

> Mr. Jackson affirmed his conviction that this was the first really big propaganda opportunity offered to our side for a long time. It enabled us to stress our devotion to peace, and it would enable us to counteract with real forcefulness the "hate America" campaign in the Soviet orbit and to calm anxieties elsewhere in the world by reassuring peoples everywhere of America's devotion to peace. Mr. Jackson further pointed out that if the President were to remain silent we would not only miss the opportunity he had outlined, but the very silence of the Chief Executive would be subject to misinterpretation by those who sought to misinterpret him. There was, in short, no option but to issue some kind of statement.

Treasury Secretary Humphrey supported Jackson, but Wilson opposed the idea on the ground that it might backfire if interpreted as an appeal to the Soviet people to overthrow their masters.

Foster Dulles bided his time, the minutes giving this summary:

> Secretary Dulles announced that he had no fixed opinion as to the desirability of a Presidential statement, but added that he felt there was a very great risk in whatever the President said. On balance, he felt that there was more loss than gain to be anticipated from the present text, since he agreed with Secretary Wilson

that it will be interpreted as an appeal to the Soviet people to rise up against their rulers in a period of mourning, at a time when they were bound to regard Stalin more reverentially than ordinarily. It was certainly a gamble.

That's the trouble with official minutes prepared after a meeting, "cleaned up" to take the harshness out of clashes in the debate. My notes and memory give a more accurate description of what took place.

Secretary Dulles' position became more fixed. Regardless of when Stalin's death became official, the United States should do absolutely nothing. We should adopt a "wait and see" stance while the Kremlin bureaucrats jockeyed for position. We should remain aloof, no matter who the new leader or leaders turned out to be. We dared not give the slightest hint that we favored any of them, since this could be interpreted as weakness on our part and tacit approval of the Communist method of choosing its leaders.

His posture did not surprise me, the blind spot of his hatred of Communism dictating his guiding premise that sealing off Russia and her Iron Curtain satellites would keep them from contaminating the rest of the world.

> During the course of this exercise the President suggested that for courtesy's sake Secretary Dulles should telephone the Soviet Embassy in Washington to inquire about the situation and to express concern. Also, a message was sent to the meeting by the Under Secretary of State, indicating that the Soviet Embassy was calling in the press at eleven o'clock, which General Smith thought indicated that "Stalin was dead as hell." In any case, said the President, it was necessary that his own statement be got out at once, since it was now a few minutes before eleven.

The next entry fails to do justice to a main part of our two-and-one-half hour debate:

> . . . Mr. Cutler proposed various other actions for Council consideration with respect to the implications of Stalin's disappearance from power. These included an intelligence estimate by the Central Intelligence Agency, a policy estimate by the Department of State, and a psychological estimate by the Psychological Strategy Board in consultation with Mr. Jackson.

The "implications of Stalin's disappearance from power" concerned the whole world.

We first tackled the question of *who* might succeed Stalin.

Allen Dulles told us that, quite frankly, the CIA could offer no solid evidence whatsoever on Stalin's successor. Nor could military intelligence, General Vandenberg reported on behalf of the Joint Chiefs of Staff. This left us to speculate.

A number of names surfaced.

I could offer some first-hand background on Vyacheslav Mikhaylovich Molotov with whom I negotiated long and hard at the founding meeting of the United Nations in San Francisco in 1945.

For years before and during the war, Molotov carried out Stalin's foreign policies. No one knew his exact role in devising these policies. I found him little more than a messenger in San Francisco. Short, about five-foot-three, and stocky, Molotov always dug in his heels on any position his superiors in Moscow ordered him to take. He remained adamant until Moscow released him to assume another stance. Occasionally, he showed a sense of humor. His number-one lieutenant, Andrei Gromyko, spoke English well in social conversation, and acted more pleasant and courteous than Molotov.

I could not see Molotov taking Stalin's place. Always the faithful order-follower, I doubted his ability to shift into the role of order-giver. He impressed me as afraid to make decisions, but could carry out the will of his superiors with great efficiency.

Lavrenty Beria's name came next. Both he and Stalin came from Georgia, both from poor families, although Beria obtained a degree in architecture. Too young at eighteen to be a key actor in the 1917 Revolution, he joined the secret police in 1921. Beria then went to Moscow as Stalin's purger of police, after the police conducted their own great purges on the party and army in the late '30s.

Now, in 1953, Beria ran the Soviet A-bomb projects and the slave labor camps, said to hold somewhere between twelve and fourteen million prisoners, most of them political.

We considered Beria a strong candidate because of his hold over the secret police.

We moved to Nikolai Alexandrovich Bulganin. As minister of war and boss of the army, navy, and air force, no one could rule for long without his support. His strange background in business and finance before assuming his army posts during the War—eventually he rose to the rank of marshal—made him the best all-around candidate on the basis of merit; but in Russia, substantive qualifications played second fiddle to Party position and raw power.

My notes do not show who suggested Lazar Moiseyevich Kaganovich. Someone described him as a sort of "roving troubleshooter" for Stalin, which meant he carried considerable clout as long as Stalin lived, but he also suffered a liability he could never overcome. He towered above Stalin in height, some estimates putting him at six feet, some above. With Stalin gone, he might shed this physical impediment to his political success, but the many enemies he made while doing Stalin's hatchet jobs could probably pool their strength against him, making a broad base of support unlikely.

Then came Georgi Maximilianovich Malenkov, who for years served as Stalin's alter ego. During the War, he ran Russia's airplane factories. Afterward, Stalin named him director of reconstruction, where he performed his duties without the slightest regard for human cost or misery. By 1946 he stood on Stalin's immediate right atop Lenin's tomb at the May Day parade, the Soviet way to show official Party rank and tell the world who held the power.

That's about as far as we could go that March morning, when we still did not even know for sure if Stalin lived, or when he might die.

Next, we moved to Eisenhower's more important questions: What changes did Stalin's death portend for our relationship with Russia? What steps should we take as soon as his death became a matter of record?

On one thing we all agreed: Stalin's reign proved him the cruelest, most powerful tyrant in all history. His orbit reached further than that of Ivan the Terrible or Peter the Great, Russia's other bloody czars. His slaughter of innocent people used the prosaic techniques of the gun, the hangman's rope, and starvation. Through intimidation and lust for power, he forced a personal loyalty from his lieutenants that wiped out any hint of morality, sensitivity, or humanity.

Despite all this, his propagandist machine—less sophisticated but just as effective as Hitler's—made him into a demigod: "Our Father," "Uncle Joe," "Our Leader," "Our Teacher," obtaining a cult worship to replace the Church that Marx labeled "the opium of the people."

They reached their goals by painting Stalin as the savior of the Russian nation from the ogre Hitler and as a man of peace. But peace from the Russian perspective meant one thing only—the motherland must never, ever again be invaded, no matter what the cost.

To help drive home their simple message, they built great museums in every major city to honor the twenty million victims of Hitler, and created massive statues towering more than a hundred feet in the air to call the nation to love of country and a patriotism centered on a love of Stalin.

We also reached consensus on another premise: Throughout history, a period of turmoil normally follows the death of powerful rulers who try, without success, to continue their reigns from the grave; but we did not know if Stalin left a "last will and testament" to pass on his rule to a chosen deputy. At one time or other, Molotov, Beria, Bulganin, and Malenkov all bloomed as Stalin's heirs apparent, at least in the eyes of Western Moscow-watchers; but each of their stars dimmed, as far as Western experts could tell.

As our discussion continued, the NSC minutes report:

> Mr. Dulles registered his agreement with the Vice President's opinion that the situation might very well be worse after Stalin's death.
>
> The President also agreed with this view, and said that it was his conviction that at the end of the last war Stalin would have preferred an easing of the tension between the Soviet Union and the Western powers, but the Politburo had insisted on heightening the tempo of the cold war and Stalin had been obliged to make concessions to this view.

"I want to reach out to the Russians—the people and the Politburo—to see if we can't somehow crack the Iron Curtain and thaw out the Cold War," the President said.

By noon, he instructed Jim Hagerty to send the message much as originally drafted.

Although not then recognized by the public or even now by most historians and biographers, this move became the

161

President's first official break with Dulles, the first time he formally overruled the Secretary's specific recommendations.

The Kremlin announced Stalin's death on March 5th, the next evening, with a spate of hyperbole that could come only from fear and insecurity. The propagandists glorified Stalin:

> The heart of the comrade and inspired continuer of Lenin's will, the wise leader and teacher of the Communist Party and the Soviet people—Joseph Vissarionovich Stalin—has stopped beating.
>
> Dear comrades and friends . . . The steel-like unity and monolithic unity of the ranks of the party constitutes the main condition for its strength and might . . . Long live the great and all-conquering teachings of Marx, Engels, Lenin and Stalin!
>
> Long live our mighty Socialist Motherland!
>
> Long live our heroic Soviet people!

The order of the eulogizers at Stalin's funeral four days later told the story of who held power as Stalin's successor:

> Malenkov—delivered the main message: The Soviet Union's struggle for peace and coexistence with the capitalist world would continue—but Russia would keep its army strong.
>
> Beria—said that Russia's socialist system would win out against the West. In the meantime, Russia must remain "firm" with no hint of "lack of unity."
>
> Molotov—said that Stalin's legacy of peace and love of the Motherland would grow stronger through the memory of the noble leader who died in the service of the Soviet people.

Over the next several days, I worked closely with Jackson and the other members of the Psychological Strategy Board to prepare for the next National Security Council meeting on March 11, when the President expected detailed recommendations on how best to respond to Stalin's death. We settled back into routine at the March 11 meeting. Allen Dulles opened with an intelligence briefing on world reaction to Stalin's death, but with practically nothing of significance from Russia itself.

> At the conclusion of Mr. [Allen] Dulles' estimate, the President reiterated a belief which he had stated earlier to the Council, that Stalin had never actually been undisputed ruler of the Soviet Union.
>
> Contrary to the views of many of our intelligence agencies, the President persisted in believing that the government of the Soviet Union had always been something of a committee government. From personal experience the President believed that had Stalin, at the end of the war, been able to do what he wanted with his colleagues in the Kremlin, Russia would have sought more peaceful and normal relations with the rest of the world. The fact that the Soviet Union instead chose cold war seemed to the President an indication that, in some degree at least, Stalin had had to come to terms with other members of the Kremlin ruling circle.

Most of the remainder of the session revolved around Jackson's creative proposal to introduce an entirely new policy direction toward the Soviet Union in a major speech by President Eisenhower no later than the next week or two.

As during the campaign, I worked closely with Jackson on the preliminary draft of the speech that would launch this new course. The March 11 NSC minutes reveal:

... The point of departure in the plan was an address by the President to be made as early as possible and not later, he hoped, than the first of next week. The draft of such a presidential address had been prepared. It contained no mere pious platitudes, but a real bite.

We knew full well that our call for a meeting of the Big Four Foreign Ministers (Russia, France, England, and the United States) would call forth objections by Secretary Dulles, but we thought the issue critical enough to raise with the President and provoke NSC debate. The minutes continue:

Notably, it had the President call for a Foreign Ministers Conference of the Big Four, in the course of which the United States would set forth its desire to negotiate all the major outstanding issues between the free world and the Soviet bloc, including the unification of Germany and disarmament. However, said Mr. Jackson, everything in the plan was to flow from the initial move, the President's address. . . .

Mr. Jackson then noted that of course objections to his plan had been raised in the course of putting it together. Most of the objections centered in the Department of State. Mr. Jackson proposed to discuss these objections, but Secretary Dulles interposed to say that perhaps this task had best be done by him.

The Secretary's comments surprised no one. We all knew his entrenched belief that he, and he alone, should be the voice of American foreign policy.

Mr. Jackson readily agreed, but said he did wish to point out that we are, as he put it, ready to shoot. He was convinced that this was the greatest opportunity presented to the United States in many years to seize the initiative, and that that initiative ought to be seized even if this Government had to proceed unilaterally.

164

The plan which he had drafted, said Mr. Jackson, was in line with the views that President Eisenhower had set forth in the course of his campaign, as well as the views during the same period enunciated by Secretary Dulles. There was nothing in it new and strange and nothing which, it seemed to him, would not fit into the framework of this Administration's thinking on psychological strategy.

Jackson followed the tactics we had worked out in advance. Label the change in policy direction "psychological" instead of substantively "diplomatic," and emphasize that it contained only those concepts already expressed by both the President and Secretary Dulles.

The next segment in the formal minutes does not do justice to Foster Dulles' brilliant lecture on Stalin's role in keeping the satellite countries in line and bound to Russia. I wish we could present it verbatim.

Secretary Dulles began his statement by observing that he personally did not endorse all the objections to Mr. Jackson's plan which had been raised in the State Department. He agreed, for example, that Stalin's death did afford the United States an opportunity to effect changes in the Communist world which might well reduce the threat which the Soviet world presented to the free world.

As he saw it, the present menace of the USSR consisted in the complete control of a vast area by a handful of men who could use their power with impunity. This terrible concentration of power had largely been created, according to Secretary Dulles, by a process in which the normal urges of nationalism in the satellite states had been channelled and transformed into virtual worship of Stalin as a demi-god.

As a result of this process, the Communist leaders in the satellite countries had been able to hand over to Stalin control of their countries without conscious loss of the national prestige. All this was possible while Stalin lived; but the Communist leaders in the satellites would experience far greater difficulty today in subordinating the impulse of nationalism in their respective countries to the relatively unknown individual who had taken Stalin's place.

Therefore, what we must do, continued the Secretary, was to play up this nationalism and discontent for all it was worth, to seize every opportunity by this device to break down the monolithic Soviet control over the satellite states.

Dulles next turned to his "wait and see" stance:

> ... [I]t seemed especially doubtful to the Secretary of State as to whether this was the appropriate moment to carry the offensive direct to the Soviet Union. The Soviet was now involved in a family funeral, and it might be best to wait until the corpse was buried and the mourners gone off to their homes to read the will, before we begin our campaign to create discord in the family. If we moved precipitately we might very well enhance Soviet family loyalty and disrupt the free world's.

Dulles seemed to speak out of both sides of his mouth, admitting that a wonderful opportunity presented itself, but discouraging plans to take advantage of it:

> Furthermore, Secretary Dulles stated his belief that another consideration should be uppermost in our minds at this time. This was a moment in history when the people of the United States and of the free world generally feel that some great new effort should be made to stake out a new course. We mustn't let this opportunity pass or let our people down.
>
> We certainly cannot be totally negative in our reactions to what had occurred in Russia, but whatever we

166

do decide to do must be done carefully and with equal consideration as to its effect on the USSR and on the free world.

Accordingly, with regard to Mr. Jackson's specific proposal of a meeting of the Foreign Ministers, Secretary Dulles could not but feel that such a meeting would have quite disastrous effects on our ties with our allies unless we obtained their prior consent to the agenda for such a meeting. They would believe our leadership erratic, venturous, and arbitrary.

Secretary Dulles said he felt especially concerned at the proposal in Mr. Jackson's plan, to place discussion of German unity on the agenda for such a Foreign Ministers meeting. Discussion of German unity in such a forum at this time would ruin every prospect of ratification of the European Defense Community by the parliamentarians of the several states. It would undermine the positions of Chancellor Adenauer and of Prime Ministers Mayer and De Gasperi, who had actually staked their futures on the ratification of the EDC treaties.

The Secretary finally presented a plan of his own to shift the emphasis from Europe to Asia, one which Jackson and I had talked about only in passing, quickly discarding it as totally impracticable.

Turning now, Secretary Dulles said, to something positive and constructive, he suggested that the President's speech should substitute, for the proposal of a Foreign Ministers Conference, a call for the end of hostilities in Asia generally, and in Korea and Indo-China specifically, under appropriate safeguards. If the new Soviet regime could be persuaded to agree to something like this, the path would be open to further negotiations on other matters.

Such an approach seemed to the Secretary of State better than to begin from the European end. But in any case enough should be done now to satisfy American opinion that no attempt to cause the Soviet to change its spots had been left unexplored.

When the Secretary of State had concluded his opening remarks, the President asked him in what form he would present his ideas to the world.

Secretary Dulles replied that he agreed that the opening gun should be a speech by the President. Mr. Jackson added that this could be done over television, the address to be directed, on the one hand, to the peoples of the Soviet Union and, on the other, to the peoples of the United States and the free world.

The President then presented his own plan of action:

The President then informed the Council that he had received some days ago, and prior to the death of Stalin, a suggestion for a speech from Mr. Sam Lubell [syndicated columnist], for whose opinions the President had considerable respect.

Lubell had written the President of his belief that in our efforts to influence the Soviets as well as the people of the free world, we should give up any more appeals with regard to specific issues, such as Korea, and concentrate instead on our determination to raise the general standard of living throughout the world; to suggest, for instance, that no more than 10% of the resources of the different countries of the world should be devoted to armaments, and all the rest to the provision of food, shelter, and consumers goods.

The President noted that the peoples of the Soviet Union had for years now been promised, after the completion of each successive Five-Year Plan, that their own personal needs and aspirations would be considered by their government. They had been disappointed in each case.

Accordingly, what we should now do is propose that the standard of living throughout the world be raised at once, not at some indefinite time in the future. Such an appeal as this might really work. . . .

The potential of the President's proposal intrigued us all, and even evoked a favorable response from Dulles:

> Secretary Dulles expressed great interest in this idea of the President's, and said that it seemed to him to be supported by the enormous difficulty experienced by the Soviet Union in keeping their satellites from participation in the Marshall Plan.
>
> Certainly, the President replied, the economic incentive would have terrific attraction in Russia if it could be got over to the ordinary people.

We presumed a consensus that the President would make the speech launching his new concepts of foreign policy, and we then concentrated on its content:

> The President again said that emphasis in the current psychological plan, and notably in his speech, must be on the simple theme of a higher living standard for all the world, and he suggested that Mr. Jackson and his colleagues take a look at this and all the other ideas which had been advanced, and come up with a new plan for the steps that we should take. The focus, the President said, should be on the common man's yearning for food, shelter, and a decent standard of living. This was a universal desire and we should respond to it.
>
> Mr. Stassen stated that plainly the country's greatest asset at this juncture was the leadership of President Eisenhower, and that every effort should be made to project the President's leadership and personality throughout the rest of the world. In addition to emphasizing the standard of living as the goal sought by the President, Mr. Jackson's plan should also stress the moral values represented in the President. . . .

Thereafter the Council discussed for some time the question of how and when, and in what forum, the President should make his address. No firm conclusions were reached on any of these points, although the President stated his own belief that the question of when and how his speech was to be delivered was almost as important as its content.

We finally decided that the best forum would be the President's scheduled appearance before the American Society of Newspaper Editors on April 16, 1953. Jackson requested input from all of us for the speech's content, and he and Emmet Hughes and I returned to our old routines of the campaign trail to get a draft ready for the President's fine editorial hand so he could convert it into "genuine Eisenhower."

As delivered, the speech made an appeal directly to the Soviets, emphasizing the main economic theme from Sam Lubell's letter of the terrible drain the armaments race put on every other facet of human endeavor:

Every gun that is made, every warship launched, every rocket fired signifies, in the final sense, a theft from those who hunger and are not fed, those who are cold and are not clothed.

This world in arms is not spending money alone.

It is spending the sweat of its laborers, the genius of its scientists, the hopes of its children.

The cost of one modern heavy bomber is this: a modern brick school in more than thirty cities.

It is two electric power plants, each serving a town of sixty thousand population.

It is two fine, fully equipped hospitals.

It is some fifty miles of concrete highway.

We pay for a single fighter plane with a half-million bushels of wheat.

We pay for a single destroyer with new homes that could have housed more than eight thousand people.

Eisenhower spoke directly to the Russians. Emmet Hughes must receive proper credit for some of his best writing in any of Eisenhower's speeches:

The Soviet system shaped by Stalin and his predecessors was born of one world war. It survived with stubborn and often amazing courage a second world war. It has lived to threaten a third.

So the new Soviet leadership now has a precious opportunity to awaken, with the rest of the world, to the point of peril reached and to help turn the tide of history.

Will it do this?

We do not yet know. Recent statements and gestures of Soviet leaders give some evidence that they may recognize this critical moment.

We welcome every honest act of peace.

We care nothing for mere rhetoric.

We are only for sincerity of peaceful purpose attested by deeds. The opportunities for such deeds are many. The performance of a great number of them waits upon no complex protocol but upon the simple will to do them. Even a few such clear and specific acts, such as the Soviet Union's signature upon an Austrian treaty or its release of thousands of prisoners still held from World War II, would be impressive signs of sincere intent. They would carry a power of persuasion not to be matched by any amount of oratory. . . .

He told the Soviets that we stood ready to enter into "solemn agreements":

171

(1) To reduce the burden of armaments through limitations of numerical strength, the production of strategic materials, the size of armies, and all weapons of great destructiveness; and

(2) For the international control of atomic energy and the prohibition of atomic weapons, with adequate safeguards including an inspection system under control of the United Nations. Everything should be designed to reduce arms expenditures so that the standard of living of all peoples in the world could rise.

He proposed "a new kind of war . . . a declared total war, not upon any human enemy, but upon the brute forces of poverty and need."

The peace we seek, founded upon decent trust and cooperative effort among nations, can be fortified, not by weapons of war but by wheat and by cotton, by milk and by wool, by meat and by timber and by rice. These are words that translate into every language on earth. These are needs that challenge this world in arms. . . .

He moved directly into the theme of Sam Lubell's letter:

This government is ready to ask its people to join with all nations in devoting a substantial percentage of the savings achieved by disarmament to a fund for world aid and reconstruction. . . .

The monuments to this new kind of war would be these: roads and schools, hospitals and homes, food and health.

We are ready, in short, to dedicate our strength to serving the *needs*, rather than the *fears*, of the world. . . .

I know of only one question upon which progress waits. It is this:

172

What is the Soviet Union ready to do?

The April 23 NSC minutes show Allen Dulles' report on the speech:

> Mr. [Allen] Dulles then summarized the world reaction to President Eisenhower's speech of April 16.
>
> With respect to the Soviet reaction, he noted that the Tass agency had quickly summarized the speech and sent out reports to the Soviet and orbit press containing 360 words. While this was all that the Soviet Union and the orbit peoples would learn of the speech from their own news sources, the coverage was nevertheless far more complete than any coverage accorded an American speech in recent years.
>
> The only detailed statement about the speech was concerned with the President's five points on disarmament. Nothing whatever was said about the President's point on the high cost and heavy burden of armament.
>
> The only gross misrepresentation of the President's words in the Tass summary was a statement that the President had wholly ignored the German problem.
>
> Turning to the free word reaction to the speech, Mr. Dulles said that it had been received nearly everywhere with great enthusiasm. The Indian Government's reaction, while hostile and neutralist initially, had subsequently changed to approval.
>
> Neither Syngman Rhee nor the Chinese Nationalists had been pleased with the President's speech.
>
> The President interrupted to observe that he did not understand what Syngman Rhee had found to kick about, since in his address the President had called for free elections in a united Korea.

A month later, Premier Malenkov presented his own peace plan, but Secretary Dulles spotted it as fostering Russia's own goals to:

(1) prevent the European Defense Community from coming into being;

(2) cause a slowdown in rearmament programs in the United States and our Allies; and

(3) protect Russia's own borders against hostile invasion by the West.

Eisenhower expressed great disappointment, but told me in several private conversations that he would keep trying to reach out to the Russian leaders. One day, we'd get through to the Russian people.

This gave me my opening to begin urging a Big Four Summit of Heads of State, not just Foreign Ministers. I knew Secretary Dulles would oppose this idea of a summit, but I wanted the President to begin to consider it seriously as perhaps his one and only forum to present his peace message directly to the Russian rulers.

Chapter 12
"Feed the Hungry Germans"

Perhaps nothing better contrasts the differences between our free-world attitudes and those of the Communists of the era than our program to feed the East Germans in the summer and early fall of 1953.

In the National Security Council meeting June 18, 1953, CIA Director Allen Dulles briefed us on the riots the preceding day in East Germany. The official "Eyes Only—Top Secret" minutes, only partially declassified in 1985, show the paucity of detailed descriptions:

> Mr. Dulles thereafter described in as much detail as possible the uprising in Berlin and East Germany, where, he pointed out, the Soviet relaxation program had likewise backfired. Mr. Dulles said that the United States had nothing whatsoever to do with inciting these riots, and that our reaction thus far had been to confine ourselves, in broadcasts which were not attributable, to expressions of sympathy and admiration, with an admixture of references to the great traditions of 1848. In summary, Mr. Dulles described what had happened as evidence of the boundless discontent and dissension behind the Iron Curtain, and added that it posed a very tough problem for the United States to know how to handle. . . .
>
> [*Paragraph blocked out as still classified*]
>
> Apropos of Mr. Allen Dulles' conclusion, Mr. Jackson [now head of the Psychological Strategy

Board] observed that while the riots certainly revealed discontent, they were more important in showing, for the first time since their enslavement, that the slaves of the Soviet Union felt that they could do something. The thing had developed past the riot stage, and was moving close to insurrection. . . .

[Two pages blocked out as still classified]

Mr. Stassen also agreed that the key areas were the European satellites. He listed all of them, and observed that in each instance the Soviet faced trouble of one kind and degree or another. It seemed plain to Mr. Stassen that there were men willing to die for their freedom in these areas, and that each of them contained indigenous armed forces. If, as had been the case in East Germany, the Russians could not trust these indigenous forces and felt compelled to bring in their own troops, this should be taken as a sign of real promise. . . .

Mr. Jackson then said that he desired the Council's guidance in pulling the East German situation together and to find a policy thread upon which he could string the actions which this Government might take. Noting the hue and cry for free elections in Germany in the course of the riots, he stressed the importance of keeping this idea of free elections alive.

In response to Mr. Jackson's request for guidance, the President suggested that the Council really needed a report from the Psychological Strategy Board outlining the possible actions that could be taken under existing policy over the next sixty days or so. He would be perfectly willing to call a special meeting of the Council to take a look at such a report when it was complete.

[Paragraph blocked out as still classified]

Dulles told us how East German workers moved into the streets, threw stones at Russian Red Army tanks, attacked official government buildings, and set fires to offices, not only in East Berlin but all over East Germany. A critical shortage of basic foods triggered the riots and the people vented their anger against Russian oppression generally. Hunger often sparks rebellion.

Our NSC one-hour debate on the U.S. response to the food riots divided itself into two vigorous camps.

One side wanted to sit back and do nothing, and let the East Germans suffer ever more under Russia's oppressive policies. In our Cold War, as in any war, they contended, you do not feed your enemy. If we did send food, the East German people would not get it. The Russians would seize it for their own army, and we would end up supporting their occupation.

I led the other view. In keeping with America's humanitarian traditions, we should send food. Food would further our aim to win the Cold War and keep it from turning into a hot one. Food for the subjugated peoples would be in keeping with the President's policy of reaching out in his search for a formula for world peace. I felt that the East Germans should be told the source of the food reaching them, and that this would show them that we in the West still remembered them, sympathized with their plight, and hoped their oppression would be short-lived.

Finally, I did not think our Judeo-Christian heritage could possibly let us sit idly by and watch other people starve while our warehouses bulged with surplus foods.

I remember Eisenhower's exact words as he brought the discussion to a close: "We will feed the hungry Germans!"

The logistics of the program fell under my jurisdiction as Director of Mutual Security, but I worked closely with C.D. Jackson and other members of the Psychological Strategy Board.

Jackson and I put our heads together to work out the food delivery program that turned on these premises:

(1) President Eisenhower should write directly to Premier Malenkov and ask his approval of our food relief program for the East Germans;

(2) We must prevent the Russians from using the relief program as an excuse for another Berlin blockade as in 1949-50, so we should enlist the support of West German Chancellor, Dr. Konrad Adenauer, in Bonn, and let the West Germans actually distribute the food through their own relief centers, already established and manned by West German personnel;

(3) We should ask Adenauer to start the food packages moving to the East Germans as soon as possible, using food stockpiles in West Berlin built up after the blockade to protect West Berlin from future shortages in the event the Russians elected to create some new mischief;

(4) We would replace these stockpiles immediately, to prevent worries of the West Germans that their food guarantees flowed out to the East Germans; and

(5) As soon as possible, we would prepare food parcels ourselves that would be marked in some way to show that they came from the United States.

On July 4, President Eisenhower made public his letter to the Russians in which the United States proposed to supply fifteen million dollars worth of food to alleviate the famine in East Germany "for humanitarian purposes." On July 7, Russian Foreign Minister Molotov rejected Eisenhower's offer, branding it an "unlawful interference into the internal affairs of East Germany." Eisenhower publicly repeated his offer July 10.

The propaganda war heated up, the whole world watching in amazement as the Russians elected to play politics with the lives of the starving East Germans.

Chancellor Adenauer wrote a public letter to Eisenhower:

> Your letter of July 10th has been conveyed to me through Ambassador [James B.] Conant [United States High Commissioner in Germany]. Your generous offer to relieve the want of the population of the Soviet zone through immediate and extensive deliveries of food-stuffs has touched me deeply.
>
> This spontaneous demonstration of humane readiness to help, which is in the best traditions of the American people, has caused great joy in all of Germany and especially has given new hope and new courage to the people in the Soviet-occupied zone of Germany. I should, therefore, like to express to you, in the name not only of the Federal Government, but also in the name of the entire German people, my heartiest thanks.
>
> It is with regret that I have learned that the Soviet Government has refused its cooperation in the relief action which you had planned. I would like to request that the delivery of foodstuffs should not as a result be withheld. On the contrary, I wish to express the hope that the foodstuffs may be placed at the disposal of the Federal Government [West Germany], which for its part will do everything to make the food available in the most effective way possible for relief of the suffering of the populations who have fallen into need as a result of the situation in the Soviet zone.

For the next three months, the whole world watched the food relief program unfold, with all its excitement, suspense, and drama, and unexpected episodes developed, all of which lay the foundations of much of what has taken place in East Germany recently. Many of the events overlap the dates of this running, day-to-day account, as they continued throughout the program's duration.

July 17—The world press headlined the loading of the U.S. freighter *American Inventor* in New York harbor with flour, milk powder, dried beans, dried peas, and lard for shipment to the West German port of Hamburg. The press labeled it part of the "$15,000,000 famine relief for East Germany program" ordered by President Eisenhower.

Technically, the shipment would replace food stockpiles in West Berlin, but this detail got lost in the fine print at the end of the news stories.

July 19—West Berlin mayor Ernst Reuter announced that in one week the West Berlin government would make available food relief packages to *all* Germans, including East Germans who visited West Berlin. At that time, West Berlin's unemployment rolls ran to 200,000. An additional 400,000 pensioners existed marginally, World War II's destructive residues still felt a full decade after Hitler's demise.

The mechanics of distribution involved issuing coupons to the East Germans, worth five marks (about $1.20) that could be exchanged for food.

Reuter's public notice brought threats from the official East German newspaper that East Berliners caught with the food packages would be considered espionage agents of the West. "Do you want to be an American spy for five marks?"

Throughout the life of the program the Russians and East Germans called it "American" and "United States," even during these initial stages when the food actually came from West German sources.

The Communist press in East Germany pursued its scare techniques by printing names of East Berliners already tried for espionage.

July 21—Alarmed at the agitation still boiling in East Germany and the bitter reactions in the world press, the USSR announced that it would grant East Germany fifty-seven million dollars in credits for food, which was a tacit admission of food shortages the Communists vigorously denied existed. The fine print of the credit offer, however, described a blatant barter program that required East Germany to ship manufactured goods to Russia to ease Russia's own shortage of consumer goods at the expense of the East Germans.

Desperate East Germans defied their government's threat and crossed into the West Berlin borough of Kreuzberg to get the food packages.

July 22—Vladimir Semyenov, Soviet High Commissioner in Germany, sent Commissioner Conant a harsh note demanding that the U.S. stop delivery of the food packets and quit using "Fascist hirelings and criminal elements who on June 17 participated in arson and looting in East Berlin." He accused the U.S. of opening "special places where Fascist agents are active under the cloak of food sales," calling the food "sales" along the East-West border a breach of the "normal situation."

For the first time, Semyenov conceded that the riots of June 17 caused "severe damage" in the Soviet zone of East Berlin.

Semyenov, of course, conveniently ignored the fact that the food distribution program used West Berlin relief offices and West Berlin volunteers who, for purely humanitarian purposes, chose to help their brethren in the East.

July 23—At a news conference, President Eisenhower stated that the food shipments for East Germany would continue, regardless of the Soviet attempts to ban them. He hoped the Soviets would not penalize the suffering East Germans for the Communists' own political purposes. He repeated that while the United States will be the ultimate donor of the food, the actual administration of the relief programs rested in the hands of the West Germans.

West Berlin announced that one million food parcels would be ready for distribution to East Germans by the end of the week.

July 24—In an effort to sabotage the food delivery program, the East Germans flooded West Berlin with tens of thousands of forged coupons—"brilliant forgeries," Commissioner Conant called them—luckily discovered only from an anonymous letter telling the authorities in West Berlin that the forgery plan was intended to provoke riots in the West when thousands showed up at the distribution places, but found no food available.

The East German propaganda media continued to list names of East Germans already tried for espionage for accepting the food packages, saying that the police would keep a record of all persons suspected of participating in the food delivery program.

July 26—The Communist press rode two themes on this the day before the food program would formally begin: (1) Those who crossed over to the West to get food would be "registered" by the Americans and their names later made available to the East German police; and (2) East Germany did not really suffer from any food shortage. In fact, so much food crammed the warehouses that it would rot if the people did not use it.

We all marveled at the stupid lie and wondered how the Communists could hope that anyone in East Germany would believe it.

July 27—The crossover began, 100,000 East Germans moving into West Berlin on foot, men and women of all ages, some weak and in need of help. They carried suitcases, pushed baby carriages, pulled rusty carts and children's wagons, wore knapsacks on their backs.

Since the coupon forgeries, eligibility for a ten-pound food package could be proved by the identity cards everyone carried in the East. Some East Germans brought ID cards for other family members, one man getting 140 pounds of food for the fourteen ID cards he brought with him.

One reporter captured the pathos of the occasion. He described hundreds of men and women standing at a bridge over the Spree River, trying to decide whether to risk encounters with the Peoples Police who waited on the other side. Hunger drove most to chance the crossing.

At the end of the day, West German workers estimated the giveaway at 103,000 packets of food.

July 28—The Communists tried a new ruse to disrupt the program. They circulated bogus newspapers in West

Berlin telling all the unemployed and the pensioners to come get food at the distribution centers, hoping to jam the centers, now increased to thirty-five.

The West Berlin authorities quickly denounced the Communist fraud on radio and in their own legitimate papers.

East Germans jammed interzone trains, coming from as far away as a hundred miles to get to West Berlin. The train rides cost up to twenty East German marks (around $5.00), but the economics worked out: one two-pound can of lard cost eighteen marks if it could be found; and the recipient of a food parcel came home with not only this much lard, but beans, peas, powdered milk, and flour—thirty dollars' worth of staples for his five dollar ticket. The West Berlin newspaper *Jorgenpost* reported that 3,000 people jammed into one train coming into West Berlin, with a normal capacity of only 900.

July 29—In another unbelievable twist, East Germany's premier, Otto Grotewohl, offered to buy "$15,000,000 of food from the U.S. or even more," while other Communist bureaucrats continued to deny that any food shortages existed.

U.S. trucks rolled into West Berlin, loaded with food. People of both East and West recognized the markings of the trucks and praised their mercy missions.

Grotewohl railed against the U.S. He called the food program "impudent"; but in the same speech, he announced some concessions demanded by the rioters on June 17. Among other things, the East German Justice Department would review 18,000 cases of persons arrested, and their program of "leniency" already had resulted in 8,871 persons being released.

July 30—West Berlin relief administrators announced that by the weekend, they expected that the gifts of relief packages would reach one million persons.

The East German official paper responded with a story that those who received food from the West would be treated as members of the "Fighting Group Against Inhumanity," an anti-Communist subversive group, and all would be placed under surveillance. The story provoked quips from Germans on both sides of the border, who wondered where all the Peoples Police would come from to keep watch over a million East Germans already on the "Fighting Group" rolls.

July 31—The East German Peoples Police began to confiscate the food parcels brought back by the starving people from the distribution centers in West Berlin. The West Germans countered by messages over loud speakers in the West German railroad stations, telling the people where the police concentrated on given days, so the East Germans could take different trains for their return home.

The Communists played into Eisenhower's hands by blaming the entire food relief program on the United States, even though West Germans actually manned West German distribution centers.

Since public schools served as distribution centers, West German administrators announced a week's delay in school openings.

August 3—East Germany banned train travel to West Berlin, but it could not stop the flow of the hungry. Many boarded trains at the far borders of the Soviet zone, got off in East Berlin, then took buses or walked across the border. An estimated 120,000 made their way to the food dispensing stations.

East Germany announced that it would be illegal for anyone to give his or her ID card to anyone else, even temporarily, to keep one person from collecting food parcels for another.

Unconfirmed reports came in to West Berlin that Soviet troops and tanks quelled riots in the Soviet sector similar to the disturbances June 17.

East German functionaries stepped up their anti-food program campaign, threatening East Germans returning from West Berlin with arrest unless they gave up their hard-won food gifts. "Railroad workers," the propaganda ran, "persuaded" passengers to drop their food packets into boxes on station platforms rather than be caught evading the law with their "beggars' parcels." East German bureaucrats claimed they collected a whole train load of foodstuffs from the West at railroad border stations, but when an East German government employee berated a crowd of returnees for traveling to the West, the crowd shouted her down, and she ran in fear for her life.

August 5—The border crossings continued at the rate of 100,000 per day. West Berlin relief dispensers now accepted letters of hardship from clergy, schools, churches, and social clubs in lieu of the ID cards to reduce the threat of reprisal for those who showed a need for more than one food package.

The Communists appealed to workers in the factories to dissuade everyone from participation in the food program, foolishly forgetting the factory workers' hunger.

August 6—The Communists tried another ruse to disrupt the relief program. They flooded West Berlin with thousands of letters aimed at the unemployed, urging them to storm the distribution centers and demand food parcels. West Germany quickly countered, as when the Soviets sent over the forged coupons earlier.

The distribution of 104,000 packages brought the total number of East Germans who received aid since the program began to two million.

In one of the most dramatic developments of the entire project, East German Peoples Police began to cross over to get their own food packages, one hundred asking for permanent asylum in the West. They reported increasing unrest in the Soviet zone that would possibly reach revolutionary proportions. The Russians made heavy troop relocations in anticipation of a full-blown rebellion.

August 15—Soviet zone newspapers began an intense campaign to try to shame the East Germans, the papers printing the names of persons caught with "American" lard, flour, milk, dried beans, and peas, calling them "weaklings" and "beggars." All would be fined at least 150 marks and their names kept by the police for future reference.

On it went into October when a fortunate harvest abated East Germany's acute food crisis and permitted us to let the food relief program dwindle to a close.

The physical tally of the eleven-week program is impressive. A minimum of three million East Germans came to West Berlin for the food handouts, some two and three times. This made an accurate nose count impossible. We did know that we provided five and a half million food packets to the West Germans to pass out. Those from August 7 on carried our logo of the split red-white-and-blue shield, two hands clasped in friendship in the middle, above the bold printed words: "United States of America."

We advised the people of both Berlins that we replaced West Berlin's food reserves, which in turn supplied the first relief packages to the East.

We could also tick off the cold statistics of the giveaways: 55,000 tons of flour; 5,000 tons of lard; 20,000,000 cans of milk. West Berlin officials estimated that at least eighty percent of the entire East German population received two of the food packets, with this participation spread over the entire country.

Perhaps the intangibles proved even more significant.

In the first place, the United States received a tremendous boost in world-wide prestige while the Communist image plummeted. The battle lines between the "good" and the "bad" focused sharply—"feed the multitudes" on the one side, against "the people aren't starving, or if they are, it's none of your business" on the other.

Next, almost immediately, the Russians took tanks and artillery away from the East German puppet army, fearful that if the shooting started, the East Germans would turn the heavy firepower toward the East.

When the East Germans came across the border by the tens of thousands, they visited with those in the West in what became known as "Peoples Congresses" in the streets, the coffee houses, the beer halls, and the parks. They could contrast, firsthand, the comparative brightness in the West with their own drab, glum, slave-like burdens of scarcity at home. They tasted freedom, though transitory, a glory many never knew as their days under Hitler flowed into the Communist occupation.

From the end of the food program, Communist infiltration and indoctrination into the labor unions of West Germany fell drastically. This frustrated the Soviets, who counted on their subversion of the labor unions, particularly in the coal and steel sections of the Ruhr Valley. They hoped to build enough of a Communist following to let them insist on German unification, but on their own terms of a united Germany within the Warsaw bloc.

The Soviets and their East German counterparts tried with all their might to force the East Germans to hate the Americans, but the effort failed completely. The East Germans remembered who fed them when they starved and remain grateful to this day.

There is no doubt in my mind that the window of freedom those millions of East Germans glimpsed during this period, and their brutalization by the Soviet oppressors, laid the foundations for the political events of 1989. The whole world can thank Dwight Eisenhower for reaching out to "feed the hungry Germans."

Chapter 13
Reaching Out to Labor:
Dreams of a "Solidarity"

My second personal assignment for General Eisenhower during the campaign—my first, liaison to MacArthur—involved an identical mission to organized labor.

Eisenhower knew of my early induction into the labor movement as a permitholder from the Pullman and Sleeping Car Conductors Union when I worked my way through law school as a pullman conductor in the late '20s. Both my brothers carried union cards, Bill's from the AFL Sheetmetal Workers Local in St. Paul, Arthur's from the Milk Wagon Drivers Union, the St. Paul Teamsters Local.

In my race for a third term as governor of Minnesota, I received endorsements from the AFL, CIO, and Railroad Brotherhoods. Organized labor also supported our new Labor Conciliation Act—the "Count 10" law—which provided a "cooling off" period in labor disputes, notification to a state labor conciliator ten days before a strike or lockout, and a thirty-day fact-finding committee in strikes or lockouts that threatened the public interest. The law's goal: Prevent economic loss and human suffering due to violent labor-management confrontation that plagued the state the preceding decade.

Chapter 13

The key provisions of the Minnesota Act served as the foundation for the federal Taft-Hartley law (Labor-Management Act of 1947) almost a decade later, but in some places, Taft-Hartley went too far.

My background in the labor field made me a frequent speaker before labor groups all over the country, but my acceptance by organized labor caused me problems with many of the Old Guard of my own party. "Big Labor must be curbed, cut down to size," they proclaimed in such strident tones that labor feared them as dedicated "union busters."

When we visited together as university presidents before his return to Europe as NATO commander, Eisenhower expressed his strong view on labor's mistake of tying itself completely to either party, at that time to the Democrats. The union leaders supposedly knew collective bargaining, but they couldn't do much horse trading when one party knew it would get labor's votes automatically.

After the nomination, Eisenhower asked me to carry his message to top labor leaders, among them George Meany of the AFL and Walter Reuther of the CIO, both of whom I knew well. He hoped to work with them to develop a balanced program that would honor the worker, put him on a level playing field with business, manufacturing, finance, and agriculture, and give him a fair shake in the economic results of his labor. At the same time, the worker should be able to speak with a democratic voice in running his union. He also needed protection from unscrupulous leaders and racketeers who controlled some of the major unions. Eisenhower worried specifically about reports that greedy union bigwigs, notably in the Teamsters, looted pension funds, risking the retirement security of thousands of laborers.

I agreed to make these contacts, even though we both knew that every major labor union in the country vigorously supported Adlai Stevenson. The unions poured millions of dollars from their treasuries into the Democratic campaign and into congressional races everywhere to elect Democratic majorities in both houses of Congress.

I must confess that I don't know any way to measure whether my liaison efforts to labor produced votes-in-hand for Eisenhower; but on my first visit with him at Morningside Heights after the election, I suggested that he consider appointing a prominent union leader as Secretary of Labor. It would be a bold move to break the Democrats' stranglehold on the unions. This would be almost unheard of for the Republicans, but it made sense. The post of Secretary of Commerce always went to someone from business or industry. Why not Labor to a labor leader?

Eisenhower agreed and charged me with the task of finding some outstanding labor man with a sound, balanced reputation and a clear record of integrity. I began my search by running down the membership list of the Executive Council of the AFL, then talked confidentially with half-a-dozen of labor's top officials.

Martin Durkin's name surfaced. His biographical sheet read:

> DURKIN, Martin Patrick. Born in Chicago, Ill., March 18, 1894; son of James J. Durkin, stationary engineer, and Mary Catherine (Higgins) Durkin; Roman Catholic; married Anna H. McNicholas on August 29, 1921; father of Martin P., William J., and John F.; attended parochial schools; took courses in heating and ventilation engineering; worked in packing house; became steamfitter's helper in 1911, and after six years made journeyman in the union; served as private in U.S. Army in France during World War I; elected assistant business agent of Steamfitters Local 597, United Association of Journeymen and Apprentices of the Plumbing and Pipe Fitting Industry of the U.S. and Canada, 1921-1933; was vice-president of

Chicago Building Trades Council, 1927-1933; made state director of labor for Illinois, 1933-1941; president of international Association of Governmental Labor Officials, 1933-1955; was national secretary-treasurer of United Association of Plumbers and Steamfitters, AFL, in 1941. and was elected president in 1943.

He seemed tailor-made for the job. Three things particularly impressed Eisenhower: his position as vice president of the Catholic Conference on Industrial Problems, his directorships of the Union Labor Life Insurance and the National Safety Council, and his experience in government as Industrial Commissioner for the State of Illinois.

I passed his name on to Herbert Brownell and General Lucius Clay, Eisenhower's top advisors on cabinet choices. Durkin cleared the automatic FBI investigation without the slightest spot on his record and Eisenhower invited him to Morningside Heights for a conference.

Durkin reacted with shock when he heard of the possibility of a cabinet offer, and laid his concerns on the line. He did not know how his fellow union workers would react to what they might consider a "turncoat" move. He took pride in being a life-long Democrat, worked hard for Stevenson's election, and supported the AFL's call for total repeal of the Taft-Hartley Act.

Eisenhower replied with equal candor. He would not advocate repeal of Taft-Hartley, but believed that the Act could be amended to give satisfaction to both labor and management. Further, he would expect his Secretary of Labor to be his "ambassador" to the union leaders to show them that not all Republicans grew horns, or meant to "bust" the unions and drive them back half a century.

In addition, he would expect Durkin to be more than an advocate of labor. He would want him, like other cabinet members, to look at the broader picture of what is best for the country as a whole, not just one segment.

Durkin asked for time, then agreed to accept the appointment. When announced, Durkin issued a statement saying that he took the post because he believed that the new President "will treat labor fairly, and with full and complete consideration."

AFL president George Meany called it "a splendid appointment," going on to say:

> Mr. Durkin, an outstanding trade unionist practically all his life, made a fine record as Industrial Commissioner of the State of Illinois under Governor Horner.
>
> He is ideally fitted by training, experience, ability and temperament for his new post.
>
> Mr. Durkin's appointment will inspire confidence among the ranks of organized labor in the expressed desire and determination of President Eisenhower to be fair to the nation's workers.

But Senator Taft's explosion made block headlines in every paper in the country. *The New York Times* titled its two-column, front-page story:

> Taft Breaks Truce By Calling Durkin "Incredible" Choice—Senator Indignant—Says A.F.L. Man Named as Labor Secretary Is "a Truman Partisan"—Sees "a Union Affront"—Declares Selection Ignores "Eisenhower Democrats" in the North and the South

Taft vented his continuing fury in a long news release:

> The appointment of Mr. Durkin is an incredible appointment. This is no reflection on the character or ability of Mr. Durkin.

I had a number of talks with Mr. Brownell, who has been the key man in Cabinet appointments, and made several recommendations of qualified men. It was never even suggested that a man would be appointed who has always been a partisan Truman Democrat, who fought General Eisenhower's selection, and advocated the repeal of the Taft-Hartley law.

It is an affront to millions of union members and officers, who had the courage to defy the edict of officials like Mr. Durkin that they vote for Stevenson.

This appointment leaves without representation in the Cabinet those millions of Democrats, North and South, who left their party to support General Eisenhower, and gives representation to their most bitter opponents.

"My appointment is not nearly as 'incredible' as Taft's statement," Eisenhower told me. "How does he think the Republicans can ever reach out to labor after a performance like that?"

Ten top CIO officials joined the fray, sending Durkin a congratulatory telegram:

The executive officers and vice presidents of the Congress of Industrial Organizations, speaking for our Fourteenth Constitutional Convention, warmly congratulate you upon your appointment as Secretary of Labor.

We feel certain that you, with a long and honorable record of experience in the trade union movement, will fill a great and constructive role in the new Administration. You may feel confident of the complete and whole-hearted cooperation and support of the Congress of Industrial Organizations in these tasks.

One of them told the press: "Usually what's bad for Taft is good for us."

Durkin handled the fracas well. He sent both the AFL and CIO telegrams saying that he looked forward to working with them on a forward-looking labor program. He wisely refused to let the media draw him into a dogfight with Taft.

Most editorial opinion across the country supported the appointment, calling Taft the loser.

"I don't give a damn about winners or losers," Eisenhower fumed. "I'm trying to make labor see that they can get friends inside the Republican party."

Durkin's confirmation cleared the Senate with a minimum of difficulty, but then months of wrangling took place over filling the posts of the assistant Secretaries of Labor and over amendments to the Taft-Hartley Act. Labor wanted these amendments but Taft, as majority leader in the Senate, blocked them.

In the meantime, Eisenhower, Durkin, and I tried to develop practical programs to reach out to labor unions overseas.

Our foreign operations programs delivered billions of dollars of goods and materials overseas where poorly paid, almost enslaved, native laborers unloaded and transported them to their distribution points.

Labor unions in these underdeveloped and Iron Curtain countries fell into three broad categories:

(1) Those dominated by totalitarian Communist control;

(2) Those under the totalitarian control of right-wing military dictators; and

(3) Fledgling independent unions that struggled between some degree of freedom and effectiveness and the danger of being gobbled up by either the Communists or the military dictators.

Our challenge: How to use our economic power and moral leadership to strengthen the independent unions so that oppressed, underpaid workers could gain enough power to improve social, economic, and eventually, political conditions.

The President expressed his enthusiasm when I formed a broad-based citizens advisory committee to get this plan rolling. I named as members the President of the U.S. Chamber of Commerce, the president of the National Association of Manufacturers, the president of the League of Women Voters, the American Farm Bureau, head of the PTA, and top business executives. The President reacted most favorably when Meany and Reuther agreed to serve.

We decided that while we in the Mutual Security Administration (later Foreign Operations Administration) could put into effect a few minimum requirements that would be helpful to the overseas unions, real, long range changes could only come from labor in this country reaching out directly to help labor in the other countries.

Durkin launched the program formally in a speech May 20 to the International Garment Workers Union, AFL, in Chicago. Reviewing the fact that the United States representation in world labor groups came through a tripartite delegation from government, industry, and labor, he urged that compacts with labor groups in other countries, as well as our own, weed out Communist infiltrators so that "Freedom is not in any way infringed."

Later, Walter Reuther addressed the Third World Congress of the International Confederation of Free Trade Unions in Stockholm, saying the free labor movements would prove to be "the most reliable ally of democracy," and punched home the theme:

> The recent uprising in East Germany indicates that
> the workers are the very core of the struggle against

Eisenhower as Commander-in-Chief of NATO when Harold Stassen visited him December 12, 1951, to urge Eisenhower to run for President as a Republican. *(Photograph courtesy of the Dwight D. Eisenhower Library)*

Dear General:—

It was grand to see you Your remarkable accomplishment in one year in Western Europe is thrilling to note and an inspiration to observe.

I am writing this forthright letter to you because I believe it is desirable that you have this specific information as 1952 begins. Of course no reply is expected nor appropriate.

Eisenhower and his longtime friend, deputy commander, and confidant, General Alfred Gruenther, when Gruenther succeeded Eisenhower as NATO commander. *(UPI/Bettmann)*

Left: First page of Stassen's handwritten letter to Eisenhower on Hotel de Crillon stationery, in which Stassen summarizes his conference with Eisenhower three days earlier, outlines the political situation at home, and explains the challenge of Taft's powerful drive for the nomination. (See page 9.)

Republican convention, Chicago Stockyards, July 11, 1952. Warren Burger and Dan Gainey, Stassen's floor managers, confer after receiving the "thumbs up" signal from Bernard Shanley, seated in the balcony above the Stockyards Arena. *(Photograph reprinted with permission of Warren E. Burger)*

Burger tells U.S. Senator Ed Thye, Minnesota delegation chairman, that the count of delegates showed that Minnesota could put Eisenhower over the top by shifting all its votes to Eisenhower immediately after the roll call ended. *(Photograph reprinted with permission of Warren E. Burger)*

By prearrangement with convention chairman Joseph Martin, Senator Thye waves his banner for recognition so that he can announce Minnesota's vote shift. *(Photograph reprinted with permission of Warren E. Burger)*

The convention explodes at Thye's announcement, which gives Eisenhower the nomination on the first ballot. *(Photograph reprinted with permission of Warren E. Burger)*

Eisenhower confers with Secretary of State John Foster Dulles, his first cabinet appointee, and Harold Stassen, Director of Mutual Security (later, Foreign Operations Administration) on their key foreign policy roles. (*AP-Wide World Photos*)

Eisenhower confers with Attorney General Herbert Brownell. During the presidential election campaign Eisenhower appointed Brownell, C.D. Jackson, and Stassen as a special advisory committee to supervise the writing of all speeches and to chart the general philosophical course of the campaign. *(UPI/Bettmann)*

C.D. Jackson, *Time-Life* executive, receives his commission as Special Assistant to the President and Chairman of the Psychological Strategy Board (later Operations Coordinating Board). Jackson played a creative role both in the campaign and later in the White House. *(AP-Wide World Photos)*

Pre-inaugural cabinet meeting, January 13, 1952, Commodore Hotel. Front, left to right: Brownell (Justice), Humphrey (Treasury), Nixon, Eisenhower, Dulles (State), Wilson (Defense). Back: Dodge (Budget), Hobby (Federal Security Administration—later Health, Education and Welfare), Adams (Chief of Staff), Weeks (Commerce), McKay (Interior), Summerfield (Post Office), Benson (Agriculture), Durkin (Labor), Lodge (United Nations), Stassen (Mutual Security). *(AP-Wide World Photos)*

Protocol dictates the seating arrangement in the cabinet room. Clockwise: Lodge, McKay, Humphrey, Nixon, Brownell, Weeks, Hobby, Adams, Dodge, Flemming (Defense Mobilization), Durkin, Summerfield, Dulles, Eisenhower, Wilson, Benson, and Stassen. At National Security Council meetings, Stassen moved up to Benson's seat next to Wilson. (AP-Wide World Photos)

At the White House, Eisenhower wishes Dulles and Stassen bon voyage on January 30, 1953, as they prepare to leave for a tour of Europe to explain Eisenhower's policies and plans for continued U.S. economic and military involvement on the continent. *(UPI/Bettmann)*

Eisenhower's first State of the Union message which Stassen helped write. The President specifically wanted Dulles and Stassen in Europe at the time of the speech's February 2 delivery to interpret the speech's main themes correctly and to be sure no one distorted its message.
(AP-Wide World Photos)

Eisenhower delivers his "Chance for Peace" speech April 16, 1953, to the American Society of Newspaper Editors. In this first major policy statement after Stalin's death, he reached out to the Soviet leaders and people in an effort to break through the Iron Curtain and give U.S. foreign policy a new, affirmative direction. *(UPI/Bettmann)*

Always a sports fan—football player and coach, baseball player, and avid golfer—Eisenhower prepares to throw out the first ball to open the 1953 baseball season. Onlookers around the President include Democratic majority leader in the Senate, Lyndon Johnson; Chief Justice Earl Warren; House Speaker Joe Martin; Vice President Nixon. To the President's immediate left: Clark Griffith, owner of the Washington Senators; Buckey Harris and Casey Stengel, baseball managers. *(National Park Service)*

Stassen, Treasury Secretary Humphrey, John Foster Dulles, and Defense Secretary Wilson attend a NATO conference in Paris in April, 1953. *(UPI/Bettmann)*

Cabinet wives. Front, left to right: Mrs. Durkin (Labor), McKay (Interior), Nixon, Eisenhower, Wilson (Defense), Brownell (Justice), Stassen (Mutual Security). Back: Weeks (Commerce), Humphrey (Treasury), Hobby (Secretary, HEW), Adams (Chief of Staff), Summerfield (Post Office), Lodge (United Nations), Dodge (Budget). *(UPI/Bettmann)*

Dulles and Stassen (left side of table) face British Chancellor of the Exchequer Rob Butler and Foreign Secretary Anthony Eden in economic conference in Washington in mid-1953. (*UPI/Bettmann*)

The President and Press Secretary Jim Hagerty after a press conference in the Executive Office Building (EOB). The two men considered their relationship to the media adversarial, but Eisenhower thought it bad taste and poor judgment to deliberately try to mislead reporters. *(UPI/Bettmann)*

Eisenhower developed his Casey Stengelese style of replying to reporters' questions he did not want to answer definitively. He never used "no comment," saying that this would alert reporters to a story not ready for public release. *(AP-Wide World Photos)*

Stassen and Secretary Wilson in the buffet line at Camp David.
(National Park Service)

Esther Stassen at Camp David talking to Eisenhower (back to camera) and Labor Secretary Mitchell. An accomplished artist, Mrs. Stassen shared with Eisenhower a mutual interest in painting. She led a group of cabinet wives who studied painting, which the President encouraged. *(National Park Service)*

Eisenhower briefs Walter Robertson, Assistant Secretary of State for Far Eastern Affairs, on his mission to Korea to tell President Rhee that he must accept the terms of the armistice Eisenhower worked out; otherwise, Korea would be left to go it alone. *(National Park Service)*

Eisenhower explains to his old deputy commander, lifelong friend, and Army Chief of Staff General Matthew Ridgway that he must accept Eisenhower's "New Look" for the military, and think in terms of the need for a truly national defense posture, not just as an advocate for the army. This policy statement accompanied the President's early warning of the dangers of a powerful military-industrial complex that could cripple the economy. *(National Park Service)*

Eisenhower presents famed golfer, course designer, and lawyer Bobby Jones with a portrait the President painted of Jones. Painting, golf, and bridge gave Eisenhower his ways to "let go" when the pressures of his office became stifling, as during the Korean Armistice and the China crisis. *(AP-Wide World Photos)*

Eisenhower used golf not only for personal relaxation, but to show the public that the Commander-in-Chief was confident and in control. *(AP-Wide World Photos)*

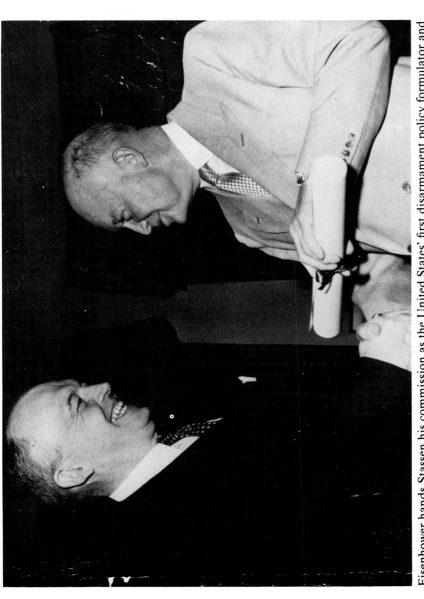

Eisenhower hands Stassen his commission as the United States' first disarmament policy formulator and negotiator, a role the media labeled "Secretary for Peace." Stassen was the only person ever to hold such a post. The appointment reflected Eisenhower's intuition to reach out to the Soviets in efforts to turn the world away from the Cold War and toward peace. (*National Park Service*)

Senators Richard Russell (Georgia), Lyndon Johnson (Texas), and Walter George (Georgia, Chairman of the Foreign Relations Committee) talk to reporters after meeting with the President to express bipartisan support for his foreign policy. Senator George's private letter to Eisenhower (sent at Stassen's recommendation) helped convince the President to overrule Secretary Dulles and move for the 1955 Geneva Summit. *(National Park Service)*

Dulles and Eisenhower confer on the Geneva Summit. Dulles ever held that all foreign policy matters should be conducted at the foreign ministry level, and not by heads of state. (*UPI/Bettmann*)

The July 21, 1955 summit session in the Palais des Nations in Geneva where Eisenhower overruled Dulles and announced his "Open Skies" proposal, first suggested by General Doolittle and written by Stassen. The arrow (left) shows Stassen's seat directly behind and between Eisenhower and Dulles during Marshal Bulganin's opening speech, when Eisenhower turned to Dulles and Stassen and said: "Harold's right. I'm going to put it in!" *(AP-Wide World Photos)*

The Big Four at Geneva: Eisenhower, Bulganin, Faure, and Eden.
(UPI/Bettmann)

Eisenhower talks with Lieutenant General James H. Doolittle after Doolittle received the Oak Leaf Cluster at Versailles, January 25, 1945. The concept of Eisenhower's "Open Skies" proposal came directly from General Doolittle, through Harold Stassen, the National Security Council, and finally the President, who announced it at Geneva. *(Photograph courtesy of the Dwight D. Eisenhower Library.)*

The President and General Doolittle at the White House nine years later. *(AP-Wide World Photos)*

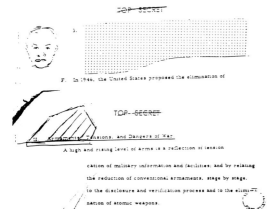

F. In 1946, the United States proposed the elimination of

H. Armaments, Tensions, and Dangers of War

A high and rising level of arms is a reflection of tension

cation of military information and facilities; and by relating

the reduction of conventional armaments, stage by stage,

to the disclosure and verification process and to the elimi-

nation of atomic weapons.

G. Since the development of a thermonuclear weapon, and since the

changes in nuclear technology began radically to transform

the prospects for international control of atomic energy,

United States policy on arms control has been under intensive

Eisenhower's doodles on pages of his copy of the "Progress Report" on disarmament given by Stassen at the May 26, 1955 meeting of the National Security Council. Stassen knew the President's doodling to be a good sign. It meant that he listened intently to the speaker, shutting out everything but the speaker's words. The Eisenhower Library seal on the right guarantees the authenticity of its documents.

One of Eisenhower's doodles at Geneva, perhaps of one of his Russian counterparts. Stassen picked it up after the July 21 session on disarmament at which Eisenhower announced the "Open Skies" concept.

Secret JL   July 19, 1955

Draft of ~~Statement~~ of President
Eisenhower on the subject of Disarmament.

~~Mr. President~~

Mr. Chairman; Gentlemen; -

~~Other statement~~

~~with intent to~~ The statements made
in this session and ~~on~~ the preceding
~~days~~ days of this conference, on the
subject of ~~disarmament~~ by each of you
have been followed by me with
close interest.

It is the most important
subject on our agenda. It is also the
most difficult. ~~In recent years~~ ~~the~~ scientists have discovered
methods of making weapons many ~~times~~
many times more destructive of ~~home~~
~~and industries and~~ opposing armed forces,
but also of homes, ~~and industries~~, and
lives, than ever known ~~by~~ or even
imagined before. These same scientific discoveries,
have made more complex the problems
of limitation and control ~~and~~ reduction
of armaments.

The first page of Stassen's longhand draft of the President's proposal on disarmament, which included General Doolittle's "Open Skies" idea. (See page 326.)

inspection and reporting methods.

I announce to you now that for the purposes of designing and testing an inspection and reporting system which will serve this magnificent objective of disarmament and peace, my government is ready in principle to permit trial inspection of units of our armed forces if other countries will do the same. My government is ready in principle to permit test aerial photographic inspection if other countries will do the same. My government is ready in principle to test inspection on the ground in specified comparable zones if other countries will do the same.

We are ready to proceed in the study and testing of a reliable system of inspections and reporting, and when that system is designed, then to reduce armaments together to the extent that the system will provide assured results.

This exploration could be conducted in two broad areas. One could be between those nations possessing global military forces. The other could involve those nations having regional forces in Europe or elsewhere.

The successful working out of such a system would do much to develop the mutual confidence which will open wide the avenues of progress for all our peoples.

Secretary Dulles' copy of the typed Stassen disarmament draft on which Dulles crossed out the mutual aerial photography proposal that a clever reporter later labeled "Open Skies." (See pages 334 and 335.)

Stassen and Eisenhower discuss the Geneva Summit, Stassen encouraging Eisenhower to write the post-summit personal letter to Bulganin. *(National Park Service)*

Eisenhower and Marshal Bulganin talk at Geneva, the President making his personal attempt to reach out in an effort to break the stalemate of the Cold War and to turn the world toward peace. (Interpreters are off-camera.) *(UPI/Bettmann)*

Eisenhower's expressive face.

communistic tyranny, the same as free labor was the core of the struggle against fascism.

On Labor Day, September 5, the CIO began a series of "public service" broadcasts on ABC radio that it hoped would eventually reach all countries behind the Iron Curtain. The series preached the role of free unions in raising the standard of living of people everywhere.

Martin Durkin built his Labor Day message around an international text, expressing sympathy for the workers behind the Iron Curtain, offering them "fellowship," and pledging to join hands with them in the fight against the "ugly specters of dictatorship and communism":

> The workers of East Germany and of Czechoslovakia have struck out against the despots seeking to enslave them, in the world's most recent examples of man's long struggle for freedom.
>
> The June graves of their martyrs are already hallowed shrines in the hearts of freedom-loving people everywhere.
>
> On this Labor Day in America we pray for labor's strength and progress.

In a similar thrust, David Morse, director general of the International Labor Office, said that the uniting of the American Labor movement with the workers' movements in other lands could go a long way toward solving many of the world's problems of poverty, hunger, disease, ignorance, and conflict, and help lay the foundations of world peace.

The President's own Labor Day message, beamed throughout both the free and Communist worlds, assaulted totalitarians wherever they held power:

The workers of America are witnesses, before the world, of the strength, the pride and the prosperity that alone can be won by free labor.

They are strong in their independent unions. They are proud beyond the temptations of political subservience. They are an indestructible bulwark of free government.

These witnesses to freedom's blessings give the lie to the sly evil of the promises of totalitarianism. They mock the false insinuation that economic well-being can be purchased only at the cost of political freedom.

They are the final answer to those who prate freedom and practice slavery, who excuse terror and aggression in the name of concern for the very workers whose lives they stifle.

Free American labor has won for itself the enjoyment of a standard of living unmatched in history. The contemporary world knows no comparison with it. There is only brutal contrast to it.

To this, there is no more pitiful and dramatic testimony than the food which this free people has been able to send to feed hundreds of thousands suffering the peculiar torments of the proletarian government of Eastern Germany.

This is a day sincerely to salute American labor: Its freedom, its dignity, its matchless productive genius—and the lesson it records for all men to read, for all time to come.

At the President's urging, we began a campaign to get the United Nations to study the plight of workers around the world. Finally, on December 7, the General Assembly voted forty to five, overruling the Soviet bloc, to air a report that found workers in Iron Curtain countries exploited for economic and political ends. The resolution denounced the sending of political dissidents to slave labor camps and called for an accounting of some 400,000 citizens of West Germany and Italy missing behind the Iron Curtain.

The Soviet delegate unwittingly gave emphasis to the report's significance by his loud attack on it. He called it "slanderous," "biased," and the "product of traitors" who "fled" the Soviet Union to avoid prosecution for their crimes.

Unfortunately, our efforts to reach out to the unions overseas did not receive total support at home. Even within the cabinet, international business interests opposed any consideration of the subject, saying that what happened to the workers in other countries concerned those countries only. We must not meddle in their internal affairs.

This meant that United Fruit, for example, could continue its unbridled operations in Central America, and the great mining companies and other international cartels did not want to open up the possibility of wage increases around the world. These business interests remained completely immune to any social, moral, or political considerations, thinking only in terms of profit and loss statements.

"Greed! Greed! Greed!" Eisenhower told me after a cabinet meeting in which Durkin and I discussed our efforts to improve the conditions in the foreign unions. "That's the real plague of mankind. Think of it! If you could change man's greed, all the rest of his problems would go away."

Martin Durkin resigned October 8, 1953, a little over eight months after he took office.

In the early days, we all found him jolly, congenial, and witty. He did not speak frequently in cabinet meetings; but when he did, everyone listened. I particularly valued his support of my efforts to build pro-union requirements into our system for delivery of American goods to foreign countries.

Perhaps around August, possibly earlier, Martin's personality underwent a complete change. He became hostile, belligerent, and downright rude, even to the President, finally saying that he felt completely out of place in the cabinet. He now appreciated the cartoons that showed the cabinet as "ten millionaires and one plumber." The plumber did not belong. He made a serious mistake when he thought for a minute that he could do anything to change "Republican thinking," which hated labor and always would.

He delivered one last effective speech October 4 before the National Conference of Catholic Charities, after his resignation but before he left office:

> Labor unions are striving to maintain and develop in man his God-given self-respect. . . .
>
> The trade union movement of America is no synthetic institution created in test tubes by philosophers in the controlled conditions of their lecture rooms.
>
> Instead, it is a concerted effort by men and women to achieve through their common effort that innate self-respect which is everyone's birthright.
>
> Collective bargaining gives wage earners the physical means of possessing self-respect. This result gives real meaning to the benefits of economic and political freedom.

Less than a year later, we learned the real cause of Durkin's mental deterioration that happened right before our eyes in the cabinet room: a brain tumor that caused his tragic death, after two unsuccessful surgeries.

Eisenhower wrote out his own compassionate message to Mrs. Durkin:

> The word of Martin's death is deeply distressing to me, as it must be to all those who had the privilege of friendship and association with him over the years.
>
> His career was marked by an unfaltering devotion to high ideals and to the service of his fellowmen. He will be greatly missed by those who knew him.

Martin's dedication to his religious faith and to the welfare of his fellow man made his life both exemplary and purposeful. He was a good and distinguished American.

Mrs. Eisenhower joins me in extending our deepest sympathy to you and your family.

Eisenhower's reference to Durkin's faith reflected his genuine respect for those who shared his own deep belief in God, no matter the form through which they practiced that belief. His attitudes toward God are no better shown than in the unprecedented prayer he used to open his inaugural address. He composed it himself without consulting anyone but close family members after their return from an early morning service at the National Presbyterian Church:

Almighty God, as we stand here at this moment my future associates in the executive branch of government join me in beseeching that Thou will make full and complete our dedication to the service of the people in this throng, and their fellow citizens everywhere.

Give us, we pray, the power to discern clearly right from wrong, and allow all our words and actions to be governed thereby, and by the laws of this land. Especially we pray that our concern shall be for all the people regardless of station, race, or calling.

May cooperation be permitted and be the mutual aim of those who, under the concepts of our Constitution, hold to differing political faiths; so that all may work for the good of our beloved country and Thy glory. Amen.

When we discussed Martin Durkin's short cabinet service, Eisenhower told me that his legacy would not be the amendments to Taft-Hartley, or legislation on unemployment insurance compensation, or broadening the conciliation and mediation services. Rather, it would be his efforts to carry out Eisenhower's mission to reach out to world labor unions as part of Eisenhower's broad-based dreams of penetrating the Iron Curtain countries.

Unfortunately, Dwight Eisenhower did not live to see the evolution of the Solidarity labor movement in Poland that led to that country's march toward freedom, but his early vision planted its seed. It's a shame that later administrations did not follow through more aggressively, and let Solidarity come about years earlier.

Chapter 14
Progress Through Compromise:
The Korean Armistice

From January through July 1953, the Korean War occupied more space in the minutes of the National Security Council than any other subject. I do not propose to rehash the great body of literature already grown up around the moves for an armistice; but I think a synopsis important to show:

(1) Eisenhower's actions and restraints as perfect examples of his belief expressed in his October 16, 1952, letter to Swede Hazlett that "leadership in the political as well as in other spheres consists largely in making progress through compromise—but it does not mean compromise with basic principles"; and

(2) How his firm control throughout resulted in an achievement that no other leader in the world could pull off.

We must remember that Korea presented only one of several crises fermenting around the world that Eisenhower faced as he moved to establish his interlocking policies of Communist physical containment and a vigorous global economy in which every country of the world would participate, Communist as well as free.

An excerpt from the June 19, 1953 National Security Council's partially declassified minutes gives a thumbnail sketch of the most serious trouble spots:

The National Security Council:

a. Noted an oral briefing by the Director of Central Intelligence on the events leading up to the recent East German and Czechoslovakian riots, and the implications thereof for Soviet policy.

b. Discussed alternative courses of action open to the United States as a result of this evidence of popular opposition to Soviet control within the satellites, as presented by Mr. C. D. Jackson.

c. Noted that the President confirmed his authorization to proceed with the development of the Volunteer Freedom Corps (NSC 143/2) at such time as might be agreed upon by the Secretary of State and Mr. C. D. Jackson.

d. Agreed that the Secretary of State should:

(1) Inquire of Chancellor Adenauer as to his need for additional arms for the West German police forces.

(2) Consider raising in the United Nations the Soviet repression of the popular demonstrations in East Germany.

(3) Continue intensified efforts to persuade our allies to refrain from relaxing their controls on trade with Communist China in the event of a Korean armistice.

e. Requested the Psychological Strategy Board to prepare, for urgent Council consideration, at a special meeting if necessary, recommendations as to policies and actions to be taken during the next sixty days to exploit the unrest in the satellite states revealed by the recent East German and Czechoslovakian riots.

Immediately after taking office, Eisenhower ordered the Joint Chiefs to make comprehensive studies of the military consequences in Korea—including casualties, costs, manpower and equipment needs, and time frames—of the different options then available:

(1) Maintain the current stalemate, with sporadic to intense fighting along the front, and daily casualties;

(2) Withdraw all UN forces (including U.S.) and leave Korea to the Republic of Korea (ROK) army south of the battle lines, with the Communists—including perhaps half-a-million Chinese—above the lines;

(3) Attempt to drive militarily all the way to the Yalu River, repeating MacArthur's conquest and temporary victory two years earlier;

(4) Try to bring the Nationalist Chinese under Chiang Kai-shek, then in exile on Taiwan (Formosa), into the war against mainland China; and

(5) Broaden the war, which meant bombing parts of China and Manchuria which the British, in Laborite speeches in the House of Commons, accused us of plotting.

But if we did broaden the war, what might Russia's military responses be?

I visited Eisenhower after he digested the reports of the Joint Chiefs. He told me that a total victory appeared out, the Communists so firmly dug in with a network of tunnels and bunkers, plus adequate artillery support, that a conventional frontal assault would produce an unacceptable number of casualties. Even a behind-the-lines landing such as MacArthur pulled off at Inchon would leave us with thousands of square miles of territory we could not hold, since the Chinese would continue to pour uncounted masses into North Korea with little concern for what happened to them as they marched south.

Any hope of total victory involved saturation bombing of the enemy's staging areas and supply depots across the Yalu and their airfields in Manchuria. Eisenhower did not want to do this merely to inflict a humiliating defeat on the Communists; but he would order it if it proved the only way to save American lives. This included using atomic bombs.

The only practical way out of the war would be a negotiated truce, leaving Korea split more or less along the present front, tragically almost the same division of the country as before the war.

But how to pull it off?

In February, Eisenhower ordered UN Commander General Mark Clark to begin armistice negotiations at Panmunjon, at the battlefield level. He knew that anything resembling a "peace conference" would take months to arrange and could stall matters for years while American troops continued to die. "Peace conference" wrangling would probably move us no closer to a solution than the options available at Clark's battlefield level.

With starts and stops, ups and downs, threats and counterthreats, charges and countercharges, strategies and counter-strategies, the negotiations lasted until the armistice's signing July 27, 1953, six months after the inauguration. These tried Eisenhower's patience no end and called forth skilled diplomatic maneuvering almost daily.

The President faced profound conflicts of opinion at home and abroad, possibly unparalleled since Civil War days, the conflicts heightened by the holdover of the Truman-MacArthur controversy.

In Korea, South Korean President Syngman Rhee, a scholarly, emotional, stubborn, and patriotic leader who served as Korea's President-in-Exile during the years of Japan's brutal occupation, proclaimed to all the world that he would accept nothing less than a united Korea with all the Chinese driven out. He sought a firm treaty of military support, economic aid, and long-range assistance from the United States, with the U.S. guaranteeing Korea's borders for all time to come.

The Republican Old Guard—Senators Jenner, McCarthy, Knowland, and others—sided with Rhee, proclaiming a "battlefield settlement" unacceptable since it did not punish the Communists for their initial aggression and left them free to take over all of Asia.

The British wanted them and us out of Korea, unconcerned about the long-term effects of our withdrawal.

The armistice negotiations moved at a snail's pace on such technical points as the exact location of the battle lines, protection for each side against the other's troop build-ups for future fighting in the event no final truce could be reached, the policing of the cease-fire agreement, and the return of prisoners.

The question of prisoners proved more vexing than all others. Rhee announced from the beginning that he would never agree to a forced return to North Korea of a single prisoner who chose not to return. The Communists insisted with equal vigor that *all* prisoners must be formally exchanged.

Rhee's unilateral, precipitous actions regarding the prisoners almost caused the total collapse of the armistice talks. By way of background, the usually-punctual President arrived late for the National Security Council meeting June 18, took his seat, heard Bobby Cutler open the meeting, and then said (my paraphrase):

> Foster [Dulles] awakened me at 3:00 this morning to tell me that an emergency crisis had arisen in Korea.
>
> He just received a message that President Rhee had released all the North Korean prisoners of war in the prisoner of war camps, without notice to the UN or United States commands. This has created a very real crisis that threatens the whole effort we are making to end the Korean War.
>
> I met at 7:00 this morning with Foster, Charlie [Wilson, Secretary of Defense], Admiral Fletcher [of the Joint Chiefs], and Frank Nash [Assistant Secretary of Defense for International Affairs].
>
> Foster felt that we should send a very strong message to Rhee, castigate him for what he had done, and emphasize that if we couldn't depend on his actions in the future, we would have to withdraw from Korea.
>
> Before any message goes out, I want a complete review by the Council. My feeling is that we must send a message of some kind, but I want its wording reviewed carefully.

I thought back over my associations with Rhee. I knew he championed the cause of *all* Koreans. He desperately wanted a united Korea, all his thoughts, words, and deeds pointing in that direction. He stood ready to take risks to reach his goal.

I also looked down the table at Dulles. Ordinarily, this type of note would be drafted and sent out by the State Department, but the President moved the matter to the NSC to be sure that the note's tone and content did not undo the four months of negotiations already behind us.

Perhaps the best way to capture the flavor of the six-month debate, the problems Eisenhower faced at home and abroad, his style and his control over the negotiations is to look at the minutes of one of the important NSC sessions when it looked for a while as though the truce talks would break down, leaving us with the same unacceptable stalemate he had found on inauguration day. I insert subheadings in brackets for emphasis and readability, and a few explanatory comments.

June 19, 1953

1. <u>AGENDA FOR 150th NSC MEETING</u>   [June 18]

The opening of the Council meeting was delayed three-quarters of an hour while the President conferred with the Secretaries of State and Defense, the Chief of Naval Operations and Assistant Secretary of Defense Frank Nash, with regard to the contents of a message from the President to Syngman Rhee.

When the President entered the Cabinet Room at 10:45, Mr. Cutler suggested that, in view of the recent developments in Korea, the President might wish to postpone Council consideration of the regular agenda, since the agenda was largely concerned with items on the Far East which could not be considered until there was a clarification of the situation in South Korea.

The National Security Council:

> Agreed that, in view of the developments in Korea and East Germany, action on the items scheduled for consideration at this meeting should be deferred.

2. <u>PRESIDENT RHEE'S RELEASE OF NORTH KOREAN PRISONERS OF WAR</u>

The President's first remark concerning the release by President Rhee of North Korean prisoners of war, was that we seemed to have acquired another enemy instead of a friend. President Rhee had welched on his promise not to take unilateral action without consultation with the UN Command. Moreover, his action in freeing some 25,000 North Korean POW's was deliberate, carefully planned in advance, and carried out in defiance of the UN Command and of Rhee's own promise.

[MESSAGE IN TONE OF ULTIMATUM TO RHEE]

Of course, said the President, it left us in a most difficult position, and he and his advisers had been composing a message which, by implication, informed Rhee that if he continued in this course it was "good-bye" to Korea. General Clark, said the President, cannot undertake to fight Rhee.

[OBLIGATED TO PUBLISH MESSAGE]

Moreover, we are almost obliged to publish to the world what we are going to say in this message to Rhee. The whole free world is puzzled and dismayed.

They realize that Rhee is in no position to carry on long by himself, and therefore they blame us, however unjustly, for what has happened.

He had just heard, said the President, that there had been an uproar in the House of Commons when the news broke in London six hours ago.

[PRESIDENT SEEKS COUNCIL'S SUGGESTIONS]

The President invited any suggestions from members of the Council as to how to handle this terrible situation. He said that he had not himself wholly realized the scope and magnitude of this release of prisoners, but he was now concerned lest the possibility of an armistice be completely destroyed. The only possible mitigating circumstance in Rhee's behavior was the fact that our own people had a few weeks ago considered such a move as Rhee had now actually made.

In any case, said the President, they were drafting a very blunt telegram to President Rhee, telling him that if he did not behave himself we might have to move out.

. . . .

The President, however, said that if it proved necessary we could probably withdraw without serious loss to our own forces.

[RHEE'S MOVE OBVIOUSLY PREMEDITATED]

In response to a question from Mr. Stassen, the President made clear his conviction that Rhee's move was in no way related to the recent heavy Chinese Communist attacks, but it obviously had been planned weeks in advance.

He then pointed out that the Council must not misunderstand his proposed message to Rhee. He was not going to say that we would actually pull out of Korea, because, for one thing, we do not want the enemy to imagine such a possibility, but in certain circumstances we might have no option but to do so.

[*Paragraphs blocked out as still classified*]

[NEED CLEAR STATEMENT IF U.S. QUITTING KOREA]

Mr. Cutler observed to the President that what he was really saying to the Council was that the whole Korean venture was over and that we were getting out. If that was indeed the President's view, Mr. Cutler stressed the necessity of a clear and forceful statement by the President that the ROK Government had broken faith with the United States. Otherwise, any U. S.

withdrawal would have terrible repercussions both among our allies and among our own people.

[DULLES ANALYZES RHEE'S MOTIVES]

Secretary Dulles asked to be heard, and stated his belief that the disaster was not irreparable if from now on it were correctly handled.

It seemed plain to the Secretary of State that President Rhee was engaged in a last desperate effort to torpedo the armistice and to force the hand of the United States. If he realizes that his attempt won't work, Rhee may well feel compelled to give up.

It will then be our task to find out whether the Communists really want an armistice so badly that they will be willing to overlook the release of the 25,000 prisoners. Certainly they had reacted violently to our own earlier proposal to effect the release of the North Korean prisoners, and of course it was a question how they would react to what was now an accomplished fact.

It was Secretary Dulles' guess, however, that they were so anxious for an armistice that they would overlook what had happened. Nevertheless, we must take the strongest possible line with Rhee so that he will not imagine that he can actually run the show.

[RHEE WANTS TO KEEP FIGHTING]

The President commented that the simple fact was that President Rhee and his supporters wanted to keep on fighting. that was the long and short of it.

Mr. Jackson said that it was important to tie in what had happened in South Korea with the uprisings in East Germany and Czechoslovakia. Together, all these events provided a real chance to assay Communist strength and weakness. While we should certainly be stern with Rhee, it would be wrong not to push ahead for the armistice rather than to make any suggestion of withdrawal. The Communists themselves must be very agitated by the grave difficulties that they were confronting in East Germany and among the European satellites. We ought not ease this pressure, therefore, by any withdrawal from Korea which would provide a victory.

The President replied, facetiously, that if we were to play the game that Mr. Jackson suggested, it might be better to send a message of congratulation to President Rhee.

[MUST KEEP PRESSURE ON COMMUNISTS]

Mr. Stassen, agreeing with Mr. Jackson, said that it seemed to him vital to keep on stepping up pressure on the Communists. This pressure, which had begun to be applied by the President and Secretary Dulles five months ago, was really beginning to hurt, and cracks in the Soviet edifice were beginning to be visible. Of course, added Mr. Stassen, we will have problems to contend with as regards our allies, but we must not relax this pressure.

[EISENHOWER: WE MUST PROTEST RHEE'S ACTIONS]

While agreeing with this point of view, the President nevertheless pointed out that the United States must either assume responsibility for President Rhee's action in releasing these prisoners, or else it must strongly repudiate that action.

If we accept what has happened without protest, our allies would regard it as tantamount to abandoning the coalition.

The Communists, too, would be quick to exploit our weaknesses, for what had happened in Korea was certainly no victory. It could be interpreted to mean that

we could not even control the ROK. Communist propaganda would shout that either the United States had
no influence on the Republic of Korea, or else that the
United States was really responsible for what President
Rhee had done.

[DULLES ANTICIPATES MORE RELEASES]

Secretary Dulles pointed out that the actual release
had occurred simultaneously in four separate POW
camps, and he anticipated that it would be followed up
in two more such camps. Obviously, therefore, the
whole thing had been planned in advance.

[PROBLEMS OF MILITARY COMMANDERS IN KOREA]

The President emphasized the terrible situation
which this posed for General Taylor and General
Clark. They could not conduct the defense of South
Korea while ignorant of what the ROK forces in their
rear would do next. How could we continue to provide
ammunition for the ROK forces when we had no idea
what their next move would be?

[NIXON: U.S. MUST REMAIN IN KOREA]

The Vice President interposed to state with great
emphasis that the United States must find some way to
remain in Korea. If we got out, he insisted, it would
constitute a great Communist victory, no matter what
we said in explanation of our withdrawal.

[PRESIDENT WORRIES ABOUT
OUR NATIONAL SELF-RESPECT]

Both the President and Mr. Stassen expressed agreement with this sentiment, but the President reverted to
his offer of June 6 and again emphasized the violation
of the promise by Syngman Rhee not to take unilateral

action without consultation. Rhee had broken his word, and the President pointed out that our national self-respect was involved in what had happened.

[STASSEN SEES AFFIRMATIVE BENEFITS]

Mr. Stassen said that it was barely possible that Rhee's action was really evidence that his Government was going to accept the armistice and that the freeing of the prisoners was simply a move to save face in the course of capitulating.

I did not use the word "capitulating," but I proved to be exactly right on what Rhee would do: ten days later Rhee agreed to the armistice he previously rejected.

The President said this might be true *if* there were an armistice.

[DULLES WANTS HARD-HITTING MESSAGE]

Secretary Dulles warned that if Rhee managed to get away with this move, and unless he wholly accepts the authority of the UN Command, we could not go on, and we would certainly get no armistice. Either Rhee accepts our authority or we shall be obliged to go our separate ways. However, added Secretary Dulles, if we hit him hard now in this message, Rhee will probably elect to save face and accept an armistice.

[PRESIDENT EMPHASIZES NEED
TO GO PUBLIC WITH MESSAGE]

The President then expressed his concern again as to the repercussions on our allies, and suggested to Secretary Dulles the advisability of calling in two or three of their Ambassadors in Washington in order to inform them of the contents of the private message he was sending to President Rhee. Over and beyond this message, of course, we must make a public announcement that we are repudiating Rhee's action.

[ANALYSIS OF RHEE'S COMMITMENTS]

Mr. Stassen questioned again, as he had earlier in the discussion, whether we could properly accuse Rhee of breaking his word, in view of the fact that he had never actually agreed to the proposed processing of the North Korean prisoners of war as anticipated in the forthcoming armistice.

Secretary Dulles and the President explained again to Mr. Stassen the commitments which President Rhee had made and broken with respect to the unilateral action, and the President warned that unless we repudiated what Rhee had done we would go down as the biggest frauds in history. After all, we had been negotiating on this prisoner-of-war issue for a good many months, and we could not jeopardize our good faith in these negotiations.

[Paragraphs blocked out as still classified]

[PRESIDENT: TELL RHEE HE BROKE HIS WORD]

The President again stated that he was not, in his message to Rhee, telling him that we were going to get out if he did not capitulate, nor even that he must return the released prisoners; but we were telling him bluntly that he had broken his word and that if he would not agree to behave himself in the future we had no alternative but to make other arrangements in Korea.

[MUST TRUST RHEE IN FUTURE]

Mr. Cutler queried the wisdom of putting any faith in Rhee's future promises, especially since to do so involved risking the lives of American soldiers.

The President replied that there seemed no clear alternative to trusting Rhee, and besides, he felt reasonably sure that if it came to a showdown, a very large part of the armed forces of the Republic of Korea would elect to stay in the lines with our own forces or to stay with us in sufficient numbers so that we could at least withdraw and create a defensible perimeter around Pusan.

[IGNORANT GUARDS RELEASED PRISONERS]

Secretary Wilson observed that it seemed that the ROK prisoner guards who had permitted the release were not actually responsible to the Chief of Staff of the ROK Army, but were responsible to the Provost Marshal, who was in effect the head of the internal police and directly under President Rhee.

This statement was questioned by Mr. Allen Dulles, but Admiral Fechteler pointed out that the ignorant guards had probably in fact carried out orders from Rhee's man whether they should have done so or not.

[EXPECT NO CONSTRUCTIVE SUGGESTIONS]

There then ensued a discussion of the probable allied reaction, and especially the British reaction, to what had happened. The President said facetiously that it would probably be similar to the behavior of some of his opposition in Congress. They would curse us, but they would offer no constructive suggestions for how to meet the problem.

[EISENHOWER'S SUMMARY]

Mr. Stassen suggested that we tell the British that our Rhee is like their Mossadegh—they would certainly understand that.

The President then summed up the discussion by stating that if no one had any better suggestion, he proposed to go ahead with the present plan for issuing a public repudiation of Rhee's action and sending a very tough private message to President Rhee. By and large, he added, he was doubtful if it would be actually necessary to contemplate a withdrawal of our forces to Pusan, because Rhee wanted to advance, not to retreat.

Although the message was finally dispatched by the State Department, the President personally edited the note to Rhee and converted it into "genuine Eisenhower." It went out considerably milder than Dulles' first proposal, but still strong enough to assure our Allies and world opinion that we continued to be in control of the Korean situation, and to caution Rhee against any further unilateral actions. It purposely left vague what we might do if Rhee repeated his prisoner-release moves or anything close to it, but omitted Dulles' threat that we might withdraw.

It accomplished the further goal of letting Rhee save face. His people demonstrated in the streets on several occasions, 100,000 strong, to support Rhee's pleas for a continuation of the war for Korea's unification.

The letter to Rhee shows Eisenhower's ability to combine firmness with measured diplomacy:

I have learned with grave concern that you have ordered the release of North Korean prisoners held by the United Nations Command in camps which are under the authority of the UN Command. Responsibility for the safeguarding of these prisoners was in part entrusted by the UN Command to the military forces of the Republic of Korea. Your order has been carried out by the use of open violence by South Korean elements against the authority of the UN Command.

On July 15, 1950, you formally advised the Commander-in-Chief of the United Nations Command that in view of the joint military effort of the UN on behalf of the Republic of Korea you assigned to him and to such military commanders as may exercise UN Command authority within Korea or in adjacent seas "authority over all land, sea and air forces of the Republic of Korea during the period of the present state of hostilities". I am informed by General Clark and by General Taylor that within recent days you have given them unqualified assurance that you would take no unilateral action at variance with the foregoing without prior consultation with them.

Your present order and the action thereunder constitutes a clear violation of this assurance and creates an impossible situation for the UN Command. If continued, such a course of action can only result in the needless sacrifice of all that has been won for Korea by the blood and bravery of its magnificent fighting forces.

Persistence in your present course of action will make impractical for the UN Command to continue to operate jointly with you under the conditions which would result therefrom. Unless you are prepared immediately and unequivocally to accept the authority of the UN Command to conduct the present hostilities and to bring them to a close, it will be necessary to effect another arrangement. Accordingly, the UN Commander in Chief has now been authorized to take such steps as may become necessary in the light of your determination. . . .

As your personal friend I hope you will find an immediate way to correct this situation. Accordingly, I am not now making this message public. I am confining myself to a brief statement deploring your action which I feel compelled to do to keep faith with my own people and our Allies.

The President did not stop with his letter. He sent Assistant Secretary of State Walter Robertson to Korea to deliver a personal message to Rhee: If Rhee did not stay hitched, the United States *would* withdraw, and leave Rhee and his ROKs alone to fight it out with the Communists. Further, the United States would withhold all future foreign aid. Earlier, I had assured Rhee that we would build electric power plants in the South to replace the hydroelectric plants in the North that produced all of Korea's electricity. These plants would be left in Communist hands by an armistice and division along the current battle front.

The armistice, signed forty days later on July 27, 1953, remains in place. Korea is still divided, but the killing stopped. In view of the wildly diverse, intense, and belligerent conflicts of opinion worldwide, Eisenhower considered *any* armistice a miracle and always spoke of it as one of the most important accomplishments not only of his presidency, but of his lifetime.

Chapter 15
The Studied Show of Relaxed Leadership: Painting, Golf, Bridge

Not all cabinet meetings turned out to be exciting. Some became downright boring, particularly when Agriculture Secretary Ezra Taft Benson droned on and on about the plight of the wool growers in his home state of Utah, or the failure of egg growers everywhere to break even on the products of their layers.

We joked about the perfect agricultual answer—provide that the surplus eggs purchased by the government must be wrapped in wool, so that Benson could take care of both his wool growers and his egg producers with one program.

The design of the cabinet table is such that fourteen people can sit at it comfortably and see every other person without straining or shifting position.

My chair, the third on the President's left after Secretaries Wilson and Benson, gave me a clear, unobstructed view of the President's facial expressions, as well as his eye, hand, and body movements.

I could easily tell when he became impatient or bored with a presentation that dragged on and on, either because the presenter did not prepare adequately or could not express himself succinctly. Not all cabinet members proved articulate.

When a discussion became tedious, the President would lay his pencil on the table, either take off his glasses or take a deep breath to carefully mask a sigh, and begin to stare at the large portrait of Lincoln that hung on the north wall, directly opposite the President's chair.

My mind also wandered as I watched Eisenhower: Could he be thinking of Lincoln's own cabinet meetings, the one in which every member voted "No" on some subject, which prompted Lincoln's report of the tally: "Seven noes and one aye. The aye has it!"?

Did he think of Lincoln's own deceptively relaxed style of spinning yarns while guiding the nation through its most trying period, when no one knew for almost three years whether the new "nation conceived in liberty and dedicated to the proposition that all men are created free and equal" could hold together?

Perhaps he replayed that tragic night at Ford's theater when the crazed John Wilkes Booth pulled the trigger.

Particularly those of us who sat on the President's side of the table came to think of the Lincoln portrait as a barometer of his mood. If he doodled, wonderful; but if he stared at Lincoln, forget it!

One morning when I arrived at the cabinet room, a blank spot on the north wall drew my eye—the Lincoln portrait was gone. Others also noticed its absence, and wondered about it: Perhaps it was off to a temporary exhibit in some art gallery? Did it need cleaning or some other type of maintenance? Did whoever made such decisions plan to replace it with something else? We all missed Mr. Lincoln's sad eyes and deep thoughts.

A couple of months later, Mr. Lincoln returned to his rightful place on the north wall, making the President appear more relaxed.

Christmas, 1953, gave the solution to the puzzle of the traveling portrait: The President presented each cabinet member and top aide with a lithograph of an Eisenhower-painted copy of the cabinet-room Lincoln. I treasure it greatly.

As he told it, the President's interest in painting came by accident, while he served as Army Chief of Staff. After his first return from Europe, Thomas E. Stephens painted Eisenhower's portrait during sittings at Ft. Myer, across the Potomac from Washington in Virginia. Painter and subject discussed painting generally, Eisenhower talking about how Churchill's great interest in painting helped save his sanity during his "exile years" between the wars.

Stephens told the General that he, too, should take up painting, as a form of relaxation. Eisenhower scoffed and said he couldn't draw a straight line or a round circle.

A few years later, the Eisenhowers invited Stephens to Morningside Heights to do a portrait of Mamie. Eisenhower tells the rest of the story in his own words, reprinted with permission from his book, *At Ease: Stories I Tell My Friends* (pages 340-341).

> An artist, Thomas E. Stephens, of New York, began a portrait of Mamie. I was an interested spectator. Having completed a sitting for the day, he asked Mamie to go with him through the house so that they could agree for a proper place for the portrait, when finished.
>
> Sitting alone after the two of them left, it occurred to me that I might as well make use of the paints remaining on his palette to try poking away on my own.
>
> The problem was to find anything on which to begin. It happened then that my old companion, Sergeant Moaney, came into the room and I had an idea. "Sergeant," I said, "in my room there is a little box about

225

twelve inches on each side. Will you please knock out the sides, take any kind of white cloth you can find, and stretch it on the board by tacking the edges?" Within a matter of minutes, Moaney was back with a clean dust-cloth and the bottom of the box. Together, we fastened the cloth to the board.

The only subject I could think of was right before me—Mamie's unfinished portrait. So I started out and kept going until the two explorers came back about forty-five minutes later. I displayed my version of Mamie, weird and wonderful to behold, and we all laughed heartily.

Tom Stephens, for some reason, urged me to keep on trying. I did not even bother to argue; painting was beyond me. So when he said that he wanted my "painting" as a keepsake, I was glad to give it to him, this product of my first grand venture into "art."

A few days later a package arrived. Opening it, I found a present from Mr. Stephens: everything I could possibly need—except ability—to start painting. I looked upon the present as a wonderful gesture and a sheer waste of money. I had never had any instruction in painting; the only thing of possible help was a working knowledge of linear perspective, a subject we had studied at West Point.

I left the open package in my room. Each day I seemed to develop a little more curiosity about painting a picture. The result was that I took the plunge, to find that in spite of my complete lack of talent, the attempt to paint was absorbing.

My most urgent need at the start was a generous-sized tarpaulin to cover the floor around the easel. The one thing I could do well from the beginning was to cover hands, clothes, brush handles, chair, and floor with more paint than ever reached the canvas. With the protection provided by the tarp, and with my painting clothes always stored in a dark recess of a closet, I succeeded in avoiding total domestic resistance to my new hobby.

The penthouse retreat at Columbia was an ideal studio. A professional might have objected to its lack of north exposure and a skylight. But privacy and quiet were more important to me than lighting.

After eighteen years, I am still messy; my hands are better suited to an ax handle than a tiny brush. I attempt only simple compositions. My frustration is complete when I try for anything delicate. Even yet I refuse to refer to my productions as paintings. They are daubs, born of my love of color and in my pleasure in experimenting, nothing else. I destroy two out of each three I start.

One of the real satisfactions is finding out how closely I come to depicting what I have in mind—and many times I want to see what I am going to do and never know what it will be.

In spite of this, I have frequently wished for more daylight hours to paint. Its only defect is that it provides no exercise. I've often thought what a wonderful thing it would be to install a compact painting outfit on a golf cart.

In the White House, in bad weather, painting was one way to survive away from the desk. In a little room off the elevator on the second floor, hardly more than a closet, the easel, paints, and canvases were easy to use. Often, going to lunch, I'd stop off for ten minutes to paint.

In Gettysburg, I've tried many landscapes and still lifes but with magnificent audacity, I have tried more portraits than anything else. I've also burned more portraits than anything else. (Garden City, N.Y.: Doubleday & Company, Inc., 1967)

I am most proud of my wife Esther's accomplishments as an artist, particularly the prizes for her exhibitions, one from the Smithsonian. She and Eisenhower talked about painting whenever they met.

He always gave personal encouragement to a group of wives of cabinet members, Congressmen, diplomats, and his own staff who met twice a week in what they called their "amateur painting colony."

One evening, we enjoyed an intimate dinner in the President's private quarters on the second floor of the White House. Another somewhat noted artist, Winston Churchill, shared our pleasure. After dinner, Eisenhower asked Esther if she would like to see his "studio." "Yes, indeed," she answered, and he took her to a room off the presidential bedroom, which he could also reach quickly from the Oval Office below.

He explained that while he could barely turn around in the room, its small north window served his need for light. He'd often run up to the studio from the Oval Office, duck in for a few minutes, and dab away.

Rachel Adams, Sherm's wife and a member of Esther's group, found a portrait of Churchill in the house they rented which served as the former residence of an ambassador from Australia. She gave it to the President, who copied it and sent it to Churchill.

Another time when we visited the Eisenhowers at Gettysburg, Mamie invited Esther to visit her husband's third-floor studio. On the way up, Mamie proudly pointed to a number of Eisenhower's paintings, particularly one of geraniums that she especially liked. She took great pride in his artistic accomplishments.

During this same visit, Eisenhower and Esther looked out a first floor window across a rolling pasture. He said that he wanted to paint the scene as a landscape but it lacked a barn or farm house or any feature to break the continuous plain all the way to the horizon. Esther suggested that he imagine a barn or a farm house, possibly a tall silo—any of those would certainly be an acceptable artistic variation. He replied, "It may be an acceptable artistic variation, but it's exactly the thing some reporter would delight in saying—that it's not a genuine landscape, because I added something that didn't exist."

By this time, the President took his art seriously.

Eisenhower used two other activities for escape and relaxation: bridge and golf, both of which the media misunderstood.

Two of his regular bridge-playing cronies, Democrat George Allen and General Al Gruenther, attest to his skill, saying that he could hold his own in any duplicate tournament.

In golf, he played a respectable "social game," to use his own words, his handicap staying under wraps all the time I knew him.

When some major crisis gave the media a field day on our approach to financial "panic" or on our risk of a shooting war (as during the Chinese crisis over Quemoy and the other off-shore islands), Eisenhower would tell Jim Hagerty to issue a statement that the President played a relaxed game of bridge the night before. Or Hagerty would alert the reporters of the President's plan to visit the golf course that afternoon, where Eisenhower would pose on the first tee or in his golf cart with a broad, contrived grin.

He wanted the world to know that he sat in complete control, no need to panic, God's in his Heaven, all's right with the world. He reminded his associates of the old military adage, variously attributed to Napoleon and half-a-dozen other famous generals: "Troops won't follow a commander into battle who looks like he's about to lead them to a rout that nobody'll get out of alive. They won't follow a long-faced commander. They want to see a leader whose air of confidence tells them that they'll all come back. My troops are now the American people, and I want them to see my confidence that we'll come back, no matter what the crisis of the moment."

At one point, when it looked like the Korean armistice talks would blow up and the fighting would intensify, he told Jim Hagerty to issue a statement that he and all the Eisenhower family would be at Camp David for the weekend "doing nothing." He actually worked feverishly behind the scenes to keep the talks alive.

Many historians and biographers continue to misinterpret Eisenhower's carefully planned, easy-going public image. They call him a "do-nothing" President, a "hands-off manager" who did little more than paint, play bridge, and golf while others saved the country and his reputation. They forget that before each game of golf in either morning or late afternoon, he worked long hours, completely in control, definitely a "hands-on" operator.

The notes of Ann Whitman, the President's personal secretary, show how he used golf to stretch his mind as well as his back and legs during his most stressful times. On July 19, 1955, at the Geneva Summit, when almost every waking hour required some crucial decision, she wrote:

> The President hit golf balls this morning, was in the office at one time and apparently very unhappy that we did not have more than a few things to sign. This was when we sent off post haste to Helen to send over the things coming into our office.
>
> This was the morning he came over asking where were the cattle. The ubiquitous Schulz dashed to the

escort and they went off to see where the "moos" came from in the morning.

Incidentally, there was on the place one very large, shaggy dog, sort of an oversize English setter, that loved the President dearly. He smelled to high heaven, but his chief delight was jumping up and putting his dirty paws on the President. Accompanied by a smaller dog of some variety [of] poodle, he would gravely make a daily visit to the office.

Thomas Kirker of the History Department at Kansas State University gives these insights into what golf meant to Eisenhower. His friendship with Robert Tyre "Bobby" Jones, 1930 Grand Slam winner, lawyer, and course designer, ran deep:

Ike was always eager for advice from Jones—as well as from Ed Dudley, the pro at Augusta—but while Jones was ready with playing tips, he was more concerned with Ike's overly determined attitude on the course. Jones knew that Ike was a fierce competitor, but he also knew that Ike was unlikely to improve beyond an 85-90 shooter because of a knee injury he'd suffered playing football many years earlier. In effect, Ike had no left side to hit against; Roberts once termed Ike "a congenital slicer." Jones felt, therefore, that Ike would enjoy the game more were he to play within his physical limitations. Jones' counsel made for an interesting exchange [of letters].

October 18, 1954

Dear Mr. President,

I think I realize how important it is for you to get the most possible enjoyment out of your golf.

. . . I understand from Cliff [Roberts] that you have allowed some of your friends to more or less badger you into the idea of setting up competitions on the basis of your 18-hole medal score.

I want to suggest to you very seriously that this idea of playing for an 18-hole medal score can produce mental and nervous pressures to which you should not be subjected on the golf course. A four ball best ball game giving you the opportunity to fail to finish a hole every now and then would be more relaxing and give you every bit of the atmosphere of competition which I know you desire. If I were in your place I would make up my mind that I would certainly never take a triple bogey and rarely a double bogey. I would just pick the darn thing up before that happens.

As ever,

/s/Bob

October 25, 1954

Dear Bob,

I know, of course, that your advice is at least aca-demically sound. Whether I can put it into practice is another story. I promise to try.

As ever,

/s/Ike

Chapter 16
Early Warnings on the
Military-Industrial Complex

When the President asked me to "sit quietly" in a meeting with the Secretary of Defense and the Joint Chiefs in early December 1954, I could not anticipate its full, long-range significance.

I made my way to the end of the cabinet table before anyone else arrived, there to observe, record, and later serve as the President's sounding board. Also, my Foreign Operations Administration supplied the weapons and other defense needs to our allies around the world, which made my presence relevant.

I greeted each participant as he entered—Nathan Twining, Chief of Staff of the Air Force, the first, at twelve minutes before the hour. He cut an impressive figure in his light blue uniform backlit by the sun coming through the windows from the Rose Garden. His wide and long panel of ribbons proclaimed thirty-seven years of service, first in the army, then in the U.S. Army Air Corps in 1924, long before a separate Air Force came into being. They called him "the brain," and he was indispensible in high-level planning sessions.

General Lemuel Shepherd, Commandant of the Marines, arrived almost on Twining's heels: tall and athletically built, his own chest of ribbons reflected a similar career of courage and command, when the Marines became equal partners with the other services during World War II.

Six minutes later, Admiral Arthur Radford, Chairman of the Joint Chiefs, walked in, enough braid on his navy blue uniform to confirm his thirty-eight years on the sea and in the air.

Admiral Robert Carney, Chief of Naval Operations and Chief of Staff when I served under Halsey during the Pacific War, followed Radford. He was a witty and charming man.

General Matthew Ridgway, Army Chief of Staff, perhaps the most imposing of them all in physical appearance, completed the group. Eisenhower felt a special affinity toward Ridgway, who jumped into Normandy behind Nazi lines with his 82nd Airborne Division on D-day. He later led the 18th Airborne Corps across the Netherlands, Belgium, and Germany, and took MacArthur's place in Korea when Truman called MacArthur home.

Three minutes before the hour, they moved behind their chairs along the north side of the table, Radford in the center, flanked by Ridgway and Twining on his right, Carney and Shepherd on his left. All fell silent, the air heavy with anticipation. Colonel Andrew Goodpaster, on special assignment as Eisenhower's White House aide, came in and greeted us all.

Exactly on the hour, the President, wearing a dark brown suit and blue tie, entered from the Oval Office, trailed by Secretary Wilson and Deputy Defense Secretary Roger Kyes.

He smiled, said "Good morning," and took his seat.

It flashed through my mind that here in this single room sat the managers of the most powerful military force in the world, with a destructive power unmatched in history. At one time or another, each of these commanders either saw active duty under Eisenhower or worked in association with him. They all, at one time, called him "Ike." Now, they appeared in different roles, the Commander-in-Chief included. The atmosphere was formal but open, all addressing the man opposite Radford as "Mr. President."

On that day I think Eisenhower stood at the peak of his self-confidence in his positions as president and commander-in-chief. His past two years in office included the successful handling of the crisis in Korea, feeding the East Germans, and considerable progress in domestic affairs.

I do not propose to give any details that would violate security regulations thirty-six years later, but I do want to report Eisenhower's statements of his general philosophy expressed in that meeting.

He began by inviting all those present to interrupt him whenever they wished. He preferred to stay away from intricate budget details and wished to talk only about his concept of what some called the "New Look" in defense. On these matters of substance, I am confident of the accuracy of my paraphrases:

> As you know, I have been carrying on, personally and through the National Security Council—and its Planning Board—extensive reviews. You've all participated in these, and I've drawn in the views of other officers, other individuals, and leading scientists, as well as some of our trusted Allied leaders.
>
> I've got the reports of the task groups on military policy, and on domestic policy, and on diplomatic policy. I want to give you my conclusions about our military doctrines. And as you will see, there's no way that you can separate military policy from economic policy.

He spoke in what we called his "command tone," firm but not strident, while he fixed those across the table with his "command look."

I want to emphasize first that our military doctrine and my deep personal conviction is that a third world war is *not* inevitable. We must stress this wherever we get a chance.

At the same time, it must be our military philosophy that a third world war *could* come upon us, but if it does, it will be only through the outreach of an opposing power.

He spoke fluently, without the aid of notes, barely stopping to catch his breath, exactly as I imagined him performing in staff meetings during World War II or at NATO.

These are the fundamentals of our approach in this "New Look," if you prefer to call it that.

This means that we should not be doing our planning or procurement on the speculation of a certain D-day, a certain number of years hence. It's not like D-day in Europe where we knew it would come one day in June.

We must be now, and continually, both powerful and alert, but on a basis that we can carry it on for the long-range future, for the next half-century or more.

I looked at his listeners, trying to guess who might be the first to interrupt; but none seemed inclined.

This also means that our national security will depend as much upon our economic strength as our military strength.

This, in my view, is very much a part of the military doctrine that we should adopt now, and follow it for this year, for the next year, and for the years ahead.

Furthermore, in view of the joint importance of our economic strength and our military strength, our military establishment must take on some responsibility for our economic strength. We must have a dynamic industrial base.

But the industrial base must never dominate our military establishment, nor should it ever be the other way around. And this is extremely important—and I'm not sure anyone can see down the road far enough at this stage—if the military and our industry leaders ever team up, they can dictate to the whole economy and the whole country. And they will end up with too much power. And that will be bad.

I, of course, could not anticipate at that session that he then laid the foundations for the warnings against the dangers of the military-industrial base that he would issue as a sort of farewell address before leaving office six years later.

Further, it should be basic military doctrine that the United States will never start a war. In this age of nuclear weapons, we all know that no rational objective can be served by deliberately starting a war of any kind. I hope the Chinese Communists learned this in Korea where everyone ended back almost exactly where they started, after all the loss of life and waste and destruction.

He next worked in his familiar text on greed, one I heard him express over and over again to many different audiences:

The entire military establishment must stand firm against greed, against corruption, against narrow favoritism, and against monopoly. There's a real danger of the military ganging up with powerful industrial leaders, and parceling out the contracts for weapons and research and all kinds of products and services. Bigness means lots of money to hand out—and that's dangerous, dangerous.

He moved to his main theme, deterrence:

237

Deterrence poses our major challenge. We must deter anyone from starting a war. We must deter them this year, next year, and for the next fifty years.

We must see to it that all military and political leaders everywhere know what a nuclear war would mean, and know that we are and will continue to be in a posture in which we cannot be defeated in a nuclear war, even though we recognize that no one can really be considered a winner in a nuclear war.

No one seemed the least bit interested in interrupting with either question or comment, all mesmerized by his extemporaneous lecture.

Deterring a potential enemy from starting a war needs concentrated attention. If we do it successfully, I repeat that we should think in terms of fifty years, of reaching for fifty years of peace. I know well the pressure of the events of today, and of the current year, but we've got to make a special effort for long-range thinking. This is crucial.

He next touched upon a favorite subject of mine because of my background at the United Nations founding conference in San Francisco.

The UN can and must make a contribution to peace, but it can never be the sole course of our national security; nor can it deter war unless the U.S. deters war. It's a fact of life that as of right now, the UN is no stronger than the U.S., nor does it have much will of its own, outside what the U.S. pushes it to.

I don't have to remind you that I've been involved with military budgets all my life. I know that none of the services ever thinks it has enough money to do its job, but the one thing I want to urge on you all today is that you must look beyond the needs of your own service. You've got to begin to think like planners for the country as a whole—for the defense establishment as a whole—and not just be advocates for your own special branch of service.

General Ridgway broke into the President's lecture first, saying that Air Force expansions cut too deeply into our position in Europe, leaving us without enough divisions to stop a Soviet attack. Even worse, our posture in the United States left us without back-up divisions if the Russians decided to take over the rest of Europe.

The President answered his old comrade of the battlefield:

Air force budget expansion is essential to make clear and real that our deterrent force is worldwide. If the Soviets should launch a mass attack in Europe, that attack must be met with a nuclear defense, and it will be. There is no other logical answer.

Ridgway pressed. A nuclear war would leave a vast vacuum of destroyed territory that we could not fill.

The President responded:

Our concentration must be on preventing any major war, and not trying to anticipate post-war vacuums. War can and must be prevented.

We must reject the concept of inevitable war, and must thoroughly consider all phases of prevention.

There are many facets to it. We must exercise care that we don't place other countries in a position in which they can start a war and drag us into it. We need to convince other countries that they cannot get by with military aggression, but do so without humiliating them so that they feel they've got to start a war to save face. That's partly what caused World War I.

We worked out of that horrible situation in Korea. We do now have a creditable NATO situation in Europe.

Twining answered Ridgway's objections logically. He knew they all thought the Air Force's budget had expanded disproportionately, but he wanted them to remember that missiles accounted for the major portion of this expansion. His delegation of authority to the scientific community moved that money outside the ordinary Air Force structure, even though it appeared as Air Force appropriations.

Admiral Carney told the President that he felt strongly that the real deterrent strength of the navy remained unrecognized. Within the year, naval scientists assured him that we would be able to launch ballistics missiles with nuclear warheads from submarines. This would let the navy place secret "launching pads" any place in the world, and stand guard in a deterrent posture.

The President continued:

> I not only want to be fair to each of you, and to your respective services, but I want to be damn sure that we cover all bases in this so-called "New Look."
>
> I'll continue to be available to each one of you singly, and to you as a group, to consider any new or additional concepts of strategy. But I want you to know where I stand in my general philosophies of military doctrine, how closely it meshes with the economic policies of the country, and how we've got to keep the military and industry balanced and apart, so they don't team up for monopolies—and too much power.

He closed with a final admonition, something of a corollary to his prior statements, yet important enough to stand on its own:

> Another important part of our military doctrine should be that we must endeavor to not let anyone think that they can successfully attempt a surprise attack upon us—never give the people of any country a

chance to feel that they can cripple us with a surprise attack so that we would be unable to respond and do them grave damage.

He asked me to follow him into the Oval Office. Among other things, he said:

> I'm continually amazed how few people in almost any walk of life can look at the broad, long-range picture.
>
> Arthur Radford can do it. I remember that only a few years ago, he championed the navy and the navy's needs, and to hell with the other services.
>
> My old and good friend, Matt Ridgway—no greater soldier and gentleman ever lived—is having great problems making the adjustment. He's the army's greatest advocate—wants the army to do it all, or at least, most of it.
>
> I upset him. He gets disappointed in me. Thinks I'm letting him down and my own branch of service down. I regret it, but I can't let old friendships and personal feelings get in the way of what I deeply feel we must do to preserve the peace.
>
> My branch of service is now all of America, and beyond.

Chapter 17
Senator McCarthy:
The Courage to Be Patient

The literature on Wisconsin Senator Joseph McCarthy and his offspring, "McCarthyism," is vast. I do not need to rehash it; but it infuriates me to see Eisenhower's handling of the McCarthy issue misrepresented by historians and biographers, and especially by Harry Truman. In *Where the Buck Stops: The Personal and Private Writings of Harry S. Truman*, Margaret Truman quotes her father as saying:

> But I think the ugliest and the dumbest thing that Eisenhower did during his administration . . . was the cowardly way he ducked the whole question of McCarthyism even when good, decent people around him were being hurt more and more by that awful and horrible man. McCarthy first began to make himself noticeable during my administration, and I recognized him immediately as a fake and a phony and as a real menace to our principles of freedom and decency. I realized that he didn't really believe the stuff he was spouting about Communists taking over the country any more than I did, and that he was just whipping up hysteria without any evidence at all because it was getting him headlines and the hope of maybe taking over the country himself. . . .
>
> I let my staff and the Congress and the rest of the world know how I felt about McCarthy every chance I got. (New York: Warner Books, Inc., 1989)

I knew McCarthy as a Midwest neighbor and one of my supporters in my serious 1948 run for the Republican nomination. I also knew him as a friendly, outgoing, likeable fellow with a warm smile and pleasant gift of gab. A former Marine, impulsive, outwardly fearless, overly ambitious, he lacked intellectual depth and possessed only a tenuous grasp of political reality. He thought only in terms of today or tonight, never even as much as a week ahead.

I make no effort to analyze his initial motives; but at some point, he went off the deep end in his belief that Communists riddled the entire federal bureaucracy, particularly the State Department and the military. He became obsessed with the belief that Heaven willed him to save the world from this unspeakable evil.

In a Lincoln's Birthday speech before the Republicans in Wheeling, West Virginia, in 1950, McCarthy claimed to hold a list of 205 card-carrying Communists in the State Department. The media saw the charge as an arresting, attention-holding, long-running serial, and played the story to the hilt.

President Truman fell for the bait, and immediately took issue with McCarthy, eventually calling him "gangster," "liar," "purveyor of the big lie," and other typical Trumanisms.

McCarthy basked in the attention the media lavished on him, suddenly becoming not only a national, but an international figure. His charges became progressively more reckless: Johns Hopkins professor Owen Lattimore and dozens of others in academia followed the Communist line and caused us to "lose China"; all Hollywood marched to the Communist drummer—its writers, producers and some leading stars; the "Reds" ran the National Council of Churches; our libraries overseas held pro-Communist and anti-American books that should be thrown out—I don't remember if he actually used the word "burned."

Thanks to the media, McCarthy's wild accusations whipped up such a national anti-Communist frenzy that he got himself named chairman of the Permanent Investigations Subcommittee of the Senate Committee on Governmental Operations. From this forum, he sent out investigators, subpoenaed witnesses, browbeat them, insulted them, ruined their reputations with the unsupported insinuations in his loaded questions, and called for contempt citations against those who stood up to him by refusing to answer.

The media continued to publicize McCarthy with front-page stories and hour-by-hour radio and TV coverage of his subcommittee hearings. Soon, a great segment of the listening public learned to recognize his voice after about three words.

Truman, Stevenson, and other Democrats tried to make "McCarthyism" a prime issue of the '52 presidential campaign, adding still more to the Senator's image. Unfortunately, at that time, polls showed that as many as sixty to sixty-five percent of the public approved of McCarthy's goal to rid government and all phases of society of the "Reds," without serious worry about his tactics.

Eisenhower's plan for handling the McCarthy "issue" rested on three fundamental premises to which he held firmly:

(1) McCarthy served as a duly elected senator, and under our form of government of separation of powers, only the Senate could effectively handle his excesses or other misconduct;

(2) A direct name-calling attack by Eisenhower would only intensify McCarthy's news value, give him a larger audience, and postpone his ultimate eclipse; and

(3) The Constitution imposed upon the executive branch, not the legislature, the duty to weed out disloyal government employees; and the task must be carried out

with due respect for constitutional rights, not by irresponsible, reckless character assignation without solid proof.

Eisenhower not only deplored McCarthy's indecent tactics, but believed that those efforts violated the doctrine of separation of powers, to which he stood committed.

I think Eisenhower's statement in the first State of the Union Message remains a classic on the subject of handling employee disloyalty:

> Our vast world responsibility accents with urgency our people's elemental right to a government whose clear qualities are: loyalty, security, efficiency, economy and integrity.
>
> The safety of America and the trust of the people alike demand that the personnel of the federal government be loyal in their motives and reliable in the discharge of their duties. Only a combination of both loyalty and reliability promises genuine security.
>
> To state this principle is easy: to apply it can be difficult. But this security we must and shall have. By way of example, all principal new appointees to departments and agencies have been investigated at their own request by the Federal Bureau of Investigation.
>
> Confident of your understanding and cooperation, I know that the primary responsibility for keeping out the disloyal and the dangerous rests squarely upon the Executive Branch. When this Branch so conducts itself as to require policing by another Branch of the government, it invites its own disorder and confusion.
>
> I am determined to meet this responsibility of the Executive. The heads of all Executive departments and agencies have been instructed to initiate at once effective programs of security with respect to their personnel. The Attorney General will advise and guide the

departments and agencies in the shaping of these programs, designed at once to govern the employment of new personnel and to review speedily any derogatory information concerning incumbent personnel.

To carry out these programs, I believe that the powers of the Executive Branch under existing law are sufficient. If they should prove inadequate, the necessary legislation will be requested.

These programs will be both fair to the rights of the individual and effective for the safety of the Nation. They will, with care and justice, apply the basic principle that public employment is not a right but a privilege.

All these measures have two clear purposes. Their first purpose is to make certain that this nation's security is not jeopardized by false servants. Their second purpose is to clear the atmosphere of that unreasoned suspicion that accepts rumor and gossip as substitutes for evidence.

My first encounter with McCarthy's Committee came in March, 1953, when my acting deputy in the Mutual Security Administration, Kenneth Hanson, told me that McCarthy investigators visited him to ask questions and examine files about a controversy held over from the Truman Administration: Were Greek ships (purchased as surplus from the United States after the war, many still mortgaged to our government) carrying strategic supplies to ports around the world from which these shipments eventually reached Communist China, North Korea, and Iron Curtain countries through transshipment? Hanson also told me that the Committee investigators served him with a subpoena to come before McCarthy on March 31. I at once checked with Tom Naughtin [Mutual Security personnel director], who assured me of Hanson's clean record.

I went to see President Eisenhower, told him of Hanson's report and subpoena, and said that I intended to go with Hanson to the Committee hearings. I would tell McCarthy that Hanson worked for me, under my direct supervision, so I would answer the Committee's questions instead of Hanson. I did not propose to let McCarthy browbeat Hanson or any Mutual Security employees the way he did other witnesses.

Eisenhower's response and instructions to me, which I can paraphrase accurately as to substance, tell the whole story of his feelings about McCarthy, and explain his course of action:

> I, as you know, was in Europe when the McCarthy thing really got going. I didn't hear much about it until I returned home last June. Of course, I couldn't escape it then or in the campaign.
>
> I did some studying on McCarthy, read a lot about him, and talked it over with Cabot Lodge and Milton.
>
> So far as I am concerned, Harry Truman really created Joe McCarthy. If Truman had ignored those charges McCarthy made down there in West Virginia about all those Communists in the State Department, the matter would have died out soon enough, even though McCarthy yelped a time or two more.
>
> Once Truman jumped in with both feet, that made McCarthy.
>
> Now, you go on up there with your man, Hanson, and you can protect him, and do whatever you think is smart. But be sure everyone knows you're speaking for yourself and not for me.
>
> There's nothing that McCarthy and the reporters would like more than to get me matched up in a dog-fight with McCarthy. That would be the same kind of mistake that Truman made.

I watched to see when to break off the conversation, or when he would end it; but he only warmed to the subject:

> I loathe McCarthy and what he stands for. He makes me feel dirty to be around him. But he won't last. He'll thrash himself out, if we don't give him some more publicity that gives him a new spurt of life.
>
> Some writers and professors are yelling for me to put him in his place, "fire McCarthy." How the hell can I "fire" a United States Senator. That's up to the Senate—if they want to discipline one of their members.
>
> This McCarthy thing is for the Senate to handle, not for me.

I did go up to the McCarthy hearing with Kenneth Hanson and sat by him. When McCarthy asked him the first question, I stepped in and answered.

McCarthy said, "I am asking my question of Hanson."

I replied, "Senator, I am answering you because I am in charge of the Foreign Operations Administration."

This caused a clash which the media reported at length, highlighting my statement that McCarthy's claimed "negotiations" with owners of 242 Greek ships "undermined" our legitimate executive negotiations with these same carriers. I said further that McCarthy's dallying invaded the executive's duty to handle foreign policy and added confusion rather than light.

In his next press conference, Eisenhower said that he thought my statement to McCarthy would be more accurate if we substituted the word "infringe" for "undermined." Neither McCarthy nor anyone else in Congress could "undermine" the executive branch of government. They might try to "infringe"; but they couldn't "undermine."

Writers, analysts, Truman, other Democrats, and later historians seized this play on semantics to assert that the substitution of "infringe" for "undermine" showed Eisenhower knuckling under to McCarthy. Nothing could be further from the truth, as he told me in the the the Oval Office when I reported on my appearance before McCarthy:

> I don't want any misunderstanding about what's happened.
>
> You're in charge of the Mutual Security Administration. You report to me; and I'm in charge of all the executive branches.
>
> You apparently protected your man from the kind of attacks McCarthy's been giving other witnesses. I approve of that.
>
> Foster thinks that "undermine" is too strong a word. He thinks it should be "infringe." He's afraid that your fight with McCarthy might have a bad effect on foreign appropriations later on.

I replied, "Mr. President, 'infringe' is okay by me, as long as McCarthy and the others on the Hill know that any time they try to 'infringe' or 'undermine' one of my employees, I'll confront them."

Thus are mountains of character diminution built from semantic molehills!

McCarthy continued his rantings until his fellow senators censured him by resolution December 2, 1954; but this did not quite finish him off, as both Eisenhower and I learned just a month before the Geneva Summit.

On June 22, 1955, in an effort to keep the Big Four Summit from taking place, McCarthy introduced a Senate resolution to require Eisenhower to demand that the Soviets commit themselves *in advance* to negotiate on the political status of the East European satellites. The resolution labeled this demand a *precondition* to the summit.

Even if this did not kill off the summit completely, it would seriously limit Eisenhower's flexibility at Geneva and send a message to the Soviets, as well as the British and French, that the President did not control his own foreign policy.

On Eisenhower's instructions, I went to see Senator Walter George, Chairman of the Foreign Relations Committee, and Lyndon Johnson of Texas, then majority leader in the Senate. They agreed on the folly of McCarthy's resolution. The Republican Old Guard, who did not want to oppose McCarthy even after his censure, saw that the resolution did not stand a chance of passing the full Senate. Senator Knowland from California, then Republican minority leader, moved the Foreign Relations Committee to table it.

We did not want this, since a motion to table leaves a matter in abeyance, subject to resurrection at some future time. We believed the President's hand would be stronger at Geneva if the full Senate slapped down McCarthy and his resolution.

By a partisan Democratic majority of eight to seven, the Committee defeated Knowland's motion to table, *all seven Republicans voting with Knowland*; then by a fourteen to zero vote, they sent the resolution to the Senate floor recommending its rejection, which happened quickly.

This became McCarthy's swan song, proving the wisdom of the policies that Eisenhower had described to me two years earlier:

> The only way to bury McCarthy is to let him do it himself, kill himself off. That's exactly what he'll do. It may not come as fast as any of us would like, but it'll come a lot quicker than if I give him new life by personally getting into a public braying contest with him.

The McCarthy affair is a tragic blot on American history. I make no effort to explain it in depth. But in addition to the character and intellectual limitations McCarthy worked with, his excessive drinking increased his tendencies toward paranoia, dimmed his analytical factors, and left him at the mercy of his staff. His two key manipulators, Roy Cohn and G. David Schine, personified irresponsibility and evil. McCarthy let them range totally out of control because they, in effect, controlled him.

The McCarthy affair also grew from a deep-seated fear of the inevitability of World War III, a product of the bankrupt Truman-Acheson policies. We survived it, not without substantial scars, because of Eisenhower's "courage to be patient," a trait that some of his predecessors and successors did not exhibit.

Chapter 18
Hands-On Crisis Management:
"I Alone Will Make the Decisions"

Nothing better demonstrates Eisenhower's "hands-on" management style than his control of the nine-month crisis with Red China over the off-shore islands in the Formosa Strait. I do not propose to present anything like a detailed military, political, or diplomatic history of that explosive period; rather, I suggest that a study of fourteen days in January and February of 1955 will highlight Eisenhower's management skills.

The background involves both geography and at least four years of modern history.

The island of Formosa (Taiwan) is slightly larger than the combined areas of Connecticut and Massachusetts and lies in the South China Sea some one hundred miles east of China's mainland. The body of water in between is the Formosa Strait, which holds the Pescadores Islands just west of Formosa and the Quemoy island group farther west. Some of the Quemoy islands actually lie in the mainland harbor of Amoy.

One hundred miles farther up the coast, the Matsu group lies ten miles east of the mainland port of Foochow; and still another one hundred miles to the north, the comparatively unimportant Tachen group juts out into the East China Sea.

When Nationalist leader Generalissimo Chiang Kai-shek retreated to Formosa after his defeat by Mao's Communists in 1949, he also garrisoned the Quemoys, Matsus, and Tachens, claiming them as part of his Nationalist domain.

Until the end of World War II, Japan ruled the entire area, including the islands that it took from China at the end of the Sino-Japanese War (1894-95) and the parts of the mainland taken by conquests which started in the '30s. The Japanese peace treaty in 1951 ended Japanese rule of the islands, but did not formally cede them to either Mao's Communist "China" or Chiang's Nationalist "China," leaving the actual ownership in a state of limbo.

For some five years, Mao and Chiang and their underlings hurled insults and threats at each other across the Formosa Strait, both claiming title to the islands. Mao called for the "liberation of Formosa." Chiang pledged a return to the mainland, which meant he would need not only Formosa but all the off-shore islands as his launching pads. The British called the fight for the islands an internal squabble from which the rest of the world should remain apart.

From the days of World War II, we considered Chiang our ally; and while we did not propose to help him regain the mainland, our Seventh Fleet patrolled the waters around Formosa to prevent Mao's Communists from swallowing up Formosa.

The war of words between the two Chinas evolved into a shooting war on September 3, 1954, when the Communists began heavy and sustained artillery bombardments of Quemoy. Pessimists called those the first shots of World War III. The Joint Chiefs split over what to do, Nathan Twining and Rob Carney urging the President to defend the islands immediately and join the Nationalists in bombing the mainland. Ridgway dissented—in his view, our strategic needs did not include holding the off-shore islands.

Eisenhower agreed with Ridgway. He would not risk going to the brink of World War III. If we ever did attack the mainland, it would be without any restraints on our forces. He would not repeat the impossible situation our troops labored under in Korea.

The Communists next shelled Matsu, and on November 1, they bombed the Tachens. We waited for their amphibious assaults to come while the Old Guard in Congress called for us to blockade the entire China coast, some repeating Twining and Carney's advice to bomb the mainland. During this period, Eisenhower again used his often quoted statement that "it takes courage to be patient."

The assault finally came January 18, 1955, when the Communists captured the island of Ichiang in the Tachen group, heating up the crisis.

The best window on the President's firm crisis management is through the minutes of the National Security Council, beginning with the January 20, 1955 session. I insert subheadings and explanatory comments for emphasis and readability:

> Mr. [Allen] Dulles began with a prediction that the loss of Ichiang Island in the Tachens group to the Chinese Communists would shortly be followed by Chinese Communist attacks on the main group of the Tachen Islands.

[COMMUNISTS HANDLED ACTION WITH SKILL]

> In the action against Ichiang, Mr. Dulles said that the Communist forces had consisted of one regiment and two battalions of Chinese Communist troops, numbering between 3000 and 4000. Against this force the Nationalist garrison on Ichiang had consisted of just under 1000 guerrillas. The island had been captured after about two hours of fighting.
>
> The Communists had handled the action with considerable skill. They had had very careful cover so that

there had been little warning, either of the landing forces or of the Communist air sorties, which had numbered 60.

All U. S. personnel on the Tachens, numbering eight, had been evacuated except one individual.

With the capture of the island, Mr. Dulles pointed out, the Chinese Communists were in a good position to shell the main Tachen Islands, which were only seven and a half miles distant from Ichiang.

[FURTHER NATIONALIST LOSSES EXPECTED]

The Nationalists were obviously preparing to risk further losses of naval vessels in order to support the garrison on the main Tachen Islands. This move was necessary, however, if the morale of the garrison, which was not very good in any case, was to be kept up.

As in all NSC and cabinet meetings, the President listened well, seldom interrupting the speakers, even when they became rambling and tedious. He sought the facts always, and hoped to learn new ways to present or use that information, striving to "make theories out of facts."

[POSSIBILITY OF EVACUATION]

According to other reports, the Generalissimo was now considering the desirability of evacuating the Chinese Nationalist forces from the remainder of the Tachen Islands. Unfortunately, there was some question as to whether he would be able to withdraw these garrisons even if he desired to, except in the unlikely event that the Chinese Communists voluntarily permitted these forces to be evacuated. In any event, the loss of the Tachen Islands would have a very unfortunate effect on the morale of the Chinese Nationalists.

[BRITISH VESSEL SUNK]

Mr. Dulles indicated that the Nationalists had retaliated yesterday for the attack on Ichiang, by a series of air strikes on Communist ports and shipping, especially in Swatow, where they had apparently sunk a British flag vessel of some 1700 tons. From Quemoy the Nationalists had yesterday bombarded two adjacent islands held by the Chinese Communists. There had been no substantial Chinese Communist attacks on Quemoy during the last few days.

The President maintained eye contact with most speakers, sometimes using his "command look," sometimes his inscrutable "bridge-playing" expression.

Secretary Dulles next gave his grave assessment:

Secretary Dulles said that he was sorry indeed to have to inaugurate the second year of the Eisenhower Administration with a recital of serious problems. However, he had come to the conclusion, over the last few days and hours, that the situation in the Tachens and on the other islands held by the Chinese Nationalists had deteriorated so rapidly that it was very unlikely that any of these islands could be defended against Chinese Communist attack in the absence of U. S. armed support on a very considerable scale.

[NEED TO REASSESS POLICY]

Since the United States had not proposed to offer the Chinese Nationalists any assistance in the defense of these islands which would involve the armed forces of the United States, the time had come for a reconsideration of our policy of refusing to participate in the military defense of *any* of the Nationalist-held offshore islands.

257

[LOSS OF TACHEN MUST BE OFFSET
BY CLEAR STATEMENT OF U.S. INTENTIONS]

The loss of the Tachen group of islands would have very serious psychological effects not only on the Chinese Nationalists, but in other areas of the Far East such as Korea, Japan, and the Philippines, unless this loss were accompanied by a clearer indication than was now available of United States intentions and where we stood ourselves. If it were indicated that the Communists were free to seize all these offshore islands, the result would be very bad indeed.

[ISLANDS ATTACK
PART OF COMMUNIST "LIBERATION" PLAN]

Accordingly, continued Secretary Dulles, it had seemed to him wise to suggest that the evacuation of the Tachen island group should be offset by a stated willingness on the part of the United States to assist with its armed forces in holding the Quemoy Islands and possibly the Matsu group.

These two groups of islands covered the harbor entrance of Amoy and Foochow, respectively, whence a Chinese Communist invasion of Formosa would probably be mounted. Moreover, the Chinese Communists invariably related their attacks on these offshore islands to their determination ultimately to "liberate" Formosa.

[GRAVE EFFECT ON U.S. POSITION THROUGHOUT ASIA]

So, said Secretary Dulles, the United States is faced with what is in fact a series of Communist military operations which are ultimately directed toward the capture of Formosa. He therefore concluded that it would have a very grave effect throughout all the nations of free Asia if we were to clarify a U. S. position which in effect amounted to abandonment of all the Nationalist-held offshore islands.

People would of course pose the question of why it is necessary for the United States to clarify its position on these islands. We had decided not to do so up to the present in the hope of confusing the Chinese Communists as to our real intentions vis-a-vis these islands.

[POLICY OF OBSCURING INTENTIONS NOW BACKFIRING]

This policy of obscuring our intentions had, however, begun to backfire, and the Chinese Communists were apparently confident in the belief that the United States was unwilling to fight in order to save any of these islands.

Accordingly, Secretary Dulles could see no further advantage in the policy of obscuring our intentions, and insisted that further pursuit of it would embarrass U. S. prestige in the Far East.

[UNSOUND TO TRY TO DEFEND TACHENS]

This being so, the next question was what to do. It seemed to him, said Secretary Dulles, fundamentally unsound for the United States to try to assist the Chinese Nationalists to hold the northern groups of islands. The Tachens and the other islands in this area were simply too difficult to defend. On the other hand, Quemoy and the Matsu group could be readily protected by U. S. air power, including such air power based on Formosa.

259

[SHOULD HELP DEFEND QUEMOY AND MATSU]

Accordingly, the Administration might well consider a new policy which would involve (1) the use of U. S. armed forces to assist the Chinese Nationalists to evacuate their garrisons from the northernmost islands, and (2) support of the Chinese Nationalists in the defense of Quemoy and perhaps the Matsu Islands, so long as the Chinese Communists professed to be preparing to attack Formosa.

[NEED A QUICK MUTUAL DEFENSE TREATY WITH FORMOSA]

If we could make this proposal clear and at the same time push through quickly the mutual defense treaty with Formosa, and if we are truly determined to hold Formosa and related areas needed in order to hold Formosa, all this would be the best possible way to avoid a steady deterioration of the U. S. position in the general area, and specifically would provide the best means of defending Formosa and the Pescadores.

Dulles continued about the President's powers to make these key defensive moves without specific authorization from Congress. Eisenhower's intuition told him when debates ran their useful course, and he performed the role of a good presiding officer in bringing them to a close.

The President said that a decision by the United States to give up the Tachen Islands, which the Joint Chiefs of Staff were already on record as having said were not vital to the defense of Formosa, would at least have the merit of showing the world that the United States was trying to maintain a decent posture.

At the same time, the proposed policy would make clear that this U.S. concession with respect to the Tachens would not mean that the United States was prepared to make any concessions with respect to Formosa and the Pescadores.

Eisenhower always weighed the military pros and cons in any foreign policy debate.

> The particular problem, continued the President, with respect to the defense of the Tachens was the lack of a safe port for our ships in this area. As a result, it would be very difficult for us to sustain the garrisons in the Tachen Islands.

> All in all, concluded the President, an announcement of a decision to evacuate the Tachens garrison, together with a statement of our determination to hold Formosa and the islands "in front of it" (Quemoy and the Matsus), would appear to be the best course of action.

Eisenhower could distinguish between the "courage of patience" required by some situations, and the fallacy of "dangerous drift."

> The President commented that unless we were prepared "completely to discount Formosa", further delay in making up our minds would result in rapid and serious deterioration of the situation. He still insisted that the chances of general war with Communist China would be less under the course of action now proposed by the Secretary of State than the "dangerous drift" which we are now in.

Suddenly, the debate took on new life and vigor when Secretaries Wilson and Humphrey jumped in. All told, it went on for three hours, everyone tense at the thought that what we

261

decided that morning could either trigger or prevent World War III.

> Governor Stassen expressed agreement with the policy advocated by the Secretary of State, not only for the reasons which Secretary Dulles had given, but for other reasons as well. As the Chinese Communists continued to build up their power and prestige and took more and more of these islands, they inevitably set in motion a deterioration of the position. He greatly feared the psychological effect on the free nations of Asia of the gradual loss of all these islands.
>
> The President intervened to say that it seemed clear to him that Quemoy and the Matsus were the outposts for the defense of Formosa.

We explored tactics, the President calling on Admiral Radford to discuss naval deployment, and what our position would be if Chiang Kai-shek elected to give up the off-shore islands.

The President always gave his summary of the conclusions of the meetings, speaking without notes:

> The President explained his opinion that it was not that any of these offshore islands was going to be easy to defend, but that the psychological consequences of abandoning these islands were so serious. It had long been the general policy of this Administration to help build up indigenous forces to defend on the ground against Chinese Communist attacks. It would be the role of the United States merely to supply air and naval support in the event of overt Communist aggression. We were now confronting a concrete test of this policy, and we must be concerned with the morale of those soldiers who might well be called upon to defend Formosa if the Chinese Communists attacked it. . . .

Summing up, the President suggested that the following was the best course of action for the Council: Arrange another short meeting of the Council between nine and ten tomorrow morning before the Cabinet meeting, and have ready for his consideration the precise sequence of actions to be taken to carry out Secretary Dulles' proposal, as well as the list of individuals who were to carry out these actions. By tomorrow morning the President believed that Secretary Dulles could produce such documents, since he would have heard from both Yeh [National Chinese Foreign Minister] and Eden. The President said he did very much want the British to go along with us because, after all, in a crisis they were good sturdy old allies. Moreover, upon thinking it over, Chiang Kai-shek himself might come to have a different feeling over the abandonment of some of these islands, inasmuch as by this new course of action he would have the United States firmly tied in with him.

At the special session of the NSC the next morning, Secretary Dulles described his meeting the previous afternoon with the British Ambassador, who advised against the proposed action, fearing that a public commitment to defend *any* of the off-shore islands might lead us to a point of no return—the use of atomic weapons against mainland China.

The discussion returned to whether the President should ask for any specific authorization from Congress. Even though he might not technically need it, he wanted it so that he could bring the entire country into the discussions and rally them behind him.

[MUST AVOID ANOTHER YALU RIVER SITUATION]

The President went on to say that in talking this matter over with the Secretary of State, he and the Secretary had believed that they could do a lot of things as a mere matter of course, but that we must at all costs avoid another Yalu River sanctuary situation in any struggle over Quemoy.

[MUST HAVE LINE OF ACTION CLEARLY IN MIND]

The President said he was absolutely determined on this point. Accordingly, he had concluded that we must get a line of action clearly in mind, including all the sequential steps. He believed that we could do what we wanted to do with regard to these islands without being too specific in the statement to Congress.

On the specific side, the President said that if we went to Congress for authority to defend the Formosa area generally, the proposal would have a tremendous effect. This would also provide time in which to let the UN action get off the ground. If the UN does not get off the ground in time, we will have to follow up with this new policy decision.

[MUST ADVISE CHINESE NATIONALISTS]

In any case, we will have to let the Chinese nationalists know about this decision. The President then inquired whether anything had been heard as yet from Foreign Minister Yeh. Secretary Dulles replied that nothing but an unofficial radio report had been heard from the Foreign Minister.

[KEEP MIND ON REAL OBJECTIVES]

Secretary Humphrey said that it was clear in his mind that the President's intention was to withdraw from the Tachen Islands. But do we withdraw from Quemoy and the other offshore islands?

The President explained to Secretary Humphrey that our ultimate objective was to defend Formosa and the Pescadores. The other offshore islands were incidental to this objective. He therefore contemplated no permanent extension of the defense area of Formosa. We will continue to defend these islands until some other arrangements can be made to quiet the Formosa area. We would then get out of the offshore islands.

[EMPHASIZE OBJECTIVE OF STABILITY IN FAR EAST]

Governor Stassen suggested that it might be wise to emphasize that our ultimate objective is stability in the Far East, with Formosa in friendly hands.

The President replied to Governor Stassen in the affirmative, and then proceeded to read the opening sentences of a draft statement to the Congress which had been prepared by Secretary Dulles.

[DID NOT NEED AUTHORITY TO EVACUATE ISLANDS]

He interrupted his reading to state that he did not feel he needed additional authority in order to evacuate Chinese Nationalist garrisons from certain of the offshore islands. However, if in the course of such action we were obliged to attack the Chinese Communists, the President felt that he might need additional authority.

On the other hand, he did not wish to specify the precise details of why he needed such extra authority.

[CONTINUE STUDY OF DRAFT STATEMENT OF CONGRESS]

In some anxiety, the Attorney General inquired whether the President intended to change his plan to seek additional authority from the Congress. The Attorney General thought it still highly desirable to seek this authority.

The President assured the Attorney General that he had not changed his ideas on this subject, and asked the Secretary of State to go on reading the draft statement to the Congress. . . .

[PRESIDENT PLANS FINAL EDITING]

Secretary Dulles then proceeded to read the remainder of the proposed statement by the President, concluding his reading amidst murmurs of approval.

The President said that of course the document would need a little more editing. He hadn't seen this version until last midnight.

Words were extremely important in this cold war situation.

The Presidential statement must be temperate and exact, but also it must reveal our firm intention. That's the best kind of a notice before the world, and if it gets genuine support from the Congress, such support would be worth a lot of additional armed forces. Accordingly we must be very careful in our choice of words.

[UN ACTION ONLY IMPORTANT FOR WORLD OPINION]

After the President and other members of the Council had discussed certain sentences in the proposed statement, Secretary Humphrey inquired of the President how long it would take the UN to reach a decision if the UN did undertake action to stabilize the situation. Would it be a matter of weeks or months?

Secretary Dulles said that such UN action would take at least a month. The President expressed the belief that a UN action would not have much influence on the course of action that the United States would have to undertake at once. On the other hand, such UN action would have great influence on world opinion.

[MUST KEEP MAIN OBJECTIVE IN MIND]

Secretary Humphrey insisted that the Quemoy problem had got to be settled. That was the dagger point.

The President replied that Secretary Humphrey made a mistake in assuming that Quemoy was the Chinese Communist objective. It was not; they were after Formosa.

Secretary Humphrey denied this, and said that he was assuming, rather, that Quemoy was a point which the United States would find it impossible to defend for any great length of time.

The President said that it would be OK with him if the UN succeeds in achieving a solution which will enable the United States to get out of Quemoy without risk to Formosa. Secretary Humphrey replied that it was still going to be hard to explain to the American people why we were finding it necessary to hold on to Quemoy.

In some exasperation, the President said to Secretary Humphrey that he sat in this room time after time with the maps all around him, and a look at the geography of the area would explain why we have to hold Quemoy.

[MUST QUELL FEARS STATEMENT CAN PRODUCE]

Dr. Flemming commented that no matter how the Presidential statement were worded, the action that the President proposed to take was of an extraordinary and momentous character. He was accordingly much concerned about the inflationary and similar influences which the President's statement would set in motion in the country as soon as its text became public. Dr. Flemming therefore advised that language should be put into the statement to indicate that the proposed action would not involve any stepping up in the currently-approved level of the armed forces or in currently-approved mobilization measures.

The President agreed heartily with Dr. Flemming's suggestion.

[PRESIDENT APPROVES DRAFT OF JOINT RESOLUTION]

After further discussion of various points made in the draft statement, Secretary Dulles turned to a draft, which had been prepared by Mr. Pfleger, chief law officer of the State Department, and Assistant Attorney General Rankin, of the Congressional resolution.

The President thought the draft of the proposed joint resolution was a good one, although it contained no hint as to actions that had been taken hitherto in using our armed forces to defend Formosa since President Truman had decreed this in his order to the Seventh Fleet. The President, in the course of a discussion of the text of the joint resolution, said he favored keeping its text general enough to allow him the necessary freedom of action.

[AVOID SPLIT IN PUBLIC OPINION]

Governor Stassen said he was fearful lest there be any unnecessary limitation of the powers of the Commander-in-Chief, in view of the contingencies that the United States faced in the future.

The President said he agreed with this, but reminded Governor Stassen that it was also essential, if possible, to avoid a split in Congressional and public opinion. The President said that all might be sure of one thing—namely, that he would do in an emergency whatever had to be done to protect the vital interests of the United States. He would do this even if his actions should be interpreted as acts of war. He would rather be impeached than fail to do his duty.

With the foundation solidly laid in the National Security Council and the Congressional leadership carefully briefed by Admiral Radford, Secretary Dulles, and the President himself, events moved rapidly over the next twelve days:

January 21—Eisenhower instructed Jim Hagerty to brief the media on the crisis—give them all the facts and explain the risks; but emphasize that while there are always risks, the goal is to prevent a major conflict. This briefing produced *The New York Times* headline: "Aim Is to Prevent Start of Big War—Administration Thinks This Can Be Done by Making U.S. Intentions Clear."

January 22—The President ordered all forces in the Pacific put on battle-alert status, and directed that all orders from the Pentagon be personally cleared with him.

January 24—The President sent a special message to the Congress, which read in part:

> The most important objective of our nation's foreign policy is to safeguard the security of the United States by establishing and preserving a just and honorable peace. In the western Pacific a situation is developing in the Formosa Straits that seriously imperils the peace and our security.
>
> Since the end of Japanese hostilities in 1945, Formosa and the Pescadores have been in the friendly hands of our loyal ally, the Republic of China. We have recognized that it was important that these islands should remain in friendly hands.
>
> In unfriendly hands, Formosa and the Pescadores would seriously dislocate the existing, even if unstable, balance of moral, economic and military forces upon which the peace of the Pacific depends.
>
> . . . .

269

The United States and the friendly Government of the Republic of China, and indeed all the free nations, have a common interest that Formosa and the Pescadores should not fall into the control of aggressive Communist forces.

He detailed the Red Chinese "pattern of aggressive purpose," the artillery fire and seizure of Ichiang, the request to the UN to try to end hostilities, the actions the United States needed to take while awaiting UN action, the fact that his moves involved no new ventures in foreign policy, and his authority as Commander-in-Chief to act in this situation.

But he wanted to show the world that the Congress and the people stood behind his resolve:

However, a suitable Congressional resolution would clearly and publicly establish the authority of the President as Commander in Chief to employ the armed forces of this nation promptly and effectively for the purpose indicated if in his judgment it became necessary. It would make clear the unified and serious intentions of our Government, our Congress and our people.

Thus it will reduce the possibility that the Chinese Communists, misjudging our firm purpose and national unity, might be disposed to challenge the position of the United States, and precipitate a major crisis which even they would neither anticipate nor desire.

He closed with a reaffirmation of purposes:

Our purpose is peace. That cause will be served if, with your help, we demonstrate our unity and our determination. In all that we do we shall remain faithful to our obligations as a member of the United Nations to be ready to settle our international disputes

270

by peaceful means in such a manner that international peace and security, and justice, are not endangered.

For the reasons outlined in this message, I respectfully request that the Congress take appropriate action to carry out the recommendations contained herein.

The resolution accompanying the message and introduced into the Congress contained five introductory "Whereas" paragraphs describing the Communists' actions. Then came the action resolves:

Therefore, be it resolved by the Senate and House of Representatives of the United States of America in Congress assembled

That the President of the United States be and he hereby is authorized to employ the armed forces of the United States as he deems necessary for the specific purpose of securing and protecting Formosa and the Pescadores against armed attack, this authority to include the securing and protection of such related positions and territories of that area now in friendly hands and the taking of such other measures as he judges to be required or appropriate in assuring the defense of Formosa and the Pescadores.

This resolution shall expire when the President shall determine that the peace and security of the area is reasonably assured by the international conditions, created by action of the United Nations or otherwise, and shall so report to the Congress.

January 25—Red China's Premier Chou En-lai fired off his response, calling the President's message a "war cry," and adding:

The Government of the People's Republic of China [the Communist regime] has repeatedly and in solemn

271

terms declared to the world that the Chinese people are determined to liberate their own territory of Taiwan [Formosa].

Since the recent successful liberation of Yikiang Island by the Chinese people, the United States Government has stepped up its military operations to make war provocations and has, on the other hand, been engineering a conspiracy for a so-called cease-fire through the United Nations to intervene in the Chinese people's liberation of Taiwan.

Taiwan is an inalienable part of China's territory.

The liberation of Taiwan is a matter of China's sovereignty and internal affairs. No outside interference is allowed.

At about the same time Chou issued his blast, the House passed the President's requested Resolution 409 to 3 with the President thanking the members for their prompt show of national will.

January 26—The Democrats attempted to make a partisan issue out of the Formosa affair. Former Secretary of State Dean Acheson, Truman foreign policy advisor Paul Nitze, the chairman of the Democratic Party, and several Senate Democrats opposed the President's request for the Resolution and attempted a delaying action in the Senate.

Senator Walter George, Democrat from Georgia and Chairman of the Foreign Relations committee, squelched them by asking each: "What is the President's alternative?"

January 27—British Foreign Secretary Anthony Eden called on Moscow to intervene in the Far East "to prevent any incident which might lead to general hostilities." His quid pro quo offer: Seat "both Chinas" in the UN, something we knew Chiang would never agree to. Nor could we in view of our commitments to him.

The President announced publicly that "I alone will make all decisions regarding the Far East, specifically about Formosa and the off-shore islands," to silence criticisms that some subordinate or admiral would blunder us into World War III.

January 28—The Senate passed the President's requested Resolution by a vote of eighty-five to three.

A review of intelligence reports in a National Security Council meeting indicates that the Communists' activities against the off-shore islands slowed appreciably.

In part, the NSC minutes read:

Governor Stassen said that his explanation as to why the Soviets were apparently egging on the Chinese Communists was as follows: The Soviets may fear that if the Chinese Communists permit themselves to be involved in friendlier relations with the Western world, the Soviets may not be able to control the Chinese so effectively. If this were so, the most desirable course of action for the United States was to try to separate the Chinese and the Russians.

Admiral Radford observed that while it was true that the Russians had had ups and downs in their policy toward Europe since 1945, they had made steady progress since that year in their program to subjugate the Far East. The only way to put an end to this steady progress and to secure peace and stability in Asia, was to carry out faithfully the policy which the President had announced to the Congress last week.

Governor Stassen expressed great skepticism as to the likelihood that the Chinese Communists would make serious attacks on Formosa or on the offshore islands which the United States would assist in defending. If this proved to be the case, and after a certain amount of noise the Chinese Communists subsided and took to peaceful ways, this was the moment for the United States to try to broaden our trade with Communist China and to explore other possibilities of opening up contact with them designed to wean them away from their alliance with the Soviets.

January 29—Jim Hagerty's diary shows another of Eisenhower's contrived moves to show the public that he sat in firm control of the situation, the tension relieved:

President and Mrs. Eisenhower left Washington for Augusta on Saturday morning, January 29, and arrived at Augusta National Golf Club at 11:40.

Needing to "let go," Eisenhower wrote General Gruenther a six-page, single-spaced typed letter summarizing the China crisis. I include it as Appendix 6 to show Eisenhower's logical approach to problems, and as another example of his letter-writing abilities.

As more classified materials at Abilene are declassified, I hope the historians and biographers will delve deeper into Eisenhower's skills as a crisis manager. All occupants of the White House can learn much from them.

Chapter 19
Secretary for Peace

Once I got to sleep, I always slept soundly when I traveled, a wake-up call a must for an early departure. I reached for the ringing phone in my hotel room in Karachi, presuming it to be the operator telling me to get up, but the clock on the bedside table said 1:00 a.m. This confused me as I picked up the decrepit instrument and answered.

"I am the night Communications Officer at the embassy," a young male voice told me. "A secret message just came in addressed 'Eyes Only for Governor Stassen from the President.' I know you are scheduled to fly out later this morning, and I thought you might want this message before you go to the airport. I have already decoded it, so it's here for you any time you want to pick it up."

I thanked him for his thoughtfulness and told him I would come right over to the embassy. He offered to send the embassy night car for me, saying the driver could be at my hotel in ten to fifteen minutes.

As I began dressing, my mind raced to probe the reason for an "Eyes Only" message from the President. Normally, this designation applied only to urgent communications sent to cabinet members and top aides, to make sure that none in the lower levels of the bureaucracy delayed delivery or attempted to handle the matter without the addressee ever becoming aware of the subject matter.

275

I paced the sidewalk in front of the hotel in the brisk early-morning air, presuming that the message related to some development in Turkey, the next stop in my annual inspection tour of foreign operations in our seventy-one countries. We considered Turkey a critical member of NATO. It bordered the Soviets on the south, providing Russia's all-weather port in the Black Sea. Turkey was a nation with sizeable military forces, but with internal political divisions that produced almost weekly parliamentary crises. I visualized some threat that I should prepare for before my arrival in Istanbul.

The embassy car with its Pakistani driver arrived, and in a few minutes I accepted the salute of the Marine guard at the front door of the embassy. He directed me to the Communications room, where the clerk handed me the message. I found a chair in the corner, sat down, and began to read, immediately discovering that it did not concern Turkey at all:

> You are aware of my conviction that some individual, on behalf of the President and the State Department, must develop within the Administration and the nation and also before the world a firm and single basic policy toward the question of disarmament.

I knew Eisenhower's frustration over the rifts within the administration on the touchy subject of disarmament, and the lack of new approaches toward the Russians to lessen Cold War tensions.

Secretary Wilson, George Humphrey, Admiral Radford, and the other Joint Chiefs all backed Dulles in his confrontational stance, which called for more arms, not less. The Atomic Energy Commission only reluctantly accepted Eisenhower's offer to place the development of nuclear energy under United Nations control, including the giving away of radioactive isotopes for peaceful uses. Some said that we dared not disclose any scientific knowledge in the nuclear field. Allen Dulles and the CIA straddled the issue, saying that our intelligence on Russia's leaders remained too uncertain to permit any safe conclusions about Soviet intentions since Stalin's death. Even though Marshal Bulganin remained as front man, many plotted and schemed behind his back. Several coveted a Stalin-type "strong man" role, but none felt sure enough of his power base to risk a play for the top spot.

The Russians drifted in a state of uncertainty, and Eisenhower feared we did the same, missing opportunities to break through the defensive barriers of their paranoia about being invaded another time.

I continued to read:

> This is the problem which the peoples of all the world demand we should solve and the U.S. must assume leadership. I feel that such an individual must not only be a coordinator and a spokesman within the Administration, but must also spearhead efforts to inform and instruct the American people in the basic factors affecting this vital subject.

Reading between the lines, I realized that this message sent to me halfway around the world signaled the President's decision to move away from Secretary Dulles' inflexible, almost bullying posture with the Soviets.

I sensed immediately where the cable led us:

> Assuming that the FOA [Foreign Operations Administration] as such is to disappear from our governmental structure, how would you feel toward undertaking this job—serving as my special assistant for the purpose? The magnitude and complexity of the task are such that I think we should make it the primary responsibility of someone of Cabinet rank.

We planned to put into effect the recommendation by Nelson Rockefeller's Committee of Government Organization to phase out the Foreign Operations Administration. We would transfer its defense support features to the Department of Defense and the direct economic aid programs to State, many of the transfer moves already in place.

Being out of the country, I did not know that the National Security Council approved the concept of my appointment to this post on February 10, 1955, and I never learned exactly what prompted the President to send me the message in Pakistan instead of waiting until I arrived back in Washington. I suspected that some precipitous speech or action by Secretary Dulles prompted it. The President and I never discussed it. A simple explanation may be the most likely: Once he made up his mind to act, he acted, no matter what the hour or where the other participants.

I do know that media criticism of his foreign policy gnawed at him. He told me several times of his impatience with Dulles and his other aides for their failure to come up with something creative that he could present to the world obsessed with the inevitability of World War III.

The President's message concluded:

> I have come to the conclusion that I should make some reasonably early announcement along this line, and I send you this cable because I want to approach no one else until I learn of your feelings in the matter. D. D. E.

(Ann Whitman's diary shows James Bryant Conant, Harvard president and German High Commissioner, as the only other person considered for the assignment in the event I turned it down).

Without moving from my chair, stunned, I read the message through a second time. I then told the Communications

Officer that I would return to my hotel and prepare an answer which I would drop off on my way to the airport a few hours later.

As I rode back to the hotel, I tried to consider all sides of the matter raised by the President's urgent cable.

Clearly, his frustrations over Dulles' unmoving Cold War stance reached a boiling point during my absence from Washington. The President obviously wished to avoid a direct confrontation with Dulles, who still held to the premise that only the Secretary of State should formulate and execute foreign policy.

Looking back from this perspective of almost forty years, I am positive that Dulles held his strong views in good faith and in the sincere belief that he worked for the best interests of the country, and, for that matter, of the President himself. But it's hard to escape the conclusion that Dulles thought himself far more competent to move in the international arena than Eisenhower, despite Eisenhower's tremendous diplomatic achievements with the Allies in World War II and later in NATO. Deep down, I think that Dulles feared that a military man simply could not handle civilian diplomatic problems; it fell to Dulles to keep his hand on the tiller.

I repeat again that I do not question Dulles' integrity in advancing his intractable views, only that I did not agree with him then. The passage of time merely confirms my original opinions.

I realized, however, that any appointee to the role the President's cable envisioned would clash directly with the Secretary unless he parroted the Secretary's posture of brinksmanship, which the President did not wish. This confrontation would probably become public even though everyone involved, including the President, would try to hold it to in-house differences of opinion.

The hands of the clock on the night stand beside the bed showed almost 2:30 a.m. when I sat down at the rickety table, in poor light, and began to draft my reply:

> Thank you for your message 1196 of March 1, received last evening in Karachi.
>
> As you are aware my basic inclination is to accept any responsibility which you decide you wish me to carry and then to endeavor to fulfill it in the manner you desire to have it conducted. This personal guideline flows both from my deep devotion to you and your objectives and from my understanding of the full measure of the responsibility which you, as President, shoulder for our country and for mankind. This concept of mine certainly applies to the development of policy on the question of disarmament which you describe and which I have studied for many years.

With the President, I always followed the policy of laying out my deepest thoughts about any question we discussed, holding back nothing of real relevance.

> I trust you also realize that this attitude of mine would apply equally to an assignment not (repeat not) of Cabinet rank as it is the task for you and not (repeat not) the rank that is decisive.

I must confess that I did realize then that before anyone could stand up against Dulles and his supporters on the question of disarmament, he would need cabinet rank; and I knew the President recognized this, as his cable showed.

> I assume in this instance the timing you have in mind would be after I have brought the substance of the President's mutual security program for fiscal year 1956 through the Congress and have eased the transition to the form of organization determined so as to

assure continuity of effective functioning overseas in the national interest and also to reasonably safeguard the fair rights of the career personnel who have effectively, loyally, and successfully operated the President's program these two years regardless of the Congressional handicaps.

At that time, 4,200 Foreign Operations Administration men and women kept its various programs moving, a highly-skilled team of technicians in food production, agronomy, hydroelectric power, and education. They worked with a vibrant *esprit de corps* and without the slightest hint of scandal. I wanted to protect their rights as they transferred to either State or Defense as we wound down the FOA.

I am confident we can again obtain the essential substance of the program from Congress notwithstanding the usual dire predictions of some who do not (repeat not) have the responsibility, and you and Foster can continue to have the vital means of implementing your decisions.

In all of my various public and private affairs, I never made a major decision directly involving my family without first discussing the details with my wife, so I added:

If agreeable to you, I would prefer not (repeat not) to reach a firm conclusion until after discussion with you personally and with my Esther.

Am scheduled to arrive in Washington from Tokyo on the 13th of March and if this course is agreeable please fix a time—early breakfast or otherwise—for me to see you.

Almost as an afterthought, I decided to add a few words about my FOA inspection trip:

This current mission is proceeding better than anticipated and the odds are now (repeat now) at least even
that a sound Asian economic plan can be established
with Asian initiative in harmony with US policy as
specified in the NSC conclusions.

I need to emphasize that neither the President nor I ran
the FOA programs as handouts or giveaways. We geared each
one to a specific defense need, all under the direct observation
of the National Security Council.

The Governor General of Pakistan sends his best
wishes to you, as did Nehru in our concluding session
in Delhi.

With my respects and best regards.

HAROLD E. STASSEN

I referred to my dinner the preceding evening with the
Governor General and top officials of Pakistan, and to an
earlier meeting with Pandit Nehru about the particular programs designed not only to help India and Pakistan feed their
burgeoning populations and start new industries, but to ease
deadly tensions that grew from partition of the British Raj in
1947.

When I reached our embassy in Istanbul, the Communications Officer handed me another "Eyes Only for Governor
Stassen" message from the President:

My warm thanks for your splendid message. We will
have our meeting to discuss this as soon as possible
after your return.

D. D. E.

I continued on to Thailand and the Philippines, into
Korea and finally to Tokyo, inspecting our FOA programs,

and collecting data on our accomplishments and on our future objectives. Particularly, I gathered the information we would need for our budget hearings before the appropriate committees of Congress for the fiscal year 1956. But the challenge of this new assignment hovered over all my waking thoughts: How I could help the President break the tensions of the Cold War by promoting disarmament, but do it in a way that would work in tandem with Secretary Dulles, instead of clashing with him!

The night of my return to Washington, I told Esther about the President's cable, tried to outline the problems and possibilities of the new post, and asked her if she felt up to seeing me embroiled in controversy if the confrontation with Dulles and his supporters did occur. As always, she told me to use my own best judgment about accepting the post; she would be with me no matter what happened. We both thought back to another surprising message, the one President Roosevelt sent to Admiral Halsey ordering me to San Francisco ten years earlier to help draft and sign the United Nations Charter.

When I reached my office the next morning, I found a message from Ann Whitman asking me to call for the earliest appointment we could work out.

The President looked trim and fit when I entered the Oval Office that same afternoon. I planned to give him a short report on my FOA inspection tour, but he jumped immediately into his concept of the disarmament coordinator: I must not only pull together everything now being done toward disarmament in all branches of government, but also develop new and creative programs to promote peace.

When I raised the question of what Secretary Dulles would say if and when we decided that a drastic change in policy should take place, his face firmed in his "command look," his voice taking on its "command tone."

He exploded: "I think its best for the country and for the world, and that's what we'll do!"

Remember, this became the United States' first coordinated attempt at arms reduction on a cooperative, international scale that directly involved our own military position. After each of our wars, of course, we unilaterally disarmed because our people basically disliked great standing armies. We participated, mostly indirectly, in a number of naval disarmament conferences after World War I, but never before tried to lead the world into reduced, less threatening military positions.

My files contain this letter on White House stationery, dated April 6, 1955, from Press Secretary Jim Hagerty:

Dear Harold:

It occurred to me that you might want to have this original copy of the release on your new appointment.

The handwriting is the President's.

The document, with the President's handwritten "Secret" scrawled at the top, bears the title, "Preliminary Draft for Possible Release by President":

3/15/55

The massive resources required for modern armaments, the huge diversion of materials and of energy, the heavy burdens of taxation, the demands for years of service of vast numbers of men, the unprecedented destructive power of new weapons, and the international tensions which powerful armaments aggravate, have been of deep concern to me for many years.

At the same time the tragic consequences of unilateral disarmament, the reckless moves of Hitler when the United States was weak, the Korean aggression

284

when our armed strength had been rapidly diminished, and the vast extent of the armament now centered around the opposing ideology of communism, have been equally apparent to me.

The recent session of the Disarmament Commission of the United Nations has again resulted in no progress and no clear crystallization of thinking on this subject. It has an inseparable relationship to our constant objective of peace.

I have, therefore, established a position as Special Assistant to the President with responsibility for developing, on behalf of the President and the State Department, the broad studies, investigations and conclusions which, when concurred in by the National Security Council and approved by the President, will become basic policy toward the question of disarmament. The position will be of Cabinet rank. [These two sentences originally read "... will become a firm and single basic policy ... ," Eisenhower crossing out "a firm and single," and changing "This" position to "The" position.]

When indicated as desirable or appropriate under our Constitutional processes, concurrences will be secured from the Congress prior to specific action or pronouncement of policy.

I have appointed Harold Stassen as a Special Assistant for discharge of this responsibility. He will be expected to take into account the full implications of new weapons in the possession of other nations as well as the United States, to consider future probabilities of armaments, and to weigh the views of the military, the civilians, and the officials of our government and of other governments.

For the time being, and for the presentation of the Mutual Security Program to the Congress, he will also continue to discharge his responsibility as Director of the Foreign Operations Administration, but he will begin this new task promptly upon this appointment.

Writing in *Affairs of State: The Eisenhower Years*, April 1, 1955, under the title, "The Peace Plugger" (chapter 34), columnist Richard Rovere gave a somewhat sarcastic but rather accurate summary of foreign policy affairs within the administration at the time of my new appointment. I insert subheadings for readability and emphasis:

> The President last week appointed Harold E. Stassen to a newly created job of Cabinet rank that the newspapers are describing variously as Disarmament Director, Secretary of Peace, and Special Assistant to the President "with responsibility for reporting on developments in the fields of armament and disarmament."

[MORAL LEADERSHIP BOLD AND IMAGINATIVE]

> . . . The action symbolizes much that is good, bad, and indifferent about the Eisenhower administration. On the moral level, it is, of course, praiseworthy. It is even, in a way, bold, original, imaginative.

[FIRST NATION WITH "PEACE MINISTRY"]

> We who have pioneered in so many fields can now post a claim to being the first nation on earth to have a peace ministry, an anti-war department, a twenty-thousand-dollar-a-year executive working at high pressure to get rid of the guns and bombs we have labored so mightily to produce. (The day after the announcement, though, the New York *Times* carried a reassuring story headed "Military Hopeful of Arms Build-Up.") No more will we Americans have to suffer in silence while Molotov, Mao, and Krishna Menon berate us for not loving peace enough. Which of their governments has a bureau that does nothing but search around for ways of abolishing war?

Editorial writers and columnists across the country and the world built to a crescendo of criticism of what they called the administration's "vacillating" or "conflicting" foreign policy, or even "no" foreign policy.

[DULLES' SILENCE ON APPOINTMENT]

... The fact that the scheme is administrative nonsense encourages this suspicion [that it is the brainchild of administration public relations people]. Peace plans and disarmament proposals should be the business of the Secretary of State. Peace is a function of diplomacy; diplomacy is a function of peace.

Mr. Dulles has not been heard to comment on Mr. Stassen's new office, but it is perfectly safe to assume that he is not overjoyed by this development.

[CONFLICTS BETWEEN STASSEN AND DULLES]

For as long as Mr. Stassen has been head of the Foreign Operations Administration, he has been getting in Mr. Dulles's hair. Foreign aid should have been a function of diplomacy, too, but diplomats were in bad repute when the Marshall Plan was set up, and the Congress didn't want to entrust all that money to dubious characters from the State Department.

[CROSS PURPOSES OF FOREIGN AID DISPENSERS]

As a consequence, the diplomats and the foreign-aid dispensers have suffered from a lack of liaison and coordination and have often worked and talked at cross-purposes.

In recent weeks, for example, Mr. Dulles has been traveling through the Far East telling the leaders there that there is no excuse for their shilly-shallying in the face of the Communist threat, and Mr. Stassen, going over the same route, has been sympathizing deeply with the same leaders and saying that not much can be expected of them until they have more calories in their diet, more hydro-electric projects, more literacy, and so forth. Now matters will surely be worse.

[DULLES: WAR—STASSEN: PEACE]

Mr. Dulles will be threatening war, and Mr. Stassen will be threatening peace, and neither, naturally, will be happy about what the other is saying.

Eisenhower genuinely respected Dulles and knew that he reflected a considerable body of public opinion, especially among the hard-nosed hawks.

[CONFLICTS BETWEEN DULLES AND EISENHOWER]

. . . But an additional appeal of the project may well have been the opportunity it afforded to offset Mr. Dulles with Mr. Stassen. For Mr. Stassen's way of getting in Mr. Dulles's hair is as nothing compared to Mr. Dulles's way of getting in President Eisenhower's hair.

Though the Secretary of State has changed his tune a good many times since 1952, when he wrote the Republican platform and in it promised the liberation of the satellite countries and just about everything short of the establishment of a town-meeting democracy in the Soviet Union, his pronouncements still do not come even close to the President's in terms of restraint and circumspection.

[FOREIGN POLICY MORE FLEXIBLE
WHEN DULLES OUT OF COUNTRY]

If one tries to catch the rhythm of events in Washington, one observes that the periods in which our foreign policy, as it is laid down from on high, appears to reach the maximum of flexibility and sobriety are those periods when Mr. Dulles is out of the country and making the rounds of the chancelleries. Then it is the President who speaks and who gives a powerful sense of being profoundly aware not only of the danger of Communist expansion but of the danger of war. After these interludes, Mr. Dulles flies in for a few days, delivers a couple of dour Calvinist forecasts of doom and retribution, then heads back out to Bangkok or Rio or wherever.

The creation of the new post and my appointment to it triggered all manner of speculation about interpersonal relationships within the President's official circles.

[STASSEN'S CLOSENESS TO EISENHOWER]

In contrast to Mr. Dulles, Mr. Stassen, a practicing politician since early youth, is never caught lagging behind the President in any respect. It might be argued that he is not as straightforward or as tough-minded as Mr. Dulles, but if that is true it is beside the point.

Mr. Stassen listens attentively to what the leader says and catches both the spirit and the letter of it. This doubtless explains why he was chosen for the new job, and it may explain why the job itself was created.

But it does not explain everything. For the fact is that quite apart from how the President may feel about Mr. Dulles and Mr. Stassen, the whole trend of American policy these days is away from the point of view that characterized the early days of the Eisenhower administration. . . . (New York: Farrar, Straus and Cudahy, 1956)

In actuality, Eisenhower inherited the Truman-Acheson policies of confrontation and the naive idea that we could totally eliminate nuclear weapons. He knew that foreign policy traditions, commitments, goals, and strategies run deep, and involve not only diplomacy but military and economic factors. Changes in course must occur slowly, step-by-step, nudging here, prodding there, "making progress through compromise." Nothing changes miraculously overnight.

Eisenhower came to believe that Dulles' efforts to break through the stalemate of the Cold War moved far too slowly. The burden of his blind hatred of Communism precluded his shift from "brinksmanship" and containment. He simply did not move away from Truman-Acheson as fast as Eisenhower wanted to go, or in the direction Eisenhower wanted to take us.

That's my best analysis of the President's decision to give me my new assignment.

I went to see Foster Dulles at the State Department before the President's March 15 press release. I told him that I did not seek this appointment; it came as a surprise direct from the President himself. I tried to assure him that even though the appointment gave me cabinet rank and the duty to report directly to the President, I wanted to work closely with him, with Charlie Wilson at Defense, Admiral Lewis Strauss of the Atomic Energy Commission, and everyone else who could help us work out a program for disarmament to remove some of the potential dangers of World War III.

Dulles and I always talked openly about our divergent views of foreign policy. He never hinted then at any displeasure over my new assignment, although I knew that he must see me as a rival in his area of expertise where no one else should dare to tread.

I also made the rounds at Defense, including the Joint Chiefs, and the other departments and agencies, explaining how I viewed my new assignment and seeking their input.

In the President's first press conference after Jim Hagerty's release, a reporter asked:

"Mr President, would you say that Mr. Stassen is your new 'Secretary for Peace'?"

The President smiled and said, "I guess you could say that."

That label turned out to be unfortunate, and upset Dulles so much that he decided he could not live with it.

Chapter 20
Moving Toward a Summit

As the President's press release explained, I wore two hats for a period of several months, continuing as Director of the Foreign Operations Administration until we secured the appropriations from Congress for the next fiscal year, 1956. I also began my role as Special Assistant to the President for Disarmament. The media did not know what to call me, many using "Secretary for Peace," but I never used the label myself.

I remained in my original office in the Executive Office Building next door to the White House, without even a name change on the door, and appointed my FOA deputy, Robert Matteson, Director of Research for the new disarmament mission. A brilliant mind, Matteson compiled an outstanding World War II record in counterintelligence. Toward the end of the war, he led a squad up the Bavarian Alps to capture the head of the Austrian SS, Ernst Kaltenbrunner, who considered himself safe from Allied hands in his secluded mountain retreat.

I designated Ed Larson as my principal secretary. As an historical sidelight, Ed developed his shorthand and typing skills as secretary to a top executive of the Great Northern Railroad in the days when society thought it improper for female secretaries to travel with their bosses.

The President concurred in my request for the Secretary of Defense, the Army, Navy, and Air Force chiefs, the CIA Director, Chairman of the Atomic Energy Commission, and the State Department to assign competent representatives to work with me. We could not hope for in-depth experience in the processes of disarmament, since we served as the first real, coordinated pioneers in the entire field. I asked simply for persons of intelligence with creative, analytical minds, who would not be afraid to challenge the status quo of the bureaucracy, and who would be dedicated to finding workable structures and procedures for disarmament and lasting peace.

"Top Secret" page 34 of my first progress report to the National Security Council, declassified in April, 1986, lists the members of my "Special Staff":

> Edmund A. Guillion, Department of State
>
> Lawrence D. Weiler, Department of State
>
> Colonel R.B. Firehock, USA, Department of Defense
>
> Captain D.W. Gladney, USN, Department of Defense
>
> Colonel Benjamin G. Willis, USAF, Department of Defense
>
> McKay Donkin, Atomic Energy Commission
>
> Robert E. Matteson, Foreign Operations Administration
>
> John F. Lippmann, Foreign Operations Administration

One name is still blacked-out after thirty-five years: the CIA representative.

We started from scratch, without today's jargon of multiple war heads, throw weights, triads, or anything else. We could not even find the working draft of a disarmament treaty as a "form book" model, should we develop its need on short notice.

But we started immediately.

On my flight home from Tokyo, I decided that if I took the disarmament post, I would assemble a citizens advisory committee to work with us. The President approved, and I named, among others, Dr. Harold Moulton, head of the Brookings Institute; Dr. James Fisk, then president of the American Scientific Society and director of Bell Laboratories; Dr. Ernest Lawrence, a Nobel laureate in physics; and Dr. Edward Teller, known as father of the H-bomb.

I must pay special tribute to another member of this group, General James H. Doolittle. An early aviation "daredevil," he set a world speed record for land planes in 1932. In May, 1942, when Japan's fortunes soared highest, he led the daring bombing raid on Tokyo that gave Japan pause and us a psychological lift. Using an aircraft carrier as a launch pad, Doolittle's B-25s took off for their "Thirty Seconds Over Tokyo," then on to landing fields in Chiang Kai-shek's China. It won Doolittle a Congressional Medal of Honor. He later commanded our air forces in the invasion of North Africa that November, and led the 8th Air Force over Europe in 1944.

I always admired his keen ability to go immediately to the bottom-line issues. In one of our first conversations, he made the simple statement that in today's world of the most destructive weapons of all time, the most important consideration is the mutual, reciprocal fear of all nations of a *surprise attack*. Our prime goal, therefore, in this pursuit of a disarmament agreement, must be some formula to secure each nation against a surprise attack. If all nations could be protected from surprise attacks, it would quiet world tensions and go a long way toward preventing the need for a continuing increase of armaments; and it would prevent World War III—something too horrible to contemplate.

Conversely, if we could not develop some formula to prevent surprise attacks, we would end up spinning our wheels on all other disarmament discussions. The arms race would continue, each superpower trying to outdevelop and outproduce the others with ever more sophisticated and destructive weapons.

One way to calm those mutual fears of all nations, he continued, would be a formula to permit each side to *fly over* the other at any time, to be sure that no new military build-ups developed, no armies massed for movement. Such missions could verify any new runways being built, planes moved to new fields ready for takeoff, or new missile launching pads—anything new in the way of offensive weapons.

I told General Doolittle that his idea of "flyovers" impressed me greatly and would become one of our crucial disarmament "texts." I told him I would fight for his idea.

From the time of Stalin's death, I vigorously advocated a Big Four Summit, to the President privately, in National Security Council meetings, in speeches, and to everyone who would lend me an ear. With equal vigor, Foster Dulles opposed a summit, anytime, anywhere. But another event took place in April, 1955 that helped nudge us toward a summit, although I did not learn its final outcome until years later.

I appeared before the authorization bill hearings of the Senate Foreign Relations Committee to make my status report on our Foreign Operations Administration and request funding for the next fiscal year. Democratic Senator Walter George of Georgia chaired the Committee. Tall, stately, courteous, with a full head of snow-white hair, the epitome of what we used to call the "Southern Gentleman," George sat in the center of the top row of the three tiers of seats for committee members.

Secretary Dulles opened the hearing from the witness table and made a general statement that described the value of our foreign operations programs and their contribution to military, economic, and diplomatic stability throughout the free world.

I sat on Dulles' right. My presentation moved into considerably more specific goals and programs. Then my four regional deputy directors supplied the details of financial needs. The session ran without interruption all morning. As we neared the noon break, Senator George's secretary approached me at the witness table and whispered that the chairman would like to see me in his office at the end of the session.

His receptionist escorted me into the Senator's inner office as soon as I arrived. We shook hands and exchanged greetings, his soft Georgia accent always pleasant to hear. I can be confident of my general accuracy in reproducing our conversation, since it made a welcome impression.

"Governor," he opened after we both sat down, "I've been giving a great deal of thought to this question we keep reading about—of whether there should be a meeting at the summit. I've concluded that there should be. If anyone can, I think that President Eisenhower may have a very significant influence upon the leaders of the Soviet Union."

I nodded my agreement, excitement welling up inside.

"From what I can tell," he continued, "there's no single dictator in charge since Stalin died. We hear a lot about discussions going on inside the Soviet Union of what our aggressive intentions are, and what they think they have to do to be ready for what we're going to do to them. It's kinda like a dog chasing its own tail. I think it would be very important for General Eisenhower—President Eisenhower—with his own unique standing, to talk to them at considerable length. A summit would do that."

I kept nodding but chose not to interrupt until he signaled his finish.

"I've thought it over a great deal, and I've reached the conclusion that it would be very much in the interests of world peace, and in the best interests of our country, if a summit could be held. The reason I wanted to talk to you is that I'm questioning whether I should write to the President about it, or whether he might resent my interference in his own executive decision on holding a summit."

I suppressed my pleasure over the Senator's words, and went on nodding my agreement.

"Do you think I would be out of line in writing to the President? Do you think he would resent it? I know his strong feelings on separation of powers, and I share them completely. So I'm pondering if a letter from me about a summit might be counterproductive. Do you think I would need to send Secretary Dulles a copy of the letter, or also write him? I am aware that deep down, he opposes a summit."

The Senator stopped and looked at me expectantly, which I interpreted as my signal to reply, rejoicing that his direct question gave me license to express my own feelings.

"Senator," I said, "I know through my most personal conversations with the President that there is no one on Capitol Hill whom the President respects more than you. I am certain that he would welcome a letter from you. Yes, he does hold deep beliefs on the doctrine of separation of powers. He does respect the chairmen of the different congressional committees, as he works with them all the time; but yours is the type of advice that a member of the legislative branch can and should give to the President. Your private letter could carry great weight, since it will not be something you will give to the media. You could not be accused of acting for personal or partisan political advantage."

"Certainly not," he snapped, almost insulted that I could even imagine such a thought entering his mind.

"What about a copy to Dulles, or a separate letter to Dulles?" the Senator persisted, obviously concerned over protocol, taste, and propriety.

"I can only tell you to use your own instincts on that. I cannot presume to even make a suggestion on it. As you apparently know, the Secretary and I stand 180 degrees apart on holding a summit."

I did not know until Eisenhower published his memoirs two years after leaving the White House that Senator George actually did write that letter. The President credited the Senator as one of the strong influences that helped him decide to proceed with a summit.

At about this same time, Winston Churchill came out in support of a Big Four Summit, and even Anthony Eden, who replaced Churchill as prime minister in April, reversed his long-held opposition.

Two stories in the May 5, 1955, *New York Times*, page 2, put the public controversy over holding a summit in perspective:

> The British Government was reported from London to be ready to propose a conference of the heads of government of the United States, Britain, France and the Soviet Union. Foreign Secretary Macmillan will put the proposal before his Western Big Three colleagues Sunday. [The foreign ministers were meeting in Paris.]

Under the headline, "U.S. Opposes Top-Level Talk," the second story read:

> Secretary of State Dulles and President Eisenhower still oppose a Big-Four meeting "at the summit" in advance of a foreign ministers conference.
>
> United States officials said today that there had been no change in this established position. They predicted that

Mr. Dulles would turn down the reported London proposal for putting the "summit" meeting first when he talked in Paris next week-end with Harold Macmillan, British Foreign Secretary, and Antoine Pinay, French Foreign Minister.

The National Security Council session on May 19, 1955, opened routinely. After disposing of budget and a dozen other items, the minutes show:

The President answered . . . and then with a smile said that he seemed to be getting a reputation throughout the world for being a very peaceful man who was surrounded by warmongers. Amid laughter, Secretary Dulles observed that the situation the President described was not without its advantages.

We discussed at some length Allen Dulles' report on CIA analyses of an "interesting shift in the protocol positions of members of the Politburo when they appeared in public." Bulganin still occupied the front-center place but he obviously lacked Stalin's decisive control. We could not appraise the ranks of Molotov, Mikoyan, Khruschchev, and the other apparently lesser lights.

My mind raced to see whether I could work this leadership vacuum in the Kremlin into another pro-summit argument. We could jump in with a summit proposal before the Soviet power struggle settled and make a substantial diplomatic gain.

While I reviewed whether another argument by me at that time would be wise or counterproductive, no matter what tone and what words I chose, the President turned to Secretary Dulles on his right and said in the firmest "command tone" I ever heard him use, "Foster, I have decided to instruct you to proceed—to let the other countries know that if they want a summit, I am ready to go to one. I want to take the affirmative approach to bring about a summit at an early date."

"Yes, Mr. President," Secretary Dulles replied in an even voice.

The President's use of the words "instruct you" is important. We seldom heard it; more often he said, "Let's . . . ," "Why don't we . . . ," or "Shall we. . . . " He did not like to overrule an associate directly, trying not to embarrass the person with whom he disagreed. "Instruct you" always came out as an euphemism for "order you!" When coupled with the President's "command tone," there could be no doubt of his meaning.

The Secretary did not give up easily: "Mr. President, a meeting of this kind is a major undertaking. It will take months to get ready for it. We must go there with our positions firmly stated, and everything in place. It will require a lot of work."

The President saw through Dulles' effort to stall the meeting and perhaps foot-drag it into oblivion.

"We'll let the Planning Board [of the NSC] handle these details," the President continued, again using his "command tone."

We debated for over an hour the ramifications of the summit, the various topics that might come up, who could best work out our positions, when and where. The cold fleshless minutes of that heated discussion which really turned U.S. foreign policy around, declassified "2/6/86," merely report:

The National Security Council:

a. Discussed procedures for developing a U. S. position on the Four-Power Heads-of-Government meeting, in the light of the above report by the Secretary of State and suggestions by the NSC

Planning Board as reported by the Special Assistant to the President for National Security Affairs.

b.   Directed the NSC Planning Board to prepare as a matter of urgency for Council consideration, recommendations on the basic U. S. policy with respect to the Four-Power Heads-of-Government meeting, including:

   (1) The general U. S. attitude toward the purposes of the meeting and the objectives which the U. S. would seek to achieve, taking into account: British and French objectives; estimated Soviet objectives, immediate and long-term; existing or anticipated Soviet proposals and possible U. S. proposals which might be introduced at such a meeting.

   (2) Maintenance of a U. S. posture of strength and confidence before, during and after such a meeting.

   (3) Disarmament (incorporating any Council decisions based on the progress report on May 26, 1955 of the Special Assistant to the President on Disarmament).

   (4) European security, including the U. S. position toward Germany; a neutral belt of European states and its impact on trade with the Soviet bloc; the status of satellite countries; and the activities of the international Communist movement.

   (5) The U. S. position on Far Eastern issues which might be raised, including the basis for U. S. opposition to a Five-Power meeting.

c.   Noted that the Special Assistant to the President for National Security Affairs would coordinate the above-directed Planning Board activities with the

Counselor of the Department of State, who would be responsible for coordinating the arrangements for the Four-Power meeting.

/s/ S. Everett Gleason
[NSC Secretary]

The President's decision to overrule Dulles' two-and-one-half-year posture against holding a summit could not help but rankle the Secretary, but he did not give the slightest hint of disappointment, displeasure, or resentment in either facial expression or tone of voice.

I walked out of the cabinet room with Charlie Wilson. In his droll, almost flat tone, he said, "Well, I see that the Secretary for Peace won out over the Secretary of State."

I winced and replied, "Charlie, please don't say that. You know how sensitive Foster is. I'd much rather have you say that the President made the correct decision today, a good decision for everybody. I don't claim any credit for the President's actions. I'm convinced that it is what the President has wanted all along. Our job now is to see to it that this summit is worthwhile."

The next morning, May 20, I kept an appointment with Secretary Dulles at the State Department, arranged several days before the NSC meeting the day before that announced the Summit. Here is Dulles' partial report of our conference:

DEPARTMENT OF STATE

THE SECRETARY

May 20, 1955

MEMORANDUM OF CONVERSATION WITH MR. STASSEN

I said that I felt that some thought had to be given to the relationship of Stassen to the State Department. I said that I did not like his use of the title "Secretary for Peace"—not that I had any personal feeling, but that it was not good for the State Department and Foreign Service to feel that some outside agency had primary responsibility for peace. I said that we thought *we* were working for peace and that that was the stimulus of our effort. Mr. Stassen said that this had come about more or less naturally without his instigation. I said however that may be, I did not care for it and I noticed that in the prospective radio broadcast for USIS he had adopted the title as one approved by the President. Mr. Stassen said that, in view of my feeling, he would drop any use himself of this title, although he could not prevent its being used by others. He went on to say that he wanted to cooperate very closely with me and hoped I would use him as though he were a sort of special Under Secretary for this field. I said that I felt that probably until there was a United States position he had better function independently as he would be in a stronger position than if he seemed to be connected with the State Department. However, I said once there was an agreed United States position, I thought then the carrying out of it ought to be under the direction and guidance of the Secretary of State, and that he should cooperate with us and take policy guidance from us. He said this would be highly agreeable to him.

. . . .

I pointed out that while we would not have to reach any early decision on the substance of our position, we might have to reach an early position on procedure, and I thought that that should be a first concern because it might come up at the Four Power talks. Mr. Stassen said that, following the Thursday presentation, he would want to talk to the different Departments separately and would want them to talk soon and first with the Department of State. I said I would welcome this.

In conclusion, Stassen said that he wanted me to "use him" to the fullest extent possible and that I could count on his complete loyalty.

We all tend to write self-serving reports, so mine differs from the Secretary's. In the first place, he did not voice his displeasure about my using the title "Secretary for Peace" in mild and restrained tones as his memorandum indicates. In the vernacular, he chewed me out, and discounted my word that I had never used the label myself. I repeated the story of its genesis from the President's own response at the press conference after my appointment.

While I did offer my sincerest cooperation in our mutual efforts to make the summit a success, I never once hinted that my loyalties lay any place other than to the President. Nor did I ever tell him that he could "use" me or that he should consider me "a sort of special Under Secretary for this field."

Chapter 21
Disarmament: A Progress Report

On May 26, 1955, under the President's specific orders, I gave the National Security Council a one-hour "Progress Report," subtitled *Special Staff Study for the President.* I used a thirty-three-page "Top Secret" handout entitled *Proposed Policy of the United States on the Question of Disarmament.* With much technical ground to cover, I wanted everyone to follow me without the need for notetaking.

I stood at the far end of the cabinet table, two aides placing and replacing charts and graphs on an easel to illustrate my presentation as I moved along. Based on the latest intelligence data, I detailed the world's armaments with technical descriptions of their capabilities, how they might be used strategically and tactically against the United States and other countries, their limitations, the imbalances, and the ratios of different reduction proposals. We rated the control possibilities on (1) their long-range substance, and (2) the likelihood of getting the Soviets to agree to them.

Portions of that report still remain classified, but I can talk about its general philosophies and goals. Most still serve as the foundation of the ongoing arms reduction talks in Geneva and Vienna.

The report opened with a basic orientation statement:

I. The Most Important Objective.

Under the current policies and the leadership of the President, the most important objective of the United States is peace—with security, freedom, and economic well-being—for the long-term future for the people of our country. This objective must be ever in mind in considering and in implementing the policy of the United States on the question of disarmament. It has been a constant and basic factor in the study which has resulted in the progress report here presented.

II. Armaments, Tensions, and Dangers of War.

A high and rising level of arms is a reflection of tension growing out of disagreements between nations, and it is in turn a source of increased tension. An arms race is thus both effect and cause. An intelligent and sound policy on the question of disarmament must recognize this dual characteristic of heavy armament.

We stated our key aim on page 13, built around General Doolittle's text that any arms limitation program acceptable to all major powers must, of necessity, include some vehicle to eliminate the fear of surprise attack:

V. A Cardinal Aim of United States Policy.

The projected condition under which the USSR would have the capability of effective destruction of the United States through a surprise attack would be so adverse to United States survival that a cardinal aim of United States policy should be to prevent this condition from arriving and to safeguard against any surprise attack.

A.   There are three broad methods of preventing the attainment of a future total weapons capability by the USSR.

    1. Voluntary unilateral decision by the USSR.

2. Enforced unilateral action of the USSR through an ultimatum or through the use of external force.

3. Multilateral effective agreement with the USSR to limit arms.

The first is highly unlikely; the second is quite certain to mean war. Maximum concentration on the third is indicated.

B. A secondary aim of United States policy should be to dissuade third nations from attaining a nuclear weapons capability.

[Paragraphs blocked out as still classified]

I stressed General Doolittle's theme several times and then moved on to more specific proposals, emphasizing the need for verifiable inspection to keep all sides from cheating (page 18):

2. Establish an International Armaments Commission with the right to observe and inspect by land, sea, or air, with the aid of scientific instruments, all existing armaments and to communicate the observations to an international center outside the country being inspected, without interference.

3. Such inspection service to be in place and ready to function on the date fixed for stopping the arms race and to be a condition precedent.

a. Such inspection service to include specifically United States nationals within the USSR and within the entire

309

Communist area, and con-
versely to include USSR nationals within the United States in a
balanced proportion.

4. Require all nations to disclose on parallel dates in stages all existing armament
and to submit to verification of the disclosure by the inspectors.

5. Stop all nuclear weapons testing as of
the same fixed date the arms race is
stopped.

6. Require an advance report to the International Armaments Commission of
all projected movements of armed
forces in international air or waters or
in foreign air, land or waters.

Appreciation of the phrase "the right to observe and
inspect by land, sea, or *air*," is critical: It served as the base for
Eisenhower's "Open Skies" proposal at the Geneva Summit
two months later, and establishes its link from General
Doolittle, to me, to the President, to the NSC, and finally to its
public announcement at Geneva.

I knew that I held the President's attention because I
could see him doodle; his copy of the "Progress Report" in the
Library at Abilene shows his doodles, one perhaps my face.

We next departed drastically from the illusory Truman-
Acheson proposals to ban all nuclear weapons (pages 21-22):

VII. Discussion of the Proposed First Phase Plan.

The first phase plan here proposed could be characterized as the establishment of a high open-arms
plateau.

A. It would not ban nuclear weapons. This is a major change in a nine-year old policy of the United States. This is an essential change for the following reasons:

   1. A ban cannot be made effective and guaranteed [*paragraphs blocked out as still classified*]

   2. In the absence of nuclear weapons, there is no effective manner of restraining aggression by the USSR and Communist China regardless of what levels of conventional arms might be agreed upon.

   3. Even though banned, nuclear weapons could be and would be produced within a few months during the course of any war initiated with conventional weapons.

      a. Nuclear weapons are knowledge plus material. The knowledge cannot be repealed. The material is available to every major nation and on every continent.

B. Both the USSR and the United States would be stopped short of the capability of mutual annihilation and neither would be required to trust the good faith of the other.

   1. This would attain the cardinal objective of United States policy.

   2. Further disarmament results would be desirable, but none would compare in importance to this first result.

311

C. The possibility of a surprise attack on the United States would be minimized. The positioning and the reporting of inspectors and the notification of projected international movements of armed forces would make a surprise attack on the United States almost impossible.

I moved to a general statement of the benefits that would flow from our proposals:

1. The United States would forego the opportunity to launch a surprise attack upon the USSR in exchange for substantial assurance against a surprise attack upon the United States.

D. The development of a nuclear weapons capability on the part of other countries would be minimized if not prevented, with the probably [sic] exception of the United Kingdom.

E. Some reduction in the financial burden of armaments would result.

F. The openness of arms and knowledge of their movements is far more important than their precise level.

G. World tensions would be reduced.

H. The security of the United States would be improved.

I. Skillful and thorough development of public understanding throughout the free world will be necessary in such a new policy and new plan. But it is realistic and based upon hard facts. It can be understood and will be supported by the people.

J. The affirmative initiative for such a realistic and far-reaching first phase plan will be recognized throughout the world as a serious and sincere endeavor and will tend to take the initiative away from the Soviet's current neutralist drive.

K. Fundamentally, it reflects a conclusion that there is a brighter prospect for peace through a policy of agreed strength than through a policy of agreed weakness. It is not expected that the United States will renounce its belief that all men should be free, but it is expected that the United States will continue to renounce the use of aggressive force to set men free.

It is not expected that the USSR will renounce its concept that all nations should be under the communist system, but it is expected that the USSR will renounce and refrain from the use of aggressive force to communize other peoples.

In a world in which these diverse systems are in competition, weakness on the part of the United States, even though it be a mutual weakness, would be more likely to lead to war and to a lack of security. This is especially true because of the geographic location of the USSR and Communist China in the center of the Eurasian land mass where over two-thirds of the people of the world reside. It is especially true when we contemplate the unorthodox methods short of aggression which would be intensified by the communists without any effective restraint upon their center.

I stressed the reciprocal nature of the benefits to the Soviets:

VIII. The Mutual Advantage of the USSR.

The foregoing sections have emphasized the advantages of the proposed initial plan to the United States. It is obvious that an agreement will not be reached unless it is also to the mutual advantage of the USSR. It is submitted that characteristics of mutual advantage are included.

A. The answer to the mutual advantage question depends in large measure upon the intentions for the future of the rules in the Kremlin. If it is their intention to launch an aggressive war at some future timing of their choice, especially if it is their intention to do so with an initial surprise attack on the United States, then neither the proposed plan, nor any other plan acceptable to the United States will be acceptable to the USSR.

But if this is not their intention, then the plan should have advantages to the USSR, for the alternative projected capability for mutual annihilation must be unattractive to them as well as to us.

B. The prospect, in the absence of agreement, of a nuclear weapons capability in Germany, Communist China, and Japan would be especially adverse to Soviet interests and would commend the proposed plan.

1. There are many indications of extreme concern of the USSR over German rearmament. An agreed leveling off as of the date of initiating effective inspection under the United States proposal would limit future German armament to a degree and in a manner much more attractive from the Soviet viewpoint than the Western European Union Treaty, and would include USSR participation on a reciprocal basis in the inspection of German armament.

2. Japanese rearmament will also be of increasing concern to the USSR, and it

would be likewise limited by the first phase agreement contemplated.

3. The USSR will have difficulty in refusing to supply Red China with nuclear weapons in future years, and yet must have a reluctance to place such power in China with the possibility of a future clash of interests in the Far East.

C. There are numerous indications that the large burden of armament is causing at least as great, if not greater, difficulty in the communist area as it is causing in the free area. The agreed easing of this burden, even though in a small degree, may have an appeal.

D. The steady expansion of United States air bases surrounding the Soviet appear to be causing an extreme psychological reaction. The halting of this expansion of United States bases should be attractive to the USSR.

E. A nuclear war of mutual destruction would be to the disadvantage of the USSR as well as of the United States.

F. If the Soviet rulers believe in the ultimate success of communism over capitalism without war, they may consider that there is an advantage in minimizing the danger of the early outbreak of war and settling down to a long-term competition of systems.

G. The USSR appears to be eager to expand trade and to be handicapped by the East-West trade controls. Broadened and beneficial trade would be facilitated by such a first phase agreement.

H. The USSR as well as the United States would presumably benefit from an improved attitude of world opinion following such an agreement.

The rest of my presentation dealt primarily with strategy and tactics to get our policies accepted by the free world and by Russia.

The paucity of NSC minutes generally is no better illustrated than by their coverage of my one-hour presentation:

> Following the presentation by Governor Stassen and members of his staff of the progress report on U. S. policy on control of armaments, Governor Stassen asked if the members of the Council had any comments to make or questions to raise.

The President showed his intense involvement in the arms reduction issue by being the first to comment. I follow my practice of inserting subheadings for emphasis and readability:

> The President opened the discussion by commending Governor Stassen and his staff for their very effective presentation. He indicated that he was in substantial agreement with the manner in which the report had emphasized that there was little chance of eliminating the danger we faced through attempting to reach agreement on the elimination or ban on the use of nuclear and thermonuclear weapons.
>
> **[NEED TO CONTROL SYSTEMS OF DELIVERY]**
>
> The President went on to say, however, that he felt the presentation had perhaps not given sufficient attention to the development, as part of the plan, of ways to control means and systems of delivery, such as planes, submarines, and intercontinental missiles. He felt that clear agreements on this type of controls would be a very important supplementary part of any agreement.
>
> He went on to say that an international control commission should have the right not only to investigate

the sites where nuclear devices were stored or produced, but also to investigate the related means by which they could be delivered.

[REINFORCEMENT OF EARLY WARNING SYSTEM]

As an example, the President pointed out that such an international control commission should have the right to have radar establishments anywhere on any continent in any country, and that this would reinforce the early warning concept basic to the system Governor Stassen was proposing.

[LEVELING OFF LIMITS OTHER SIDE'S CAPABILITIES]

Governor Stassen replied that the President's points were good ones and important. He said that he felt such provisions were inherent in the system of control he was proposing.

He referred again to one of the basic concepts of his presentation, namely, that if you could achieve an effective leveling-off and stabilization of further development of means of delivery, then you were in effect creating the major check to any further increase in the other side's capabilities to damage you.

I continued to emphasize General Doolittle's theme of the need to protect against surprise attack:

Governor Stassen returned to comment on the relation between a leveling-off of further advancement in means of delivery and the inspection provisions of the control system.

He indicated again that the essential facet of the system, once the capabilities to inflict damage had been stabilized, was to give warning against, or to deter, any surprise attack.

[ADVANCE REPORT OF REQUIRED MILITARY MOVEMENTS]

He noted that any nation would be required to report in advance flights of planes, movements of troops, activity by submarines, and other related military movements. He said that if, for example, such movements had not been reported in advance, then one would have a very good indication of hostile intentions when they were discovered.

Secretary Dulles remained surprisingly quiet during the entire discussion, but finally showed his innate need to introduce pessimism and complexity into every problem that fell within his "exclusive" realm of diplomacy:

The Secretary of State then noted his agreement with the President on the very fine presentation made by Governor Stassen and his group.

Secretary Dulles noted that it was not a simple matter, and raised many problems.

Furthermore, he expressed the hope that during departmental consideration of Governor Stassen's plan, primary attention would be given to the main proposals, not the supplementary ones.

I tried never to oppose the Secretary directly, but feared his skilled technique of decimating programs he did not like with inserts, limitations, and boundaries:

Governor Stassen expressed his agreement with Secretary Dulles, pointing out that a particular effort had been made in developing the proposals to state in clear and precise terms its basic aspects, so that it would be easier for the departments to establish points they questioned or differed upon.

[SALIENT POINTS REVIEWED]

Governor Stassen then went on briefly to review some of these salient points brought up in his plan.

The first was that U. S. policy should no longer propose the elimination of nuclear weapons as part of a control-of-armaments system.

Another point was whether or not we should shift, in our armaments control proposal, to concentration on control of delivery systems in order to eliminate the possibility of surprise attack.

A third point concerned our willingness to accept this plan as a first phase.

Another important aspect was the firm provision for U. S., and Soviet, participation in the control and inspection commissions . . . .

The debate on the report continued for two full hours, the President finally closing it by warning against leaks that would irreparably damage our efforts, and urging me to get the document into final shape by July 1. He wanted it ready for the Geneva summit, the exact date still not determined.

Chapter 22
The Geneva Summit

"Harold, have a seat," the President said as I approached his desk in the Oval Office after my quick summons by Ann Whitman in early July of 1955.

I knew this meant a discussion of some kind, not just one of the short directives he issued while we stood before him. In the standing posture, my mind's eye always saw him in military uniform, issuing firm orders in his confident "command tone." His instruction to sit alerted me to some kind of conflict about to unfold.

I took a chair at his right while he took off his glasses, looked straight at me and said, "Harold, Foster does not want you to be at the Geneva conference."

I looked back in both surprise and disappointment.

I'm confident of the accuracy of these conversations, though naturally, I claim no verbatim report:

> Mr. President, I cannot say that I am totally taken aback. I, of course, am aware of the intensity of Foster's feelings about my continuous urging that there should be a summit, and that we should reach out toward the Soviet Union. The more you have indicated views of moving in that same direction and the more I have supported your views, the more Foster has been bothered. But I do believe that his proposed agenda does not have the faintest chance of any affirmative possibilities at all.

As always, the President and I pulled no punches as we tried to work out a solution to the problem we faced. I continued:

> As you know, I differ drastically with Foster on several basic points. His thought of having you at a summit to press the Soviet Union for unification of Germany at this time cannot possibly go anywhere. It will meet a complete, absolute stone wall. The Soviets think only of the suffering their people experienced in the war. The word "Germany" means only "Nazis" to them at this point in history.
>
> And Foster wants you to spend your time making a series of statements criticizing the Soviets. This can only chill world opinion. My great concern is that if you go to a summit with Foster's agenda and you follow the foreign policy lead that Foster proposes, you will be forced into a negative position that will be tragic for you, tragic for our country, tragic for world peace. I feel very strongly about that.

He did not break eye contact as I continued:

> You were aware, of course, of the work of my exceptional staff, and our team of outside advisers. You know our analyses of this entire matter of the interrelationships between the Soviets and the U.S., and arms control. Our proposals offer some hope for you to express your goals of reaching out to the Soviets in an effort to break the stalemate of the Cold War. I think that Foster Dulles' concept of the summit will produce the exact opposite effect, exactly what you don't want to happen.
>
> But it is your conference, Mr. President. You know that I respond to your decisions.

Then I stopped. As I watched him, I sensed he already knew how to resolve his problem, or else we would not be holding this conversation. He would simply have sent me a message telling me not to go to Geneva.

> Harold, I've been thinking about it. Would you mind going to Paris without any advance publicity? Be there quietly in a hotel. Let Andy Goodpaster know where you will be. I feel certain I will want you in Geneva, but that will, of course, depend on how the opening session goes. I don't want to force Foster on this issue right now. I think we'll work it out all right, but the better strategy is what I have in mind.

I told the President that if he wanted me in Paris, that's where I would be and I would do my best to conceal my part of the trip.

"Good!" he replied with his characteristic air of completion, "If I need you in Geneva, Colonel Goodpaster will call you, and you can get there in a few hours."

I started for the door, but then turned with these parting words:

> Mr. President, if you think you will want to talk about disarmament and arms limitations in Geneva, you should also have someone from the Department of Defense, and Admiral Radford should be there for that part of the discussions. We already have indications that Marshal Zhukov [then Russian Minister of Defense] will be in the Soviet delegation. You understand, of course, that I'm not minimizing your own competence in the field of defense, but from the standpoint of appearances, if you are to take up arms control, I suggest that your own Defense Minister and Joint Chiefs Chairman should be present.

He stood and shot back his response, almost before I finished speaking:

323

No, I don't want Charlie Wilson sitting in Paris on the uncertainty of whether I will or will not want him in Geneva. I don't think that's good form, particularly when some reporter will find out that the Secretary of Defense is biding his time in Paris and start speculating on what that means. What I'll do, I'll ask Bob Anderson [Deputy Secretary of Defense] to be over there with you; and I do think it's a good idea to have Arthur Radford in Paris, too.

A few days later, after a cabinet meeting, the President asked me to stop by the Oval Office for a minute. He said that he wanted Nelson Rockefeller, Special Assistant to the President for Cold War Strategy, also to be with our stand-by group in Paris. Dulles told Eisenhower that Nelson tried to push himself into the Geneva delegation after a State Department briefing July 11, and Dulles did not want Rockefeller to be in Geneva either.

I told the President that, of course, I would be happy to include Rockefeller in our Paris group, and made the necessary arrangements.

In the Eisenhower Library in Abilene, I found this Top Secret State Department memorandum, now declassified and open to researchers. It is another example of the need to flesh out official documents:

July 11, 1955.

TOP SECRET

Briefing by State Department on Geneva Conference.

Present: The President, the Secretary of State, Livingston Merchant, Douglas MacArthur, II, Dillon Anderson, Nelson Rockefeller, Colonel Goodpaster.

Personnel to be available in Paris during Geneva Conference.

Governor Stassen, Nelson Rockefeller, Admiral Radford and the Deputy Director of Defense, Robert Anderson, are to stay in Paris during meeting. To be available upon call. May be asked to come over for a dinner or meeting.

Military Uniforms. Swiss Government has agreed to wearing of uniforms by the President's aides.

German unification. Secretary checked with the President wording of statement now being worked on by preliminary group in Paris. Military organization of Western and Eastern German Armies to be phrased less specifically than originally.

Statement of General Principles. Secretary of State suggested that a re-affirmation of the statement recently made in San Francisco by Van Kleffens would serve the purpose. Dulles said it was a good little statement and one the Soviets particularly wanted. Foreign Ministers have agreed to it. President agreed.

Seating Arrangement. After some discussion, it was agreed that Mr. Hagerty would sit in on those conferences which the President attends; he will not sit in on those conferences which President does not attend. This arrangement will enable Mr. Hagerty to report to the press some of the color of the conference. President agreed to the seating arrangement.

Dinner to be given July 21st by the President of Switzerland. This has been agreed upon.

For the sake of secrecy, we decided to fly to Paris on July 16, the same afternoon the President left for Geneva, reasoning that the media's involvement with the President's flight and activities would let us slip out of Washington unobserved. On the evening of July 19th, Colonel Goodpaster called me in my room at the Hotel de Crillon in Paris to say that the Big Four agreed that day that the subject of disarmament would be the sole topic of the July 21st session. The

President wanted Nelson Rockefeller and me in Geneva as soon as we could get there.

I told him we would arrive early the next morning. Goodpaster also said that he thought the President would want me to prepare his talk for that July 21st session; it should reflect the studies and report of my staff to the National Security Council on May 26th. But he cautioned: "Don't say anything about writing any speech for him until he asks you to do it himself."

I thanked Andy and settled back to reflect on the situation.

I called Nelson to alert him that the President wanted us in Geneva and began to prepare the draft of the President's disarmament speech. I wrote it on long yellow sheets, my tools since law school days, and still keep that draft that evolved through the long hours of the night of July 19-20.

I began with a recognition of statements made by the other participants in the opening session, already reported in the press.

> The statements made in this session and on the preceding days of this conference on the subject of disarmament by each of you have been followed by me with close interest.

> It is the most important subject on our agenda. It is also the most difficult. In recent years the scientists have discovered methods of making weapons many, many times more destructive of opposing armed forces, but also of homes, and industries, and lives, than ever known or even imagined before. These same scientific discoveries have made more complex the problems of limitation and control and reduction of armament.

This paragraph set out the basic conclusions of all our experts in the nuclear weapons field, the real root of our major concerns.

I then discussed where we stood in 1955 as we met at the summit, taking excerpts from our Progress Report to the NSC that the President approved on May 25th:

> After our common victory in World War II, my country rapidly disarmed. Within a few years our armament was at a very low level. Then events occurred beyond our borders which caused us to realize that we had disarmed too much. For our own security and to safeguard peace we needed greater strength. Therefore we proceeded to rearm and to associate with others in a partnership for peace and for mutual security.

This, of course, referred to North Korea's attack on South Korea and the European problems caused by the Soviet Union's presence in Poland and other Eastern Europe countries. I tried to use language not too abrasive, but still factual.

I wanted to let the Soviets know immediately that we intended to remain strong, and that they should not read our overtures on disarmament as a sign of pulling back on our part:

> My country is prepared to maintain and if necessary increase this armed strength for a long period of years if this is necessary to safeguard peace and to maintain our security.

Then came a paragraph used by President Eisenhower in his April 16th, 1953 speech to the American Society of Newspaper Publishers:

> But we also know that a mutually dependable system for less armament on the part of all nations would be a

327

better way to safeguard peace and to maintain our security.

This again projected the thinking the President expressed in his April 16th, 1953 "Chance for Peace" speech:

> It would ease the fears of war in the anxious hearts of people everywhere. It would lighten the burdens upon the backs of the people. It would make it possible for every nation, great and small, developed and less developed, to advance the standards of living of its people, to attain better food, and clothing, and shelter, more of education and larger enjoyment of life.

The next paragraph of my draft read:

> Therefore my government is prepared to enter into a sound and reliable agreement for less armament. I have directed that an intensive and thorough study of this subject be made. From these studies, which are continuing, a very important principle is emerging to which I referred in my opening statement on Monday.
>
> No sound and reliable agreement can be made unless it is completely covered by an inspection and reporting system adequate to support every portion of the agreement.

This, of course, reaffirmed our main premise of providing security against surprise attack. The world learned of these intensive studies when the President announced my appointment as special assistant for disarmament in March, for the specific purpose of working out practical safeguards.

> The lessons of history teach us that disarmament agreements without inspection increase the dangers of war and do not brighten the prospects of peace.

At that time we all remembered vividly the Japanese violations of the treaties on naval armaments after World War I and the German violations of the Versailles Treaty bans on building tanks. These breaches culminated in World War II.

> Thus it is my view that the priority focus of our combined study of disarmament should be upon the subject of inspection and reporting.
>
> How effective an inspection system can be designed which would be mutually and reciprocally acceptable within our countries and the other nations of the world? How would such a system operate? What could it accomplish? Is complete certainty against surprise aggression attainable by inspection? Could important violations be discovered promptly and effectively counteracted?

That series of questions, of course, mirrored our experience with the surprise attack by Japan at Pearl Harbor, and the Nazi's blitzkrieg of the Soviet Union on June 22, 1940, in violation of Hitler's "friendship" pact with Stalin in August 1939.

> We have not as yet been able to discover any scientific or other inspection method which would make certain of the elimination of nuclear weapons and would be interested in knowing if any other nation has made such a discovery. Our study of this problem is continuing. We have not as yet been able to discover any accounting or other inspection method of being certain of the true budgetary costs of total armament. Our study of this problem is continuing.
>
> As you can see from these statements, it is our impression that many, if not all, past proposals of disarmament are more widespread than can be covered by the inspection methods suggested.

This paragraph reflected all of the lengthy statements made over the years that the complete elimination of nuclear weapons from the face of the earth clearly could not be assured by any conceivable inspection method.

> From my statements I believe you will anticipate my suggestion. It is that we instruct our representatives in the U N Subcommittee on Disarmament to give priority attention to the study of inspection and reporting. Such a study could well include a step by step testing of inspection and reporting methods.

I reached that portion of the draft concerning the fundamental need to protect against surprise attack. Disarmament could come about only after we minimized each nation's fear of surprise attack. I knew that the President considered this, by far, the most important proposal of the entire summit. It also became the center of the dramatic series of conferences within the United States delegation, and finally influenced the President's decision to present it directly to the Soviet Union in a meaningful manner:

> I announce to you now that for the purposes of designing and testing an inspection and reporting system which will serve this magnificent objective of disarmament and peace, my government is ready in principle to permit trial inspection of units of our armed forces if other countries will do the same. My government is ready in principle to permit test aerial photographic inspection if other countries will do the same. My government is ready in principle to test inspection on the ground in specified comparable zones if other countries will do the same.

> We are ready to proceed in the study and testing of a reliable system of inspections and reporting, and when that system is designed, then to reduce armaments

together to the extent that the system will provide assured results.

. . . .

The successful working out of such a system would do much to develop the mutual confidence which will open wide the avenues of progress for all our peoples.

That ended my draft. On the following day, I also added in an "Insert B" on the quest for peace that came from a report of Nelson Rockefeller's panel.

The quest for peace is the statesman's most exacting duty. Security of the nations entrusted to his care is his greatest responsibility. Practical progress to lasting peace is his fondest hope. Yet we must not betray the trust placed in us as guardians of our people's security. A sound peace *can* be achieved but only on the basis of mutual knowledge as well as mutual good will. Only by following this hard but sure road to peace can we achieve our eventual goals of security, justice, well-being, and freedom for all the people of the world.

When Nelson Rockefeller and I arrived at Geneva on the morning of July 20, Colonel Andrew Goodpaster met us and took us immediately to our rooms at the du Rhone Hotel. We checked in, left our bags, and rode with Goodpaster to the President's "Geneva White House" in the Villa Creux de Genthod on Lake Geneva, five or six miles from the Palais de Nations where the formal summit sessions took place.

Rockefeller and I met the President at 10:30 a.m. He told us a bit about the opening session the day before: The Russians sat stoney-faced and impassive while Eisenhower presided, the only participant to hold the dual rank of Chief of State and head of government.

I said, "Mr. President, when you speak on disarmament tomorrow, I strongly recommend that you have Admiral

Radford with you, and also Al Gruenther [Supreme Commander of NATO and of U.S. armed forces in Europe]."

He turned to Colonel Goodpaster and told him to get Radford and Gruenther to Geneva as soon as possible. They arrived by plane that afternoon.

As the President left, Ann Whitman told me that he wished me to meet with him and Secretary Dulles in the Palais des Nations at 3:00 p.m., just before the afternoon session of the 20th. We met, and he said to me in Foster Dulles' presence, "Harold, I want you to prepare a draft of a speech for me to make tomorrow afternoon at the session on disarmament. I want you to prepare it as promptly as you can, and then have others work it over."

I replied, "I'll proceed at once, Mr. President."

"Report back with what you've drafted at 6:00, and we'll have a general conference on the subject."

Our six o'clock meeting with the President is reported by two memoranda, now declassified in the Eisenhower Library. Secretary of the NSC Dillon Anderson's, is the most complete:

July 21, 1955

MEMORANDUM FOR THE RECORD:

At a meeting at 6:00 p.m. on Wednesday, July 20, 1955, in the President's Villa at Geneva, the following attended:

The President

The Secretary of State

Mr. Livingston Merchant,
  Assistant Secretary of State
  for European Affairs

General Alfred M. Gruenther,
  Supreme Allied Commander in Europe

Admiral Arthur W. Radford,
  Chairman, Joint Chiefs of Staff

Mr. Robert B. Anderson,
  Deputy Secretary of Defense

Mr. Harold E. Stassen,
  Special Assistant to the President
  on Disarmament

Mr. Nelson A. Rockefeller,
  Special Assistant to the President

Mr. Dillon Anderson,
  Special Assistant to the President
  for National Security Affairs

Colonel Andrew J. Goodpaster,
  White House Staff Secretary

Governor Stassen handed to the President and read a "Draft of Statement of President Eisenhower on the Subject of Disarmament". A copy of that instrument is attached to the original of this memorandum.

The President expressed himself as being entirely in agreement with the principles enunciated in the paper, particularly with reference to the importance of an effective inspection system in connection with any kind of disarmament agreement.

The Goodpaster memorandum, "Meeting at the President's Villa, 6 PM, 20 July 1955," adds:

> Governor Stassen handed out a draft statement on Disarmament, of which the most striking idea was that of indicating willingness to agree to permit overflights of the U. S. and the USSR for aerial photography as a device for inspection. Mr. Robert Anderson indicated that the furnishing of lists of military installations should be coupled with that.

A copy of the typed manuscript that I handed out at 6:00 on July 20th is in the files of the Eisenhower Library.

After a brief discussion, I suggested to the President that because of time constraints, all participants should give me their comments by 11:00 the next morning (July 21). I would work them into my original draft, perhaps ending with alternative paragraphs to give the President options from which to make this final choice. We should all meet again at 2:00 in the afternoon, only two hours before the disarmament session opened. We could not make major revisions at that time, but only do some polishing.

The President agreed, and the meeting broke up, each one taking his copy of the draft.

Early the next morning, I met with Admiral Radford and General Gruenther, who approved my draft without any changes. Two days before, during our stand-by in Paris, Admiral Radford had told me that after searching his conscience and conferring with colleagues, he now supported the concept of aerial flyover inspections.

By 11:00, I received all the suggestions from the other participants, and began working on the final draft.

We met, as scheduled, in the President's office at 2:00. I reported the different suggestions. I told him that Secretary Dulles deleted the entire section of the draft that dealt with aerial inspection and the exchange of "blueprint" information on military installations, but my copy of the draft still included it.

The President looked to Dulles, who said that he did not think it wise to make the proposal at this Conference. We would need to consult our allies and Congressional leaders in advance.

The President countered:

> I spoke preliminarily to Anthony Eden yesterday morning and told him something about Stassen's work on this, and Jimmy Doolittle's idea. He said we could easily call Premier Faure and get his support. We can call Washington and tell Speaker Rayburn and Senator George what we propose; and I think they will approve.

I remember Dulles' exact words in response: "It has not been in my thinking of what should be included in this summit meeting."

My best judgment at this late date is that Dulles thought this final argument might win him the day, since the President would be reluctant to overrule his Secretary of State on a matter of this magnitude less than two hours before the formal summit session opened, but he misread Eisenhower, who added: "I believe this is sound, and I believe I should make the proposal."

Dulles did not give up easily. He argued:

> Well, if you're going to do it you should not include it in your opening statement. Save it for the second time around, when you get your second chance to speak. Then, you can include it in your rebuttal, and no one will be able to complain about a lack of advance consultation. In other words, since this will be Marshal Bulganin's turn to be chairman, he'll open the meeting, then turn to you on his left, and let you make the first

presentation. Make your statement without the reciprocal air photography and blueprint exchange section.
Let it go 'round to France and the U.K. Bulganin will
then make his statement; and you can make your follow-up with some comments on what the others have
said—then bring in this new proposal.

I made an instant decision to counter the Secretary's argument. I spoke in as even a tone as I could muster:

Mr. President, with all due respect to Foster, from
my own experience of negotiating with the Russians,
going back to the UN Charter sessions in San Francisco, that is not the way it will work. Bulganin will take
advantage of his chairmanship; and immediately after
he calls the session to order, he will not call on you to
speak first. He'll make his presentation on behalf of the
Soviets. He'll make it in full, and will be exact and
specific. Then, he'll call on you; and then France, and
the United Kingdom. When Anthony Eden finishes for
the U.K., Bulganin will make a brief comment, then
adjourn the meeting. You won't get a second time
around. There won't be any rebuttal; so if you feel
strongly about the reciprocal air photography and
blueprint exchange section, you'd better put it in when
he gives you your first and only chance to speak. Otherwise, you will not have any other opportunity.

The President turned to Secretary Dulles. "Foster, what
do you think?"
Dulles replied evenly, "Obviously, we have a difference of
opinion on how the Soviets will proceed."
The President answered in his "command tone":

Here's what we will do. Harold, prepare the manuscript which I will use without the air photography and
blueprint section; but mark plainly on it where that
portion should come in if I decide to use it.

336

I gathered up copies of the manuscript and rushed them to the typist for the final touches. I marked Eisenhower's copy with two large arrows on each side of page four where the "Open Skies" proposal would go in, and gave this to him separately.

The President asked me to accompany him to the afternoon session held in the Council Chambers, a huge amphitheater with high, muraled ceilings.

A square, four-sided table that could comfortably seat ten delegates on each of its sides filled the great hall, with rows of chairs for staff members behind it. The United States delegation faced a glassed-in wall of offices across the room where the recording secretaries worked and where the linguists made their simultaneous translations, broadcast into the earphones of the key attendees.

I glanced to the left side of the table where Anthony Eden and his assistants nodded to the President as he led us in. Premier Faure and his retinue, in their seats immediately in front of the glass wall, did the same. On our immediate right I recognized Marshal Bulganin, Chairman of the Council of Ministers, seated in the center of the Russian delegation, flanked by Foreign Minister V.M. Molotov; Deputy Foreign Minister Andrei Gromyko; Marshall Zhukov, Eisenhower's old comrade-in-arms, now Defense Minister; and Nikita Khrushchev, then known only as a member of the Presidium of the USSR Supreme Soviet.

I nodded to Molotov and Gromyko, momentarily recalling my negotiating days with them at the UN Charter meeting in San Francisco ten years earlier. Both remained impassive.

At the President's request, I sat directly behind him and Secretary Dulles, my chair actually between them.

We tuned our earphones to the proper volume to receive the simultaneous translation of Marshal Bulganin's call to order. Without losing a breath, he continued: "I have a statement to make on this subject on behalf of the Soviet Union," and he plunged into his formal speech.

When the translation began, the President turned to Dulles and me and said, "Harold's right! I'm going to put it in!"

Dulles nodded.

Each Russian speech took twice as long as those in other languages because the translators went more slowly. The Russians also insisted that the record show an "official" translation by their skilled interpreter, Troyanovsky, who trailed the tight-knit Russian group wherever they went.

The President doodled. After the meeting adjourned, I picked up a couple of his doodle sheets containing sketches of two of the Russians, looking surprisingly like Bulganin and Molotov.

When the second Russian translation finished, Bulganin called on President Eisenhower who started down through his prepared statement. When he reached the place where my arrows on page four told him to insert the "Open Skies" section he paused, took off his glasses, and looked directly at the Soviet table, his eyes scanning Bulganin, Molotov, Khrushchev, Zhukov, and their row of assistants and interpreters.

He personalized his message, speaking directly to the Soviets. By this time, he knew from memory exactly what he wanted to say about "Open Skies," and did not need to read from the text or even refer to it. He spoke from the heart, holding the entire room in his spell, even before the translations could unfold. I have never heard him more eloquent or forceful than in this short presentation. You can feel the spontaneity in its wording, including some redundancy to give emphasis:

Gentlemen, since I have been working on this memorandum to present to this Conference, I have been searching my heart and mind for something that I could say here that could convince everyone of the great sincerity of the United States in approaching this problem of disarmament.

I should address myself for a moment principally to the Delegates from the Soviet Union, because our two great countries admittedly possess new and terrible weapons in quantities which do give rise in other parts of the world, or reciprocally, to the fears and dangers of surprise attack.

I propose, therefore, that we take a practical step, that we begin an arrangement, very quickly, as between ourselves—immediately. These steps would include:

To give each other a complete blueprint of our military establishments, from beginning to end, from one end of our countries to the other; lay out the establishments and provide the blueprints to each other.

Next, to provide within our countries facilities for aerial photography to the other country—we to provide you the facilities within our country, ample facilities for aerial reconnaissance, where you can make all the pictures you choose and take them to your own country to study, you to provide exactly the same facilities for us and we to make these examinations, and by this step to convince the world that we are providing as between ourselves against the possibility of great surprise attack, thus lessening danger and relaxing tension. Likewise we will make more easily attainable a comprehensive and effective system of inspection and disarmament, because what I propose, I assure you, would be but a beginning.

The President returned to page four of the original manuscript and completed his presentation.

When the President finished speaking, Bulganin called on Premier Faure, who declared France's eager support of the

"Open Skies" proposal. Anthony Eden, in his turn, said that Great Britain would gladly open her own skies to aerial inspection.

This brought the program back to Bulganin who surprised us all by declaring that the President's proposal seemed to be sincere and worthy of study. Then he abruptly adjourned the meeting.

Following routine, the delegates and their aides moved into the reception room, also massive, lofty, and richly decorated, for refreshments and informal talk before going to their respective dinner engagements. Usually two delegations met together each evening.

I stood next to the President when Nikita Khrushchev, his interpreter at his side and the other Russians trailing behind, sort of elbowed his way up in front of the President, butting into the President's conversation with someone.

"Mr. President," he began through Troyanovsky, "I do not agree with Chairman Bulganin."

By this time Eden, Faure, Dulles, and almost everyone in the room had formed a ring around Khrushchev and Eisenhower, straining to hear what they said, the French whispering their translations of both the English and the Russian into their own language.

The Russian delegation hung back behind Khrushchev, silent, expressionless, listening to Khrushchev's talk, but choosing not to interrupt. I think that everyone in that circle made the same discovery at about the same moment: They saw and heard the real Russian ruler, Joe Stalin's stubborn successor. It mattered not what posts the rest now held or their future roles—Molotov and Gromyko as the executioners of the Kremlins' foreign policy, Bulganin the polished, dapper front man, and the President's old friend and comrade, Zhukov, head of Defense. The real power lay with the dumpy, feisty, flamboyant man who confronted Eisenhower.

"Mr. President," Khrushchev continued, "do I understand you to indicate that if we both cut loose with these modern weapons, it would be the end of civilization?"

The room fell deadly silent, the President obviously trying to figure out whether Khruschev's question could be serious, or if he tried to lay some sort of trap.

The President spoke through Ambassador Bohlen, a brilliant linguist:

> Mr. Khrushchev, surely your scientists and your generals are telling you the same thing ours are telling us. One of these bombs would devastate any major city, and then stir up death-dealing dust that will blow with the winds around the world. As you know, these winds blow west-to-east; so if we ever cut loose with a lot of these nuclear bombs, it will be the virtual end of civilization north of the equator. The human race would have to be carried on by those who live south of that line.

All in the room came from countries north of the equator.

An aura of reflection settled in. The Russians turned and walked away. In a few minutes, the hall emptied as we made our way to our dinner engagements.

Chapter 23
Summit Aftermath

Press Secretary Jim Hagerty quickly prepared handouts of transcripts of the President's disarmament proposal which some now-forgotten reporter labeled "Open Skies." The world media zeroed in on the specifics of aerial inspection and blueprint exchange, and clamored for more information. Hagerty told me the President suggested that I hold the press briefing since I knew more about the genesis and details of the concepts than anyone else.

The Eisenhower Library at Abilene contains the complete, thirteen-page transcript of my news conference.

I began with an opening statement (edited slightly to correct punctuation errors):

> GOVERNOR STASSEN: Gentlemen, I assume this is one of these evenings when there really isn't any need of a background session because there has been so much said in the foreground that covers the situation.
>
> It was quite a dramatic moment in the session when the President began to speak on the subject of disarmament. The center of attention was upon him immediately . . . [E]ven as he made his opening remarks, I think it was very evident to all . . . that he was speaking on the subject of which he has both deep convictions and extraordinary knowledge.
>
> I haven't found out whether Jim Hagerty, in his briefing, gave you the fact that when he came down to the

paragraph that begins "Gentlemen," on page 2 of the big mimeographed sheet, that he took off his glasses and looked over directly to Premier Bulganin and spoke . . . those next five paragraphs without a manuscript.

He then came back to his manuscript, down below, "Now from my statements . . . "

Of course . . . Faure spoke . . . of the deep feeling and the significance he gave to the President's remarks. He spoke of July 21 as being a date that would have great significance.

. . . [T]hen Prime Minister Eden spoke, going around in that rotation regularly. He said he felt it was a proposal that would advance the cause of peace. He came back to Chairman Bulganin, who earlier had presented a digest in abbreviated form of their May 10th proposal, when he opened this subject on the agenda.

Then Premier Bulganin said it was a matter of what to do with these various suggestions that had been made by that time, which had a lot of meaning in them . . . [He] suggested they be referred to the Foreign Ministers to see what action they would recommend . . .

There were many references by all four to the continuation of taking up this subject in the United Nations, particularly through the subcommittee on Disarmament . . . [A]s you may have noticed in the text, the President made a very specific reference to that, coming to it, in fact, immediately after this extemporaneous portion of the total message.

The anticipation would be that sometime after a brief period of weeks, this [UN] subcommittee would become active again. You recall they last met in London for an extended session. They were in London when the Soviets' May 10 proposals were made. Perhaps with the the anticipated convening of the General Assembly of the United Nations, it may be that the subcommittee would resume its work in New York, although that has not been decided as yet.

Under questioning, I emphasized that the proposals came from the President:

Q. Well, sir, is this particular thing about the blueprint, is it correct to infer that this might be called the first public fruits of the intensified study that you and your experts have made, or is it something that developed completely apart, separate from that, an idea that was conceived to try out?

A. Well, it's not a part inseparate [sic], but I would put it this way. Everything that is said in this statement comes from President Eisenhower. In other words, this is an Eisenhower message, an Eisenhower proposal, an Eisenhower approach. Now, what he does is always based on the most effective staff work he can mobilize.

Q. I just wanted to ask a follow-up question then, sir. Are you saying . . . that this blueprint reconnaissance thing was his idea?

A. I'm saying this is his proposal.

Q. Yes, but was it his idea?

A. Well, it is his idea, when he advances it.

Q. Governor, this is what you might call a break-through in the disarmament field. Could you give us the name of the man or the group that originated the idea of aerial reconnaissance as a way of approaching the problem?

A. No. All I would give you is that it's an Eisenhower proposal.

Q. Well, Governor, will you tell us again which of these paragraphs he ad libbed? Is it the one that starts, "Gentlemen" and ends up with "Now for my statement"?

A. That's right. He said, "As you can see from these statements, it is our impression that many past proposals of disarmament are more sweeping than can be

345

assured by effective inspection." Now, that short sentence has an awful lot of meaning, when you think of all the proposals that have . . . gone on during these years at the same time these scientists have been making tremendous strides in the weapons field. At that point he took off his glasses, and he turned to Premier Bulganin and he began, "Gentlemen," and then he continued down to where he says, "What I propose, I assure you, would be but a beginning." At that point he put his glasses back on and picked up his manuscript again and went back.

As the questions continued, I left no doubt that the President's proposal differed from those advanced by the UN subcommittee, theirs multinational, with arms inspections supervised by the UN. The President's new proposal involved bilateral actions directly between the U.S. and the USSR over and above the UN approach.

World reaction to the "Open Skies" proposal was nothing short of fantastic. For the first time in half a decade, emphasis shifted from an atmosphere of gloom and Armageddon because of the Cold War confrontations to hope that openness and mutual exchange could help avoid the catastrophe of World War III. Many prophets of doom sat back to reassess their predictions that this final conflagration would occur by 1970 or 1975 and that nothing could prevent it.

The mere face-to-face meeting of the four great leaders, plus the "Open Skies" proposal, offered hope, especially to the high school and college generation who felt themselves doomed. Everywhere, you could feel the heavy air of pessimism lighten into guarded relief, almost cautious euphoria. After all, life's struggles could again be meaningful.

The President's statements at the summit, of course, included more than "Open Skies" and blueprint exchange:

In recent years the scientists have discovered methods of making weapons many, many times more destructive of opposing armed forces—but also of homes, and industries and lives— than ever known or even imagined before. These same scientific discoveries have made more complex the problems of limitation and control and reduction of armament.

After our victory as Allies in World War II, my country rapidly disarmed. Within a few years our armament was at a very low level. Then events occurred beyond our borders which caused us to realize that we had disarmed too much. For our own security and to safeguard peace we needed greater strength. Therefore we proceeded to rearm and to associate with others in a partnership for peace and for mutual security.

The American people are determined to maintain and if necessary increase this armed strength for as long a period as is necessary to safeguard peace and to maintain our security.

But we know that a mutually dependable system for less armament on the part of all nations would be a better way to safeguard peace and to maintain our security.

It would ease the fears of war in the anxious hearts of people everywhere. It would lighten the burdens upon the backs of the people. It would make it possible for every nation, great and small, developed and less developed, to advance the standards of living of its people, to attain better food, and clothing, and shelter, more of education and larger enjoyment of life.

Therefore, the United States government is prepared to enter into a sound and reliable agreement making possible the reduction of armament. . . .

. . . .

The quest for peace is the statesman's most exacting duty. Security of the nation entrusted to his care is his greatest responsibility. Practical progress to lasting peace is his fondest hope. Yet in pursuit of his hope he must not betray the trust placed in him as guardian of the people's security. A sound peace—with security, justice, wellbeing [sic], and freedom for the people of the world—*can* be achieved, but only by patiently and thoughtfully following a hard and sure and tested road.

Dulles' inflexible attitude toward the summit generally, and his obvious coolness to "Open Skies" or much else other than German reunification, never abated. It shows clearly in his July 19 memo to the President, written and delivered in Geneva, two days before the summit's plenary session on arms limitation at 4:00 p.m., July 21:

SECRET

———

THE SECRETARY OF STATE
WASHINGTON

Geneva
July 19, 1955

MEMORANDUM FOR THE PRESIDENT
THE GENEVA WHITE HOUSE

———

A talk with Molotov in the buffet makes it clear to me that he at least hopes that the Conference will drop entirely the matter of German unification and leave Adenauer without any hope on this subject except such hope as he may derive from his prospective visit to Moscow.

On the other hand, it is our policy, and it is Adenauer's hope, that we will get established here the principle that there should be an early unification of Germany and a directive to a future meeting of the Four Foreign Ministers to find a European security framework which will make German unification possible.

Unless we can accomplish this latter result, our Conference here will, I think, be a failure. I think that it should be possible to get the principle of unification adopted and to get it remitted for study at a future meeting of Foreign Ministers along the lines of the draft resolution which I showed you this afternoon.

Perhaps you will have a chance to drive this home to Zhukov, as what you say to him will carry more weight than all else that can be said around the conference table.

John Foster Dulles

After Geneva, the president's approval rating at home soared to over eighty percent, which produced an interesting commentary on human nature: Anyone who ever passed close to the "Open Skies" concept tried to claim credit for it, no one knowing that it clearly originated with General Doolittle.

Until his death, Harry Truman remained more interested in bashing Eisenhower than in any effort to discover the facts. Again, we turn to Margaret Truman's quotes of her father in *Where the Buck Stops: The Personal and Private Writings of Harry S. Truman:*

I'll list some of the things Eisenhower didn't do when he was supposed to be running the country.

In July 1955, a meeting was arranged in Geneva between Eisenhower, the leaders of Great Britain and France and three important Russians: Nikolai Bulganin, the premier of Russia; Nikita Khrushchev, the

349

head of the Communist Party; and Georgi Zhukov, Russia's defense minister.

The word was that Eisenhower was going to arrange for world disarmament, at least in a limited way; arrange for the unification of the two Germanys; and ease the Cold War tensions between the United States and Russia.

Eisenhower was also going to push a good idea that wasn't his own, of course, but had been suggested by Nelson Rockefeller and some other people: an open-skies agreement that would allow the nations at the conference to fly freely and do photographic reconnaissance freely over the other countries so that the countries involved could make sure that armament, and any agreed disarmament, was kept within promised limitations. (New York: Warner Books, Inc., 1989)

I want to give Nelson Rockefeller full credit for what he actually did propose at Geneva: exchange programs of students, teachers, scientists, business leaders, artists, dancers, singers, any group that would help us reach out to the Communists, especially in the USSR. These exchanges of people and exhibits, renewed every four years by treaties, continued until President Carter stopped them after the Afghanistan invasion.

Nelson's proposals worked their way into the final conference communique:

Development of Contacts Between East and West

The foreign ministers should by means of experts study measures, including those possible in organs and agencies of the United Nations, which could (A) bring about a progressive elimination of barriers which interfere with free communications and peaceful trade between peoples and (B) bring about such free contacts and exchanges as are to the mutual advantage of the countries and peoples concerned.

The Foreign Ministers of the four powers will meet
at Geneva during October to initiate their consideration of these questions. . . .

The Rockefeller proposals did not touch even vaguely on
"Open Skies," "blueprint exchange," or any other facet of
disarmament.

I want to take this opportunity to clear up these important
points of history, and give credit where due. First, I reiterate
that the "Open Skies" concept came from General James
Doolittle, and no one else. We can trace its origin and evolution through official records at Abilene, directly from
Doolittle to me, through my disarmament team, to the
National Security Council, to the President's personal
approval, and to his own creative pronouncement at Geneva.

Second, the decision to include "Open Skies" in the
Geneva talks flowed directly from President Eisenhower's
firm control of foreign policy, which involved overruling his
own Secretary of State and other cabinet advisors.

His basic philosophy of openness among all nations and
reaching out to all nations marked a revolutionary change in
attitude, the first major shift away from Truman's inflexible
"containment" policy, unfortunately perpetuated for two-
and-one-half years by Secretary Dulles. It started the long,
tedious process that today gives hope for genuine arms reduction all over the world, even though the USSR balked at
implementing "Open Skies" at the Foreign Ministers meeting
the following October, while Eisenhower recuperated from
his heart attack.

I further believe that the President's pronouncements at
Geneva went a long way toward putting the brakes on a
reckless plunge toward World War III. Before Geneva, the
U.S. and the USSR butted heads because of Dulles' intransi-
gent belief that we needed to rely on strength alone—even to

the point of "going to the brink" if need be—and the Soviets' deepening paranoia about being invaded.

From today's perspective, with dozens of space satellites circling the earth and photographing every military post, arms manufacturing plant, transportation center, golf course trap, and blade of grass, the Geneva proposals seem primitive; but the world then did not know space orbits, Voyager fly-bys of Mars, Jupiter, and Saturn, or cameras that could read and record a soldier's rank on his collar from eighteen miles above the earth.

Still, I'm fascinated by George Bush's revival of "Open Skies" as a major foreign policy concept, and its experimental use by both NATO and the Warsaw Pact countries as a viable way to prevent surprise attack. Its value stems from the fact that slower, low-flying aircraft with special cameras and powerful sensors can gather important intelligence information that eludes inspection by satellites.

The important tools of diplomacy are not the new developments in technology which always change, nothing remaining the same. The key elements are approaches and attitudes; and I submit that Dwight Eisenhower's legacy consists of the constants of openness, reaching out, and mutuality, all of which will serve any president well— then, now, and into the future as far as we can see.

During the next three days, the President called me to the Oval Office several times where we critiqued the summit. He expressed guarded optimism, but said he knew that full implementation of the "Open Skies" proposal would be years, perhaps decades away. Because of their backgrounds in a closed society, the Soviet leaders could not view it on its face as a genuine peace offer, one they could safely embrace. But, he continued, "They will eventually change their attitudes. I am optimistic! World War III is not inevitable and containment alone is not the answer."

We discussed the possibilities of a personal follow-up with the Soviets that he would initiate, over and above the State Department's routines which then pointed only toward the ensuing Foreign Ministers meeting.

"What do you think of my writing directly to Marshal Bulganin?" he asked. "I doubt that Foster will want this, but I have a hunch that I need to do it."

"Play your instincts," I answered. "They have served you well in the past, and if that's what you feel like doing, by all means, do it!"

Two days later, he sent Bulganin a letter that I know to be genuine Eisenhower, a letter he personally drafted without any input from the State Department. It expressed his prayerful hope for the world:

> Dear Mr. Chairman:
>
> Now that the Four Power Conference has become a part of history, I want you to know how deeply I believe that our combined efforts during the past week produced an effect that will benefit the world. Good results should certainly spring from the solemn and repeated assurances by the leaders of both East and West that we intend, hereafter, to discuss our differences in conciliatory fashion and to seek in every case an answer that may satisfy the requirements of each side.
>
> I do not minimize the gravity of the problems which must be solved before world tranquility can be achieved. In your opening statement at Geneva, you named some of the matters that so greatly trouble the Soviet Union. In turn, I specified others profoundly disturbing to the entire population of the United States. Only statesmanship of a high order and an unshakeable resolution not to revert again, on either side, to some of the practices of the past, will permit progress toward and final solution of these critical problems.

I personally feel that some of the world tensions, of which we so often spoke at Geneva, have been eased by the fact of our meeting face to face and, during that eventful week, giving to the world a record of long and meaningful discussions and debate without either side, in any single instance, challenging the sincerity of the other or resorting to invective.

Since last Saturday evening, I have been thinking over your farewell words to me, which were to the effect, "Things are going to be better; they are going to come out right." To you and to your associates, I renew my own expressions of friendly interest and intent, and my lasting appreciation of the opportunities that were mine at Geneva for joining with you, Mr. Khrushchev, Mr. Molotov and Marshal Zhukov in so many fruitful discussions.

If we can continue along this line, with earnest efforts to be fair to each other and to achieve understanding of each other's problems, then, eventually, a durable peace based on right and justice will be the monument to the work which we have begun. This is the profound hope of our Government.

Will you please convey my greetings to those who accompanied you to Geneva, and with best wishes to yourself,

Sincerely,

/s/ Dwight D. Eisenhower

His Excellency
   Nicolai A. Bulganin
      Chairman of the Council of Ministers of the
         Union of Soviet Socialist Republics
         Moscow

This personal letter to Bulganin, "genuine Eisenhower" through and through, captures his basic philosophy of "reaching out" for peace to halt the slide into World War III.

Young people today cannot appreciate the aura of gloom that hung over the world when Eisenhower took office in 1953: At least since Korea, some of our national leaders (including Truman's Secretary of the Navy in a 1950 speech) called for a "preventive war" to silence the Russian menace while we still held the power to do it. General Orville Anderson, Commandant of the Air War College, that same year announced that the Air Force stood at the ready, awaiting orders to drop its atomic bombs on Moscow.

Political columnists of different hues regularly predicted Russia's entry into the Korean stalemate, putting us at war with the USSR on worldwide battlefields. Some of Chiang Kai-shek's U.S. supporters implored us to back his invasion of the mainland to wipe out Mao's Communists before they swallowed up all of Asia. Secretary of State Dean Acheson wrote of London's fright in the wake of Prime Minister Attlee's "long withdrawing, melancholy sigh" when he thought of the world situation.

The *Bulletin of the Atomic Scientists* showed their "Doomsday Clock" set at "two minutes to midnight." Albert Einstein received world-wide attention when he said that "general annihilation beckons," the only way out "a supranational judicial and executive body."

Teachers in some schools taught their pupils to be ready to crawl under desks when they heard the sirens signal the beginning of World War III.

Doom, gloom, fear, and depression gripped the world!

Eisenhower eased it by announcing new approaches in his inaugural message, by bringing the Korean War to a close, by feeding the starving Germans, by peacefully handling the China crisis, and finally by "reaching out" at the Geneva

Summit. There, he proposed his "Open Skies" concept to abate the universal fear of all nations of surprise attack, urged effective disarmament talks, showed the world the folly of world war and the need for cooperation, and forcefully restated the United States' dedication to peace.

Notwithstanding the intervening decades of lesser tragedies, the "Eisenhower Direction" is paying off today. Pray that it continues for the decade of the '90s and for the century ahead!

Appendix 1

MY LORD Mayor, My Lords, Ladies and Gentlemen:

The high sense of distinction I feel in receiving this great honor from the City of London is inescapably mingled with feelings of profound sadness. All of us must always regret that your country and mine were ever faced with the tragic situation that compelled the appointment of an Allied commander-in-chief, the capacity in which I have just been so extravagantly commended.

Humility must always be the portion of any man who receives acclaim earned in the blood of his followers and the sacrifices of his friends. Conceivably a commander may have been professionally superior. He may have given everything of his heart and mind to meet the spiritual and physical needs of his comrades. He may have written a chapter that will glow forever in the pages of military history. Still, even such a man, if he existed, would sadly face the facts that his honors cannot hide in his memories the crosses marking the resting places of the dead. They cannot soothe the anguish of the widow or the orphan whose husband or father will not return.

The only attitude in which a commander may with satisfaction receive the tributes of his friends is in

357

humble acknowledgment that, no matter how unworthy he may be, his position is a symbol of great human forces that have labored arduously and successfully for a righteous cause. Unless he feels this symbolism and this rightness in what he has tried to do, then he is disregardful of the courage, the fortitude and devotion of the vast multitudes he has been honored to command. If all the Allied men and women that have served with me in this war can only know that it is they this august body is really honoring today then, indeed, will I be content.

This feeling of humility cannot erase, of course, my great pride in being tendered the Freedom of London. I am not a native of this land. I come from the very heart of America. In the superficial aspects by which we ordinarily recognize family relationships the town where I was born and the one where I was reared are far separated from this great city. Abilene, Kansas, and Denison, Texas, would together add in size to possibly one five hundredth part of Greater London. By your standards those towns are young, without your aged traditions that carry the roots of London back into the uncertainties of unrecorded history. To these people I am proud to belong, but I find myself today five thousand miles from that countryside, the honored guest of a city whose name stands for grandeur and size throughout the world. Hardly would it seem possible for the London Council to have gone farther afield to find a man to honor with its priceless gift of token citizenship.

Yet kinship among nations is not determined in such measurements as proximity, size and age. Rather we should turn to those inner things, call them what you will—I mean those intangibles that are the real treasures free men possess. To preserve his freedom of worship, his equality before the law, his liberty to speak and act as he sees fit, subject only to the provision that he trespass not upon similar rights of others—the Londoner will fight! So will the citizen of

Abilene! When we consider these things then the valley of the Thames draws closer to the farms of Kansas and the plains of Texas. To my mind it is clear that when two peoples will face the tragedies of war to defend the same spiritual values, the same treasured rights, then, in deepest sense those two are truly related. So, even as I proclaim my undying Americanism, I am bold enough, and exceedingly proud to claim, basic kinship to you of London.

And what man who has followed the history of this war could fail to experience inspiration from the example of this city? When the British Empire stood—alone but unconquered, almost naked but unafraid—to defy the Hitler hordes, it was on this devoted city that the first terroristic blows were launched.

Five years and eight months of war, much of it on the actual battleline! Blitzes, big and little, fly-bombs, V-bombs; all of them you took in your stride. You worked—from your needed efforts you would not be deterred. You carried on, and from your midst arose no cry for mercy, no wail of defeat. The Battle of Britain will take its place as another of your deathless traditions. And your faith and endurance have finally been rewarded.

You had been more than two years in war when Americans, in numbers, began swarming into your country. Most were mentally unprepared for the realities of war—especially as waged by the Nazis. Others believed that tales of British sacrifice had been exaggerated. Still others failed to recognize the difficulties of the task ahead.

All such doubts, questions and complacencies could not endure a single casual tour through your scarred streets and avenues. With awe our men gazed upon empty spaces where once had stood buildings erected by the toil and sweat of peaceful folk. Our eyes rounded as we saw your women serving quietly and efficiently in almost every kind of war effort, even flak batteries. We became accustomed to the warning sirens, which seemed to compel, from the native Londoner, not a single hurried step. Gradually we drew closer together until we became true partners in the war.

In London, my associates and I planned two great expeditions, that to invade the Mediterranean and later that to cross the Channel. London's hospitality to Americans, her good-humored acceptance of the added inconveniences we brought, her example of fortitude and quiet confidence in the final outcome—all these helped to make the supreme headquarters of two Allied expeditions the smooth-working organizations they became! They were composed of chosen representatives of two proud and independent peoples, each noted for its initiative and for its satisfaction with its own customs, manners and methods. Many feared that these representatives could never combine together in efficient fashion to solve the complex problems presented by modern war.

I hope you believe we proved the doubters wrong! Moreover, I hold that we proved this point not only for war—we proved that it can always be done by our two peoples, provided only both show the same good will, the same forbearance, the same objective attitude that British and Americans so amply demonstrated in nearly three years of bitter campaigning.

No one man could, alone, have brought about this result. Had I possessed the military skill of a Marlborough, the wisdom of Solomon, the understanding of Lincoln, I still would have been helpless without the loyalty, the vision, the generosity of thousands upon thousands of British and Americans. Some of them were my companions in the high command, many were enlisted men and junior officers carrying the fierce brunt of the battle, and many others were back in the U.S. and here in Great Britain, in London. Moreover, back of us were always our great national war leaders and their civil and military staffs that supported and encouraged us through every trial, every test. The whole was one great team. I know that on this special occasion, the three million American men and women serving in the Allied Expeditionary Force would want me to pay the tribute of admiration, respect and affection to their British comrades of this war.

My most cherished hope is that, after Japan joins the Nazi in utter defeat, neither my country nor yours need ever again summon its sons and daughters from their peaceful pursuits to face the tragedies of battle. But—a fact important for both of us to remember—neither London nor Abilene, sisters under the skin, will sell her birthright for physical safety, her liberty for mere existence.

No petty differences in the world of trade, traditions or national pride should ever blind us to identities in priceless values. If we keep our eyes on this guidepost then no difficulties along our path of mutual co-operation can ever be insurmountable. Moreover, when this truth has permeated to the remotest hamlet and heart of all peoples, then indeed may we beat our swords to plowshares and all nations can enjoy the fruitfulness of the earth.

My Lord Mayor, I thank you once again for an honor to me and to the American forces that will remain one of the proudest in my memories.

Appendix 2

My letter to Eisenhower following the White House announcement on April 11, 1952, that Eisenhower would be relieved of his NATO duties June 1, retired from the Army, and returned to the United States.

On the top of this copy from the Eisenhower Library the name "McCann" appears in Eisenhower's handwriting, indicating that Eisenhower read it and referred it to Kevin McCann, his aide.

HAROLD E. STASSEN
8212 ST. MARTINS LANE
PHILADELPHIA 18

April 14, 1952

General Dwight D. Eisenhower
Supreme Commander SHAPE
APO 55, Postmaster
New York, New York

Dear General:

It was great news that you will be back here June 1st.
When your letter was released I issued the following statement:

"General Eisenhower has performed a near miracle in his
one year of service in rebuilding the morale, the spirit
and the defense of Western Europe. He deserves a 'well
done' from the American people for this additional service in his illustrious career.

"We will await with interest his statements and his actions
upon his return to America on June 1st."

My attitude continues to be the same as it was last
mid-December. Senator Taft continues to be very strong within
the Republican organization but thus far has been prevented from
buttoning up sufficient strength for a nomination.

As I anticipated, my entry last December and my direct
challenge to him did spread out his effort. It led directly to
his entry into New Hampshire, whereupon I did not enter any New
Hampshire delegates and centered my effort on his bad foreign
policy record.

I am following the same course in my New Jersey speeches
and I am confident you will win a decisive victory there tomorrow.

In Pennsylvania where only your name and mine are entered you will win an overwhelming vote and I will make no anti-
campaign.

In Ohio on May 6th Taft has the big edge, but if your
local supporters back my delegates we may win a few delegates
away from him.

365

HAROLD E. STASSEN
8212 ST. MARTINS LANE
PHILADELPHIA 18

Page #2 - General Eisenhower

Having set out on my present course it seems best
that I carry it through even though it is rough. Weak though
my position is, I believe it would leave a greater vacuum
versus Taft if I dropped out, especially before June 1st.

Thus I intend to carry on through the various national
forums, stressing the issues and platform views which I hold,
and opposing Senator Taft's policies.

Perhaps after June 1st we can have another talk.
Until then, my sincere regards to you.

HES/mc

Appendix 3

CHIEF JUSTICE WARREN BURGER'S DESCRIPTION OF THE 1952 REPUBLICAN NOMINATION OF GENERAL EISENHOWER

In mid-summer, 1966, an editor of LIFE called Warren Burger, then a justice of the District of Columbia Circuit Court of Appeals, to tell him that while cleaning out LIFE's photo morgue, they found several pictures of the Justice at the end of the balloting at the 1952 Republican Convention in Chicago.

Would the Justice like them?

Burger said, "Yes," and dictated a memorandum for historical purposes to accompany the photographs. One copy came to me in 1966 and lay dormant in my files until its first public appearance here.

Subheadings are inserted for readability and emphasis.

MEMORANDUM RELATING TO *LIFE* PHOTOS DEPICTING THE SCENES OF THE BALLOTING NOMINATING GENERAL EISENHOWER AS REPUBLICAN CANDIDATE FOR PRESIDENT

[1951 MEETING AT McALPIN HOTEL]

The story behind these *LIFE* photos goes back to a meeting in December 1951 at the McAlpin Hotel in New York City. Governor Stassen had consulted with

367

several close friends beginning late in 1950 concerning the 1952 Republican prospects.

Stassen had expressed his view that General Eisenhower could secure the nomination if he wished and could be elected and that Taft, then the leading "regular" Republican contender, would probably secure the nomination if Eisenhower did not contest his claim, but that Taft would lose the election.

[STASSEN'S PARIS VISIT WITH EISENHOWER]

Stassen concluded to go to Paris late in November 1951 to express to General Eisenhower his views that a determined effort was required to prevent a Taft nomination.

Stassen went to Paris and we received word that he had seen General Eisenhower and that he wished to meet with us when he docked in New York City on the Queen Mary. We met after his delayed arrival (due to storms).

Present at the McAlpin Hotel were: Stassen, Amos Peaslee, Daniel Gainey, Bernard Shanley, Elmer Ryan and Warren E. Burger.

[FEARED TAFT NOMINATION]

Stassen reported he had a cordial visit with the General but the General neither agreed nor disagreed with his appraisal but was firm that he would not return to the United States and campaign for the nomination.

Stassen felt the General was genuinely interested in serving but not on any basis other than good faith draft.

Stassen then repeated his conclusion that if the General adhered to his position, Taft would have the nomination in his grasp before the Convention, notwithstanding the Liberals and moderates of the

GOP were against Taft. Dewey, Lodge and Stassen all preferred the General. Earl Warren's position was not clear.

[STASSEN SHOULD NOT SACRIFICE HIMSELF]

Stassen said he still could see no way to keep the Convention choice open to the General or some other moderate candidate except to enter the contest himself and oppose Taft "in the flesh" on the basis of Taft's views and force Taft into contests for delegates in as many states as possible.

Stassen felt Taft was vulnerable in certain Ohio districts, and that his weaknesses with Labor and moderates could thus be shown.

All present pointed to Stassen's lack of a political base, lack of financing, and organization. All felt the effort would damage Stassen and that he ought not sacrifice himself; two present urged him immediately, indeed that very day, to seek an understanding with those shaping up as the General's leaders, and then proceed on an agreed program.

[STASSEN SAID HE MUST BECOME "BONA FIDE CANDIDATE"]

Dewey, Brownell, Lodge and others were emerging as leaders of a "Draft Ike" movement. Stassen disagreed, pointing out he had to gain support from some people leaning to Taft and that he could not carry out the role he contemplated except as a bona fide candidate and that he would not be willing to deceive his friends who preferred Taft over Eisenhower, even though the purpose and hopeful effect of his program would be to help the General get the nomination.

[STASSEN FOOLISH TO RISK POLITICAL DESTRUCTION]

The discussion became very heated and emotional at one point with Ryan saying Stassen was foolish to risk political destruction without an understanding with the Eisenhower forces and that in any event he, Stassen, would be accused of being a stalking horse by the Taft forces.

Stassen responded by saying he would understand fully if those present immediately worked with the General's friends rather than to support his strategy and that every one was free to do so with his blessings. But he said he had a firm conviction that he could not effectively or conscientiously enter the contest unless he was in fact a free agent, even while recognizing that he had no prospects in reality.

[NEED CANDIDATE TO STOP TAFT]

Ryan, I believe, argued that Stassen would be accused of trying to position himself for a compromise in case of a deadlock between Taft and Eisenhower.

Stassen's answer was that by the time he opposed Taft in state Primaries from April to July, including Ohio, Taft would never willingly release a single delegate to him and that someone else was likely to emerge as a compromise candidate if a deadlock developed. This, said Stassen rather grimly, as I recall, would then dissolve all accusations.

All present finally agreed to support whatever program Stassen finally pursued and a larger meeting was discussed for a later date to canvass the situation after Eisenhower had a few more months to view developments and recognize that Taft would take the nomination absent active opposition.

All agreed that Dewey had shot his bolt, that only an active and determined campaign by someone like

Stassen, Lodge or Earl Warren could prevent delegates from making early commitments to Taft.

[THREE BASIC PROPOSITIONS]

When the meeting concluded Stassen summarized the day's discussion and his conclusion to enter unless some other moderate or liberal acceptable to us entered the field early in 1952.

He then said he wanted to lay down three basic and controlling propositions to guide our thinking from then until Eisenhower or some other moderate got the nomination. The three propositions were:

1. Do nothing to injure or impede an Eisenhower nomination.

2. Do nothing to aid Taft.

3. That at any time Stassen's strength, however small, added to Eisenhower's would gain a nomination, that was to be done swiftly and decisively, because Taft would be strong until defeated.

Stassen had this written and after the meeting I copied it almost verbatim and kept it with other notes on the discussion.

[DEPRESSION OVER RISKS TO STASSEN]

All present agreed to the proposed course but most of us were depressed at the personal hazards Stassen was assuming and apprehensive as to the misunderstandings which could ensue in the circumstances, absent some understanding with the General's friends.

[PAINFUL PERIOD BEFORE CONVENTION]

The three propositions laid down were faithfully adhered to once Stassen embarked on his course.

In the painful period while Stassen doggedly pursued his difficult course through the Convention in July, 1952, Ryan and Gainey chaffed [sic] at the restraints of not making some expression, however informal to Brownell or Lodge, although as July 1952 approached the latter could not have failed to see that what Stassen was doing was in the General's interests, so close was the struggle for delegates.

Stassen endured the biting criticism of some of his oldest supporters [for] entering the contest. But Stassen's analysis was that this tied Taft down with money, energy and personnel involved in protecting his own power base, and more important, showed that Taft was "wrong" on foreign policy and weak with independent voters.

[TAFT ADMITTED STASSEN WEAKENED HIM]

Few people ever grasped Stassen's strategy on this score but on one occasion Taft acidly commented to me that Stassen's contest against him weakened him with internationalists and independents whose support was vital to any Republican.

[EMOTIONAL ENCOUNTERS WITH EISENHOWER SUPPORTERS]

We pursued this course, difficult as it was; it included some emotional encounters with Eisenhower supporters in the lower echelons although there were none such with Brownell or Lodge.

[CREDENTIALS COMMITTEE VOTES: "NEUTRAL—AGAINST TAFT"]

At the Convention I went on the Credentials Committee at Stassen's urging, because he had correctly analyzed, as had Brownell, that the battle would be won or lost in that forum. Stassen, Brownell, and I conferred on my taking a place on the Credentials Committee. In keeping with our program I informed Brownell, Dewey, and Lodge that I did not want to be regarded as committed to General Eisenhower but would pursue my own course in the Credentials battles. I did so, but on three or four highly critical votes, and in debate, my position was decisive in favor of Eisenhower. Clarence Brown, Taft's Floor Manager, sarcastically, but not bitterly, described my position in the Credentials Committee as "neutral—against Taft."

In the days before the balloting I was in constant contact with Brownell, Lodge, Dewey and to some extent with Nixon, who was vainly trying to smoke out Earl Warren.

[WARREN WOULD NOT SWITCH TO EISENHOWER]

Stassen tried with no success to prevail on Earl Warren to join in a decisive swing to Eisenhower.

Stassen had designated Gainey and me as Floor Managers. Earlier I had attended a meeting of all Floor Managers in Joe Martin's office to agree on procedures and recess time. Present were Lodge, Adams, Clarence Brown, Bill Knowland, Gainey and myself.

[AGREEMENT WITH MARTIN THAT RULES PERMITTED MINNESOTA TO CHANGE VOTE]

I lingered after the meeting and asked Joe Martin if I correctly construed the Convention Rules to mean that

373

Minnesota could change its vote after casting one ballot for Stassen on the Roll Call. Martin said that until
his gavel went down announcing the first ballot vote,
any delegate or delegation could change. He smiled
and said he would keep that in mind in light of our
conversation.

[NIXON COULD NOT "SMOKE OUT" WARREN]

At 2:00 A.M. the morning of the balloting, I met with
Stassen and reported that Nixon's efforts to smoke out
Earl Warren were barren, that Knowland was noncom-
mittal to the point of rudeness.

Our floor checks, which had been more accurate on
the delegate contests than those of Lodge and Adams,
showed that the vote would be very close on the first
ballot. We agreed that our 20 odd delegates might be
decisive.

[DISTURBED BY EISENHOWER "AMATEURS"]

We were both disturbed by the excesses of the "amateur" Eisenhower followers who had made vicious
attacks on Taft with placards like the "Louisiana
Purchase" and the "Texas Steal"; we feared that the
bitterness of the Taft forces might be heightened more
if Taft lost by a hairline decision of the Convention
than if there was a decisive first ballot nomination.

[STASSEN WANTED MINNESOTA DELEGATE SHIFT
TO COME SWIFTLY]

We decided one more effort should be made to get
California to join with us and secure Eisenhower's
nomination swiftly and decisively. We reviewed the
timing of changing the vote of the Stassen delegates
and Stassen emphasized the crucial need for decisive
action on the floor. He said in case communication was
delayed or messages came through out of time or out of

374

order, the "battle plan" agreed on at the 1951 McAlpin Hotel Conference still held and he would expect us to move swiftly to shift his delegates to the General whenever that would assure his nomination.

[WARREN AND KNOWLAND WOULD NOT COOPERATE]

We agreed that I should make one more effort and offer California the option to announce a change in Stassen's votes and Warren's to clinch the General's nomination. Before the balloting I went to Bill Knowland at the Convention Hall and proposed that we do this. I tried to engage Earl Warren in the conversation but he smiled politely and walked away. Knowland, more truculent than usual, said, "We do not want the credit, or the responsibility for an Eisenhower nomination." (Sherman Adams reports this in his book and Knowland has never challenged this episode.) I should add I suggested that Knowland or Earl Warren go to the podium and make the announcement for both California and Minnesota.

[THIRD PARAGRAPH OF STASSEN "BATTLE PLAN" PUT INTO EFFECT]

The Convention then proceeded to the first ballot and when it was 80% complete it was quite clear that Eisenhower would be only a dozen votes more or less from the nomination and that the third paragraph of Stassen's "battle plan" would go into effect.

[PICTURES SHOW FINAL SECONDS OF BALLOTING]

Before Joe Martin had announced the result, we raised our standard; Martin recognized Minnesota and we responded changing all of Stassen's votes to the General. The pictures show the sequence of the final 200-300 seconds of this balloting when Gainey and I agreed on the shift and then consulted Senator Thye.

[The foregoing was prepared from notes made between December 1950 and August 1952]

/s/Warren E. Burger

Washington, D. C.
September 1966

Appendix 4

STATE OF THE UNION ADDRESS
FEBRUARY 2, 1953

DELIVERED SPEECH	DRAFT #4
TO CONGRESS	(STASSEN)

I welcome the honor of appearing before you to deliver my first message to the Congress.

It is manifestly the joint purpose of the Congressional leadership and of this Administration to justify the summons to governmental responsibility issued last November by the American people.

I welcome the honor of appearing personally before you to deliver my first message to the Congress.

The time calls for plain talk and purposeful action. The people have demanded a true and constructive change in their leadership. It is the manifest purpose of my Administration to justify their resounding call to office.

. . . .

SPEECH	DRAFT
The grand labors of this leadership will involve:	These truths tell us what must be the grand labors of leadership. They are:
Application of our influence in world affairs with such fortitude and such foresight that it will deter aggression and eventually secure peace;	To apply our strength in world affairs with such fortitude and such foresight that it will deter aggression and secure peace;
Establishment of a national administration of such integrity and such efficiency that its honor at home will ensure respect abroad;	To give to our own people a government of such integrity and such efficiency that its honor at home will ensure respect abroad;
. . . .	. . . .
Dedication to the well-being of all our citizens and to the attainment of equality of opportunity for all, so that our nation will ever act with the strength of unity in every task to which it is called.	And to foster the well-being and ensure the equality of opportunity enjoyed by all our citizens, that the freedom we enjoy may inspire free men everywhere.
The purpose of this message is to suggest certain lines along which our joint efforts may immediately be directed toward realization of these four ruling purposes.	So believing, let us see clearly the specific tasks before us.
. . . .	

SPEECH

Our country has come through a painful period of trial and disillusionment since the victory of 1945. We anticipated a world of peace and cooperation. The calculated pressures of aggressive Communism have forced us, instead, to live in a world of turmoil.

. . . .

First: Revising our customs regulations to remove procedural obstacles to profitable trade. I further recommend that the Congress take the Reciprocal Trade Agreements Act under immediate study and extend it by appropriate legislation. This objective must not ignore legitimate safeguarding of domestic industries, agriculture and labor standards. In all Executive study and recommendations on this problem, labor and management and farmers alike will be earnestly consulted.

DRAFT

Our country has come through a painful period of trial and disillusion since the joyful summer of victory in 1945. We anticipated a world of peace and productivity. The calculated aggression of Stalinism has forced us, instead, to live in a world of turmoil.

. . . .

First: This entails—as the essential beginnings—revision of our customs regulations to encourage trade and extension of the Reciprocal Trade Agreements Act. This objective need not and should not ignore legitimate protection of industries, agriculture and our labor standards. Labor, and management and farmers alike will be represented in Executive study and recommendation on this problem.

SPEECH	DRAFT
Second: Doing whatever government properly can to encourage the flow of private American investment abroad. This involves, as a serious and explicit purpose of our foreign policy, the encouragement of a hospitable climate for such investment in foreign nations.	Second: We must do all that government. . . .
Third: Availing ourselves of facilities overseas for the economical production of manufactured articles which are needed for mutual defense and which are not seriously competitive with our own normal peacetime production.	Third: We must avail ourselves. . . .
Fourth: Receiving from the rest of the world, in equitable exchange for what we supply, greater amounts of important raw materials which we do not ourselves possess in adequate quantities.	Fourth: We should receive from. . . .
In this general discussion of our foreign policy, I must make special mention of the war in Korea.	I have made, as you know, a visit to the fighting fronts of Korea.

SPEECH	DRAFT
	I increased markedly my understanding of the physical and military conditions in that unhappy region; most of what I learned beyond the scope of the normal press report falls under the prohibition of military security.
. . . .	. . . .
I am, therefore, issuing instructions that the Seventh Fleet no longer be employed to shield Communist China. This order implies no aggressive intent on our part. But we certainly have no obligation to protect a nation fighting us in Korea.	It is senseless that the United States Navy should be assuming defensive responsibilities on behalf of the Chinese Communists so that they can, with greater impunity, kill our soldiers and those of our United Nations allies, in Korea. I am, therefore, issuing instructions that the Seventh Fleet no longer be employed to shield Communist China.
. . . .	. . . .
Especially must we remember that the institutions of trade unionism and collective bargaining are monuments to the freedom that must prevail in our industrial life. They have a century of honorable achievement behind them. Our faith in them is proven, firm and final.	. . . . The institutions of trade unionism and collective bargaining are monuments to the freedom that must prevail in our industrial life. They have a century of honorable achievements behind them. Our faith in them is proven, firm and final.

381

SPEECH	DRAFT
. . . .	. . . .
I propose to use whatever authority exists in the office of the President to end segregation in the District of Columbia, including the federal government, and any segregation in the armed forces.	I propose to use whatever authority exists in the office of the President to end segregation in the District of Columbia, in the federal government, and in the armed forces.
. . . .	. . . .
There is—in our affairs at home—a middle way between untrammelled freedom of the individual and the demands for the welfare of the whole Nation. This way must avoid government by bureaucracy as carefully as it avoids neglect of the helpless.	There is—in our affairs at home—a middle way between the rights of individual freedom and the demands for governmental action.

One more example from the State of the Union Address shows Eisenhower's penchant for shortening his speeches:

DELIVERED SPEECH TO CONGRESS	DRAFT #4
(Approximately 275 words)	(Approximately 550 words)
Both military and economic objectives demand a single national military policy, proper coordination of our armed services, and effec-	Both military and economic objectives coincide. They both demand effective unification of military policy, proper coordination of our

SPEECH	DRAFT
tive consolidation of certain logistics activities.	armed services, and effective consolidation of certain logistics activities.
We must eliminate waste and duplication of effort in the armed services.	From this fact, certain basic rules of conduct follow.
We must realize clearly that size alone is not sufficient. The biggest force is not necessarily the best—and we want the best.	We must strive tirelessly to eliminate any waste and duplication of effort in our armed services.
We must not let traditions or habits of the past stand in the way of developing an efficient military force. All members of our forces must be ever mindful that they serve under a single flag and for a single cause.	We must realize clearly that size matters less than quality: The biggest force is not necessarily the best—and we want the best.
. . . .	We must not let traditions or habits of the past stand in the way of developing an efficient military force. Each individual member of our forces must be ever mindful that we fight under one flag and for one cause, that of freedom.
. . . . This record includes our inherited burden of indebtedness and obligations and deficits.	
The current year's budget, as you know, carries a 5.9 billion dollar deficit, and the budget which was presented to you before this Administration took office, indicates	-p. 16- A. THE BURDEN OF DEBTS AND DEFICITS It is important for everyone

SPEECH

a budgetary deficit of 9.9 billion for the fiscal year ending June 30, 1954. The national debt is now more than 265 billion dollars. In addition, the accumulated obligational authority of the federal government for future payment totals over 80 billion dollars. Even this amount is exclusive of large contingent liabilities, so numerous and extensive as to be almost beyond accurate description.

The bills for the payment of nearly all of the 80 billion dollars of obligations will be presented during the next four years. These bills, added to the current costs of government we must meet, make a formidable burden.

The present authorized government debt limit is 275 billion dollars. The forecast presented by the outgoing Administration with the fiscal year 1954 budget indicates that—before the end of the fiscal year and at the peak of demand for payments during the year—the total government debt may approach and even exceed that limit. Unless budgeted deficits are checked, the momentum of past programs

DRAFT

to understand that this Administration does not and cannot begin its task with a clean slate. Much already has been written on the record, beyond our power quickly to erase or to amend.

As we begin our joint responsibility of shouldering and moving forward with the task of our America we have a very serious handicap in the form of the burden left behind of indebtedness and obligations and deficits by those who preceded us.

The national debt, as you know, is now 270 billion dollars. The current year's budget, as you know, carries a 5.9 billion dollar deficit, and the budget which was presented to you before we took office, indicates a budgetary deficit of 9.9 billion for the fiscal year ending June 30, 1954. Not so well known is another serious part of the load we must carry. The accumulated additional obligational authority of the federal government, representing orders and commitments and promises for future payment, for defense production and other items, now totals

384

SPEECH	DRAFT
will force an increase of the statutory debt limit.	billion dollars. The bills for the payment of nearly all of these obligations will be presented during our Administration. Taken together, this is an unprecedented burden upon the government of our country.
Permit me this one understatement: To meet and to correct this situation will not be easy.	
Permit me this one assurance: Every Department head and I are determined to do everything we can to resolve it.	

-p. 17-

Thus, in addition to meeting the expenses of the things we do, the orders we place, the obligations we make from this day forward, we must at the same time carry, with large interest costs, or gradually pay off, this mammoth burden. We will do it. But it will not be easy. It will require the understanding support and heavy tax paying for yet a while by the citizens of the land.

You may be assured I will begin at once to do everything I can to improve this situation.

I have directed an examination of the appropriations

SPEECH

DRAFT

and expenditures of all departments in an effort to find significant amounts that may be impounded without damage to our essential responsibilities. In this way we can begin to do what has to be done—not in June 1954—but now. When such opportunities for economies are determined, they will be reported to the appropriate committees of the Congress.

The forecast presented with the fiscal year 1954 budget indicates the total government debt will approach the authorized limit of $275 billion at the end of the fiscal year 1954. Unless this deficit trend can be checked, the momentum of present programs or unforeseeable events may force a reconsideration of the statutory debt limit.

These results and possibilities cannot be modified or changed without forms of action which may be unpalatable to some of us, but is [sic] demanded by most of us. While we are prepared to take whatever action is necessary, that endeavor can proceed only with the full

SPEECH   DRAFT

understanding and cooperation of the Congress and of
all our people.

The President added new material of his own throughout
my Draft #4.

He loathed and feared waste and inefficiency in bureaucracy, in the army, in industry, in labor, in academia, and
especially in "big government." His inserts, with some later
polishing, ran:

There is more involved here than realigning the
wheels and smoothing the gears of administrative
machinery. The Congress rightfully expects the Executive to take the initiative in discovering and removing
outmoded functions and eliminating duplication.

One agency, for example, whose head has promised
early and vigorous action to provide greater efficiency
is the Post Office. . . .

There are, today, in some areas of the postal service,
both waste and incompetence to be corrected. With the
cooperation of the Congress, and taking advantage of
its accumulated experience in postal affairs, the Postmaster General will institute a program directed at
improving service while at the same time reducing
costs and decreasing deficits.

In all Departments, dedication to these basic
precepts of security and efficiency, integrity and economy can and will produce an Administration deserving
of the trust the people have placed in it.

Our people have demanded nothing less than good,
efficient government. They shall get nothing less.

. . . The best natural resources program for America
will not result from exclusive dependence on federal
bureaucracy.

. . . [T]he welfare of the people demands effective and economical performance by the government of certain indispensable social services.

. . . I shall shortly send you specific recommendations for . . . a reorganization plan defining new administrative status for all federal activities in health, education, and social security.

Appendix 5

When the pressures of the presidency built up, Eisenhower felt the need to "let go" in the form of letters to close friends and longtime associates. He dictated many of these with practically no later editing. With others, he meticulously edited and rewrote them.

I include three examples of his letter-writing style:

(1) A letter to his brother, Milton, with extensive editing, and the final version of that letter;

(2) The rough draft of a letter regarding a Trinity honorary degree; and

(3) A personal letter to Mr. and Mrs. John Hay Whitney.

January 6, 1954.

PERSONAL AND CONFIDENTIAL

Dear Milton:

Thanks very much for your note of the fourth on the matter of revising labor laws. Our attitude is that we should appeal to that "mass of American citizens who with their heads and hands produce much of the wealth of America." Most certainly we are not consciously seeking the favor of the so-called labor leader—we want to be fair to the worker. In line with this, we are giving far more effort to developing proper housing, health, old age, and unemployment insurance and

389

other programs of this kind, than we are to specific amendments to labor laws.

Maintenance of prosperity is one field of governmental concern that interests me mightily and one on which I have talked incessantly to associates, advisers, and assistants ever since last January. The first task, of course, is the determination of the scope of Federal responsibility and authority. This varies with the times; in these days I am sure that government has to be the principal coordinator and, in many cases, the actual operator for the many things that the approach of depression would demand.

In its over-all aspects, the matter falls within the advisory responsibility of the Chairman of the Council on Economic Affairs. He does not have the responsibility of developing all of the government's subsidiary and operational plans. But he does have the responsibility of watching and studying economic portents, and of assuring the President that each of the measures taken by the government is fitted to the problem and is instituted at the proper time.

In one way or another practically every Department and Agency of government is involved. Means available to the government include revision of tax laws to promote consumption; extension of credit and assuring of low interest rates; vigorous liberalization of all social security measures; extension of all kinds of reinsurance plans, as well as direct loans and grants; acceleration in construction programs involving everything from multiple purpose dams, irrigation projects, military equipment and public buildings on the one hand, to increased expenditures for soil conservation, upstream water storage and public housing on the other. There are, of course, other things the government can and would do.

Certain of the things above mentioned could be done promptly in any emergency. The Federal Reserve Board could promptly lower reserve requirements in member banks to ease credit and make money available for industrial and consumer purposes. On the other hand, everything that touches public works, if they are to be undertaken intelligently and without <u>unnecessary</u> waste, requires a vast degree of advance planning. The larger the project (and presumably, therefore, the more effective in relation to unemployment), the more extensive must be this planning and normally the longer the time required for its completion.

Suppose a multiple purpose dam is to be part of such a program. Even after legal authorization there are many, many months of design and field exploration that must precede initiation of actual construction work. Moreover, behind all <u>this</u> planning, there should have been completed, in advance, the great surveys that treat each of our main water systems as a unit. I think that a vast amount of this has been done—at least I am so assured. And I know that, without it, we will not work intelligently.

So—I would like to know the amount of coordination that has taken place between the Department of Agriculture and the Bureau of Reclamation in determining the relationship of upstream work on the whole Kaw River system and the need for great dams along the axis and on the main branches of that river system.

This one example illustrates, I think, how needful it is that planning in this one field of conservation and utilization of water resources be carried on constantly and exhaustively. The over-all program, cover[ing] all fields, would be vast. Yet it should be so carefully drawn up that we would know the exact priority in which we should attempt to take the various steps; exactly how many people would be put to work; and all of the other things that would be necessary if [we] hope—in a recession—[to] substitute effectiveness for the fumbling and bumbling of 1933.

In view of the complexity and continuing nature of this problem, I sometimes wonder whether we should not have an office in government that in the economic field would parallel the Office of Defense Mobilization in the military field.

Sometime let's talk about it.

As ever,

/s/Ike

Dr. Milton Eisenhower,
The Pennsylvania State University,
State College,
Pennsylvania.

THE WHITE HOUSE
WASHINGTON

January 6, 1954.

Personal and Confidential

Dear Milton:

Thanks very much for your note of the fourth. Our whole approach is to that "mass of American citizens who with their
heads and hands produce so much of the wealth of America."
Most certainly we are not consciously seeking the favor of
the so-called labor leader -- we merely want to be fair to
the worker. In line with this, we have given far more effort to developing proper housing, health, old age and unemployment insurance and other programs of this kind,
than we have to specific amendments to labor laws.

There is one field that interests me mightily and one on
which I have talked to associates, advisers and assistants
ever since last January. It is that of the proper use of
governmental resources and authority in preventing depression.

In its overall aspects, the matter is the responsibility
of the Chairman of the Council on Economic Affairs. He
does not have the responsibility of developing all of the subsidiary and operational plans. But he does have the responsibility of watching and studying the portents, and assuring
that the proper measure is instituted at the proper time.

In one way or another practically every Department and
Agency of government is involved. Means available to
the government include, for example, revision of tax laws
to promote consumption; extension of credit and assuring
of low interest rates; extension of all kinds of reinsurance
plans, as well as direct loans and grants; acceleration in the

Personal and Confidential

393

THE WHITE HOUSE
WASHINGTON

Personal and Confidential

Dr. Milton Eisenhower - 2

construction programs involving everything from multiple
purpose dams, irrigation projects, military equipment and
public buildings on the one hand, to increased expenditures
for soil conservation, upstream water storage, ~~and so on and
so on~~. There are, of course, other things the government can
do. ~~I am only citing a few to illustrate the point I want to make.~~

Certain of the things above mentioned can be done ~~very~~ promptly
in any emergency. ~~For example,~~ The Federal Reserve Board
can lower reserve requirements in member banks ~~and so quickly~~
ease credit and make available money for industrial and consumer
purposes. On the other hand, everything that touches public
works, to be undertaken intelligently and without unnecessary
waste, requires a vast degree of advance planning. The larger
the project - (and therefore the more effective in relation to
unemployment) -- the more extensive will be this planning and
normally the longer the time required for its completion.
~~Take, for example,~~ a multiple purpose dam. ~~Once authorized,~~
there are many, many months of design and field exploration
that must precede initiation of actual construction work. ~~But
even~~ behind all this planning, there should be completed in advance,
the great surveys that treat each of our main water systems as a
unit. I think that a vast amount of this has been done -- at least
I am so assured.

~~But what~~ I would like to know ~~is~~ the amount of coordination that
has taken place between the Department of Agriculture and the
Bureau of Reclamation in determining the, of upstream work on
the whole Kaw River system, ~~for example,~~ and the need for great
dams along the main axis and on the main branches of that river
system.

Personal and Confidential

394

THE WHITE HOUSE
WASHINGTON

Dr. Milton Eisenhower - 3.

This one example illustrates, I think, how needful it is
that this planning be carried on constantly and exhaustively.
The overall program should be so carefully drawn up that
we would know the exact priority in which we should attempt
to take the various steps;   exactly how many people would
be put to work; and all of the other things that would be
necessary if would substitute effectiveness for the fumbling
and bumbling of 1933.

In view of the complexity and continuing nature of this problem, I sometimes wonder whether we should not have an office in government that in the economic field would parallel
the Office of Defense Mobilization in the military field.

Sometime let's talk about it.

As ever,

Dr. Milton S. Eisenhower,
The Pennsylvania State University,
State College,
Pennsylvania.

ROUGH DRAFT

Dear Al:

Quite naturally, I am highly ~~flattered~~ *complimented* by the suggestion that I

~~should~~ come to Trinity next June and there receive an honorary doctorate of

the college. I ~~should~~ very much hope that you ~~would~~ convey to the *T*rustees

an expression of my very deep appreciation and ~~the~~ sense of distinction ~~I feel.~~

While still at Columbia, I made it a personal policy ~~of mine~~ to

limit my appearances at ceremonial affairs ~~at other colleges and universities~~ *in other educational institutions*

to two per year. I have ~~very~~ earnestly tried to apply that policy ever since.

However, I occasionally make an exception *expecially* when there is no speech involved

and I can be present merely as a guest.

This year I have ~~one~~ *a former* engagement of some years' standing, at

Columbia. *commencement.* I have also agreed to go to a little school in Maryland, Washington

College. On top of this, the June period promises to be a very busy one. *as a whole,*

The ~~sum~~ total of all this means that even if I could find it possible

to come to Trinity, I could not participate in the ceremonies as a speaker

(of course I ~~have~~ *would have* no objection to standing up long enough to thank the *, if there,*

397

President, Trustees, Faculty and so on, and express appreciation of the

honor~~ary degree.~~ *done me,*

Other considerations ~~have applied~~ *apply* to the problem.   For such

trips I normally use an airplane. This raises the following questions:

(a) ~~the location of~~ *is there* a suitable air field wh~~ich must, of course,~~ *will (would)*

~~be a large, fully equipped one;~~ *landing and other aids.*

(b) *what is* the distance from the air field to the college~~ and whether~~

~~or n~~ot the route necessarily leads through a populated center; *does*

(c) ~~ability to keep the purpose of party~~ *can the activities of the day be* limited strictly to

the one ceremony -- namely, the graduation exercises. (Your ceremony

being on Sunday, this should be relatively easy ~~in this case~~.)

(d) ~~ability to keep any reception or "hand-shaking" ceremony~~ *is it necessary to have   can any such*

~~within reasonable limits~~ *ceremony be kept kept under reasonable limits* and without hurting any feelings. (While

prospective hosts are ~~alway~~s ready to promise that any such ceremony *normally inserts only*   *this is sometime*

~~will be kept to~~ a very small number, the fact is that t~~hey are sometimes~~

done

~~compelled to do~~ it at the cost of making the honor guest appear rude and

unappreciative of the courtesy that people intend to pay him.   This is

a very touchy point.   I like people and like to meet them, but the burden

of numbers sometimes becomes almost overpowering ~~and the matter has~~

~~to be looked at very carefully and sympathetically before arrangements~~

~~are actually made.~~

I am writing you very fully and completely, and I hope that I

do not appear to be ~~stuffy~~ about the matter.

*I do not mean to be stuffy
or difficult. The duties of
this office become wearing at
times — energy must be conserved
where possible. So — if you
and write to me soon again,
Rex, I think we should come close
to a definite decision.*

399

THE WHITE HOUSE

WASHINGTON

April 28, 1954.

Dear Betsy and Jock:

~~It comes to me with something of a~~
~~shock to realize that I apparently~~
~~forgot to thank you for the two~~
~~handsome ties you brought to me~~
~~at Augusta.~~ As always, I am
appreciative ~~of your kindness.~~

~~I'm glad you were able to be at~~
Augusta National ~~during part of~~
~~our stay there~~

With warm regard,

Sincerely,

Mr. and Mrs. John Hay Whitney,
630 Fifth Avenue,
New York,
New York.

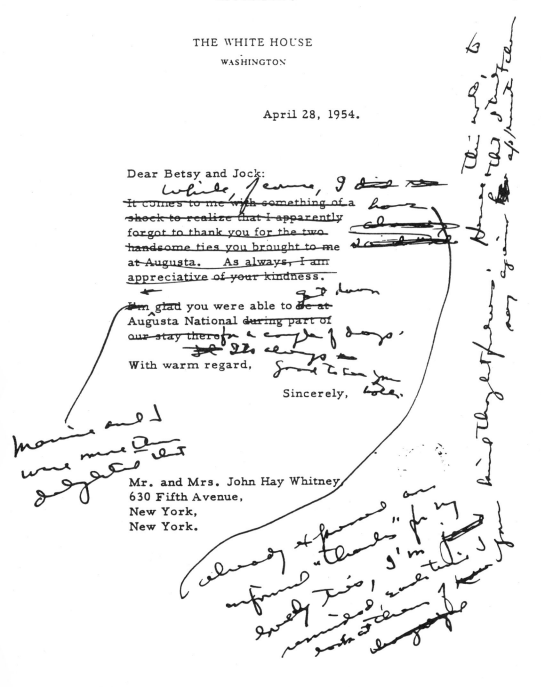

401

Appendix 6

Eisenhower's "let go" letter to General Alfred Gruenther describes the China crisis. The subheads are inserted for emphasis and readability.

February 1, 1955

Dear Al:

The past two weeks in Washington have been a period of tension—reminiscent of the numerous "flaps" that used to plague us in the old War Department.

[EFFORT TO OBTAIN PUBLIC'S SUPPORT]

The principal cause has been the Administration's effort to clarify our people's understanding of the consequences of an attack by the ChiComs on Formosa and its neighboring islands, and to obtain their expressed support of the government's plans to defend those islands effectively. An added difficulty, as is always the case, has been the extreme care with which the public relations angle of this effort had to be handled.

[THUMBNAIL SUMMARY OF BROAD WORLD PICTURE]

In the present case, we have a Europe that, speaking generally, is fearful of what some Europeans consider

403

American recklessness, impulsiveness and immaturity in the foreign field. In Red China we have a dictatorial regime which seeks every opportunity to develop among its own people and all other Asiatics a deeper and deeper hatred of the West, particularly of the United States. In Formosa we have the remnants of the Chinese Nationalists who are suspicious of any move in the Far East that does not involve an "immediate direct and destructive attack on Red China."

[BASIC CONFLICTS AT HOME]

At home we have the truculent and the timid, the jingoists and the pacifists. Underlying the whole is the most important fact of today's life—the irreconcilable conflict between the theories of the Communist dictatorship and the basic principles ["problems" crossed out and "principles" inserted in longhand] of free world existence.

[DISTINCTION BETWEEN FORMOSA AND OFFSHORE ISLANDS]

Any military man can easily make [a] clear distinction between the defense of Formosa and the defense of the so-called offshore islands. Not only are two different military problems presented, but in the one case we are talking about territories the control of which has passed from nation to nation through the years—and in the other case, about territories that have always been a part of the Chinese mainland both politically and, in effect, geographically. So the political differences are almost as plain as the military differences when we talk about the defense of these two territories.

If there were no other factors than the military to consider, you and I, for example, would study the problem and would very quickly reach a decision that we would permit <u>no</u> advance by the Communists beyond the offshore islands, but that in any struggle involving only the territory of those islands, we would see no reason for American intervention.

[POLITICAL CONSIDERATIONS]

Such a solution would infuriate the Chinese Communists because of their announced objective to take Formosa; it would infuriate the Chinese Nationalists because the retention of the offshore islands sustains their hope that one day they will go back to their homeland. It would more or less please our European friends because it implies to them a moderate attitude on our part, and the responsible officials in those countries can see the danger to all of us if Formosa should fall to the Communists. (Not that Red China, in her present state, would be a direct threat to the United States, but with international Communism having thus penetrated the island barrier in the Western Pacific and in a position to threaten the Philippines and Indonesia immediately and directly, all of us would soon be in far worse trouble than we are now.)

[WISHES OF PACIFIST ELEMENT]

At home the hypothetical solution I mention would be accepted by most merely because it is simple to describe, although there is a certain pacifist element that wants us completely out of the Western Pacific. Some people seem to think that we can surrender to the Communists the Japanese productive capacity and all the richness of the South Pacific territories and still be perfectly safe in this country. There are people who did not believe Hitler's threats any more than they now believe those of Chou and the Kremlin.

Now, if the solution we adopt should state flatly that we would defend the principal islands of the offshore group (Quemoy and the Matsus), we would now please the Chinese Nationalists, but we would frighten

405

Europe and of course even further infuriate the Chinese Communists. Not that I think this last particularly important, because they are going to be infuriated anyway.

[LONG-RANGE PROBLEMS WITH ALTERNATIVES]

By announcing this as a policy we would be compelled to maintain in the area, at great cost, forces that could assure the defense of islands that are almost within wading distance of the mainland. This defensive problem could be extremely difficult over the long term, and I think that the world in general, including some of our friends, would believe us unreasonable and practically goading the Chinese Communists into a fight. We could get badly tied down by any such inflexible public attitude.

On the other hand, as we consider the problem of defending Formosa, we understand how important to us is the morale of the Chinese forces on that island. Their willingness to fight and to keep themselves in a high state of readiness for fighting is one of the keys to the situation. Consequently, even though we clearly see that our major concern, so far as territory itself is involved, does not extend beyond Formosa and the neighboring Pescadores, yet the economical and efficient defense of these islands involves a concern for the areas from which it could most easily be attacked.

[RESOLUTION IS OUR PUBLICLY STATED POSITION]

You probably read the Resolution that was passed by the Congress, at my request. The wording, as to areas outside Formosa and the Pescadores, is vague. In view of what I have just said, you can understand why this is so.

The Resolution, then, is our publicly stated position; the problem now is how to make it work. The morale of the Chinese Nationalists still remains important to us, so they must have certain assurances with respect to the offshore islands. But these must be less binding on us than the terms of the Chino-American Treaty, now before our Senate for ratification. We must remain ready, until some better solution can be found, to move promptly against any Communist force that is manifestly preparing to attack Formosa. And we must make a distinction—(this is a difficult one)—between an attack that has <u>only</u> as its objective the capture of an offshore island and one that is <u>primarily a preliminary movement to an all-out attack on Formosa.</u>

[GREATEST CONCERN IS TO RETAIN PUBLIC CONFIDENCE]

I could go on and discuss a thousand different points, with shadings of each, that we have discussed and hashed over during the past two weeks. Basic conclusions were scarcely involved; there have never been any great differences within the Administration on fundamentals. Most of the talks centered around the question of "what can we say and how can we say it" so as to retain the greatest possible confidence of our friends and at the same time put our enemies on notice that we are not going to stand idly by to see our vital interests jeopardized.

[ANALYZES OWN APPROACH TO PROBLEMS]

Of course, only time will tell how successful we have been. Every day will bring its problems and many of these will cause much more talking and haggling—even some <u>thinking</u>! More and more I find myself, in this type of situation—and perhaps it is because of my advancing years—tending to strip each problem down to its simplest possible form. Having gotten the issue well defined in my mind, I try in the next step to determine what answer would best serve the long term advantage and welfare of the United

States and the free world. I then consider the immediate problem and what solution can we get that will best conform to the long term interests of the country and at the same time can command a sufficient approval in this country so as to secure the necessary Congressional action.

[MAY BE AN "AUTOCRAT" WITH "PHRASEOLOGY"]

When I get a problem solved on this rough basis, I merely stick to the essential answer and let associates have a field day on words and terminology. (I suppose that many of those around me would protest that even in this field I am sometimes something of an autocrat and insist upon the employment of my own phraseology when I consider the issue important.) However, I really do try to stay out of this particular job as much as my own characteristics, particularly my ego, will permit.

Whatever is now to happen, I know that nothing could be worse than global war [emphasis added].

[RUSSIA DOES NOT WANT WAR]

I do not believe that Russia wants war at this time—in fact, I do not believe that if we became engaged in rather a bitter fight along the coast of China, Russia would want to intervene with her own forces. She would, of course, pour supplies into China in the effort to exhaust us and certainly would exploit the opportunity to separate us from our major allies. But I am convinced that Russia does not want, at this moment, to experiment with means of defense against the bombing that we could conduct against her mainland. At the same time, I assume that Russia's treaty with Red China comprehends a true military alliance, which she would either have to repudiate or take the plunge. As a consequence of this kind of thinking, she would probably be in a considerable dilemma if we got into a real shooting war with China. It would not be an easy decision for the men in the Kremlin, in my opinion.

[MUST SHOW FIRMNESS]

In any event, we have got to do what we believe to be right—if we can figure out the right—and we must show no lack of firmness in a world where our political enemies exploit every sign of weakness, and are constantly attempting to disrupt the solidarity of the free world's intentions to oppose their aggressive practices.

Oddly enough I started out this letter with the complacent thought that I could point up, in one or two paragraphs, the salient features of my last two weeks' existence. Now I find that after all these words, I have only vaguely pointed out the biggest ones in this particular "can of worms."

When I see you in a couple of weeks, we can talk these things over more fully.

With love to Grace, and, of course, the best to yourself,

As ever,

/s/Ike

General Alfred M. Gruenther
Supreme Commander
Allied Powers Europe
APO 55, c/o Postmaster
New York, New York

Index

420

ing in "Chance for Peace" speech, 171-173; hits "Korea" speech theme second time, 83-84; pre-inaugural cabinet meeting, 109; problems with speeches, 51; with DDE aboard *Helena*, 99-100

Hull, Cordell, member of American delegation to UN founding, xii

Humphrey, George, debates on price and wage controls, 112-113; effort to remove Stassen, vii; pre-inaugural cabinet meeting, 109; supported Jackson after Stalin's death, 156; with DDE aboard *Helena*, 99-100

Humphreys, Robert, RNC public relations specialist, 41

-I-

Introducing Harold Stassen, vi-xvi

Iron Curtain countries, labor unions in, 197-198; Stassen committee activated "Solidarity" program, 198-203

-J-

Jackson, C.D., named campaign advisor, 44-47; policy shift toward Soviets after Stalin's death, 163; Psychological Strategy Board, 107; recommendations on Stalin's death, 155-156; with Stassen for "Korea" speech delivery to DDE, 77-78

Jenner, William (Senator), accusations

against Truman for firing MacArthur, 66; attacks on General George Marshall, 52-56; "battlefield settlement" of Korean War unacceptable, 209

Johnson, Lyndon (Senator), agreement to kill McCarthy resolution, 251

Jones, Robert Tyre ("Bobby"), DDE companion and golf mentor, 231-232; DDE host in Augusta, 91

Judd, Walter (Congressman), 1951 Stassen group meeting, 6

-K-

Kaganovich, Lazar Moiseyevich, as possible Stalin successor, 159

Kennedy, John F., defeat of Henry Cabot Lodge for US Senate, 10

Khrushchev, Nikita, power structure in USSR, 300; reaction to DDE Geneva disarmament speech, 337-339; shows who rules USSR, 340

Kirker, Thomas, insight on DDE's golf, 231-232

Knowland, William F. (Senator), effort to table McCarthy's Geneva resolution, 251; offer of substitute DDE "Korea" speech, 80;

Kohler, Walter (Governor), 1951 Stassen group meeting, 6; involvement with "Marshall" Milwaukee speech, 54; "Korea" speech by DDE, 71-85

Korean armistice, 205-222; conflicts of opinion on ending war, 208-209; DDE: combines firmness

in Korea, 143-144

New Hampshire primary, DDE victory, 31; Lodge fears Taft victory, 30; Stassen: affirmative strategy, 30-31; decides to enter, 24-25; role evaluated, 29; Taft, Adams and Stassen filings, 25; Taft directly attacks Eisenhower, 30

"New Look" for defense, 235-242; all nations must know they cannot cripple US, 240-241; economic strength equally important with military strength, 236; Joint Chiefs must plan for country as whole, 238-239; military must assume role for economic strength, 236; need dynamic industrial base, 236; need for deterrence, 237-238; neither industry nor military must dominate other, 237; no way to separate military from economic policy, 235; no winners in atomic war, 237; Ridgway protests deep cuts in army's budget, 239; Third World War could come, 236; Third World War not inevitable, 236; Twining answers Ridgway's objections, 240; UN must contribute to peace, 238; US will never start a war, 237; warnings against greed and corruption, 237

Nielsen, Aksel, hosts DDE after Convention, 41

Nimitz, Chester (Admiral), surrender ceremonies aboard *Missouri*, 60

Nitze, Paul, Democrats attempt partisan issue on China crisis, 272

Nixon, Richard, "Checkers" speech, 72; "Millionaires Club," 71; pre-inaugural cabinet meeting, 109; Secret Fund, 71-72

North Atlantic Treaty Organization (*see* NATO)

-O-

"Open Skies" proposal, Bush revives concept, 352; DDE: agreement with Stassen draft on inspection system, 333-334, basic philosophy of reaching out, 351-352, credits Doolittle for aerial inspection idea, 335, disarmament speech, 337-339, insert of aerial inspection in disarmament speech, 338-339, plan to get Stassen to Geneva Summit, 321-323, strategy to include "Open Skies" concept in disarmament speech, 336; detailed description of Geneva Summit, 321-341; disarmament speech includes Doolittle concept of aerial inspection, 330-331; Doolittle plan to prevent surprise attack, 308-310; Dulles: continuing coolness toward, 348-349, denigration of Summit's accomplishments, 348-349, opposition to Geneva inclusion, 335-336, tries to keep Stassen from Geneva Summit, 321-323; "Eisenhower direction," 356; favorable Bulganin reaction to DDE disarmament speech, 340; favor-

428